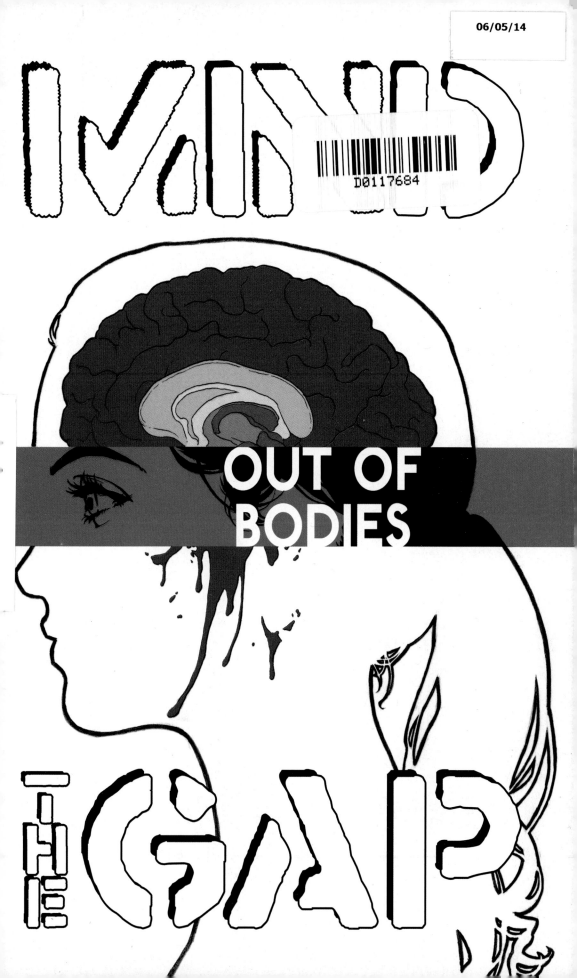

MIND

06/05/14

D0117684

OUT OF
BODIES

THE GAP

Written & Created by Jim McCann

MIND

Letters by Dave Lanphear

Production and Graphic Design by Damien Lucchese

Edited by Rob Levin

Cover by Rodin Esquejo & Arif Prianto

MIND THE GAP, VOL. 3: OUT OF BODIES
ISBN: 978-1-60706-811-2
First Printing

IMAGE COMICS, INC.
Robert Kirkman - chief operating officer
Erik Larsen - chief financial officer
Todd McFarlane - president
Marc Silvestri - chief executive officer
Jim Valentino - vice-president
www.imagecomics.com

Eric Stephenson - publisher
Ron Richards - director of business development
Jennifer de Guzman - pr & marketing director
Branwyn Bigglestone - accounts manager
Emily Miller - accounting assistant
Jamie Parreno - marketing assistant
Emilio Bautista - sales assistant

Jaemie Dudas - administrative assistant
Kevin Yuen - digital rights coordinator
Tyler Shainline - events coordinator
David Brothers - content manager
Jonathan Chan - production manager
Drew Gill - art director
Jana Cook - print manager

Monica Garcia - senior production artist
Vincent Kukua - production artist
Jenna Savage - production artist
Addison Duke - production artist

Issue 11 · Issue 12
Sami Basri · Art
Jessica Kholinne & Beny Maulana [issue 12]
of STELLAR Labs · Colors

Issue 13 · Issue 14
Rodin Esquejo · Art [Present]
Dan McDaid · Art [Past]
Arif Prianto of STELLAR Labs · Colors [Present]
Lee Loughridge · Colors [Past]

Issue 15
Rodin Esquejo · Art [Present]
Dan McDaid · Art [Past]
Jessica Kholinne of STELLAR Labs · Colors [Present]
Lee Loughridge · Colors [Past]

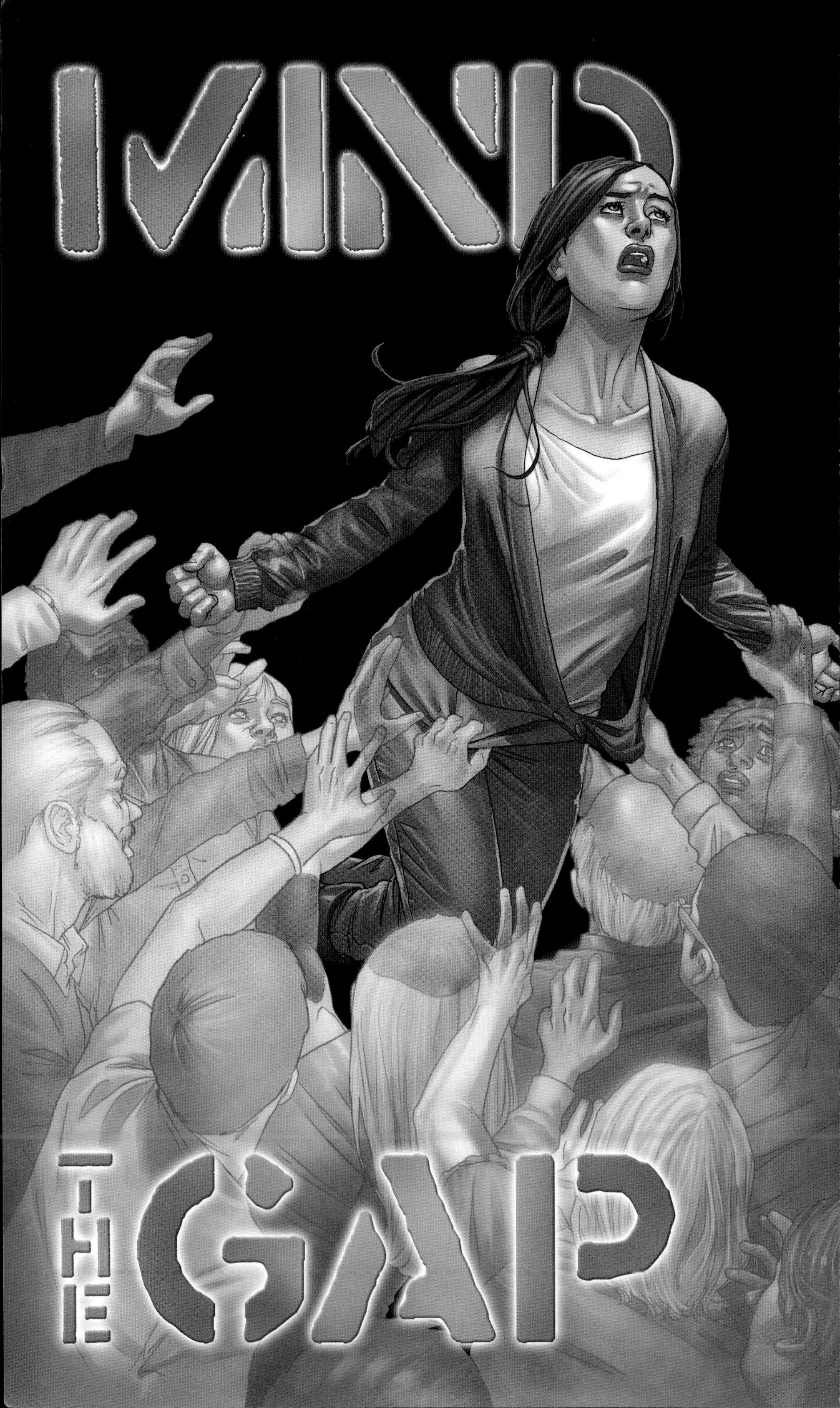
MIND
THE GAP

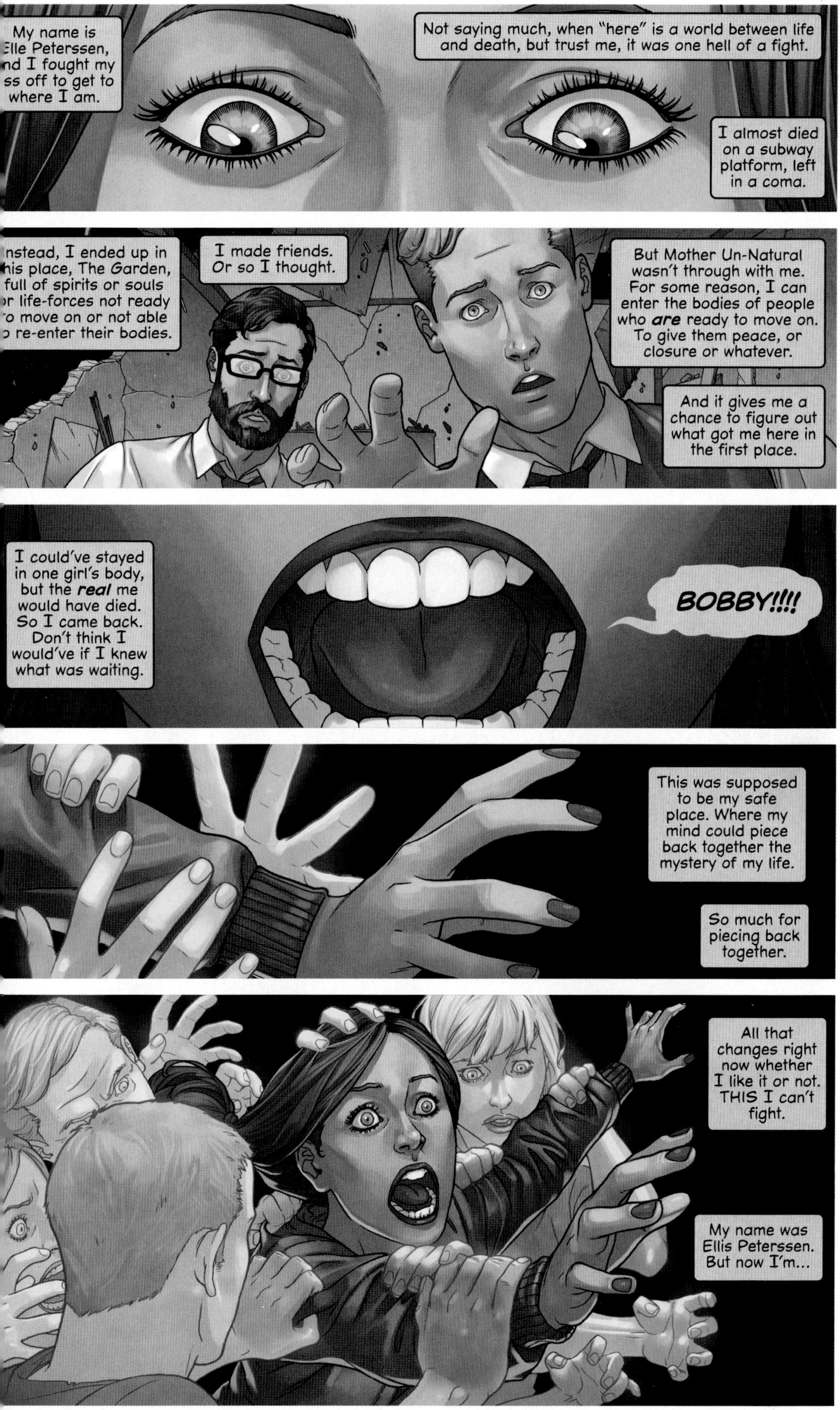

My name is lle Peterssen, nd I fought my ss off to get to where I am.
Not saying much, when "here" is a world between life and death, but trust me, it was one hell of a fight.
I almost died on a subway platform, left in a coma.
nstead, I ended up in his place, The Garden, full of spirits or souls r life-forces not ready o move on or not able re-enter their bodies.
I made friends. Or so I thought.
But Mother Un-Natural wasn't through with me. For some reason, I can enter the bodies of people who *are* ready to move on. To give them peace, or closure or whatever.
And it gives me a chance to figure out what got me here in the first place.
I could've stayed in one girl's body, but the *real* me would have died. So I came back. Don't think I would've if I knew what was waiting.
BOBBY!!!!
This was supposed to be my safe place. Where my mind could piece back together the mystery of my life.
So much for piecing back together.
All that changes right now whether I like it or not. THIS I can't fight.
My name was Ellis Peterssen. But now I'm...

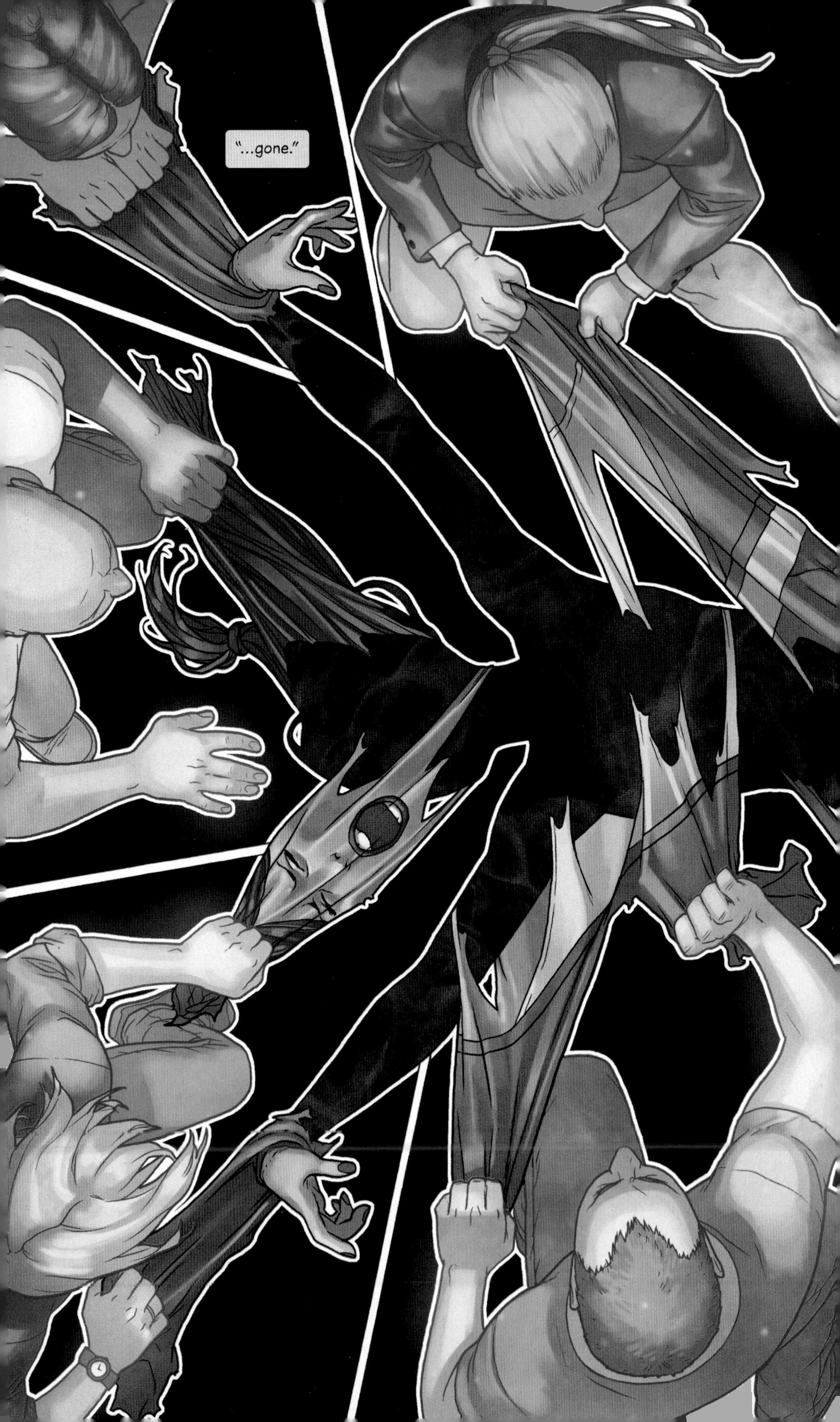
"...gone."

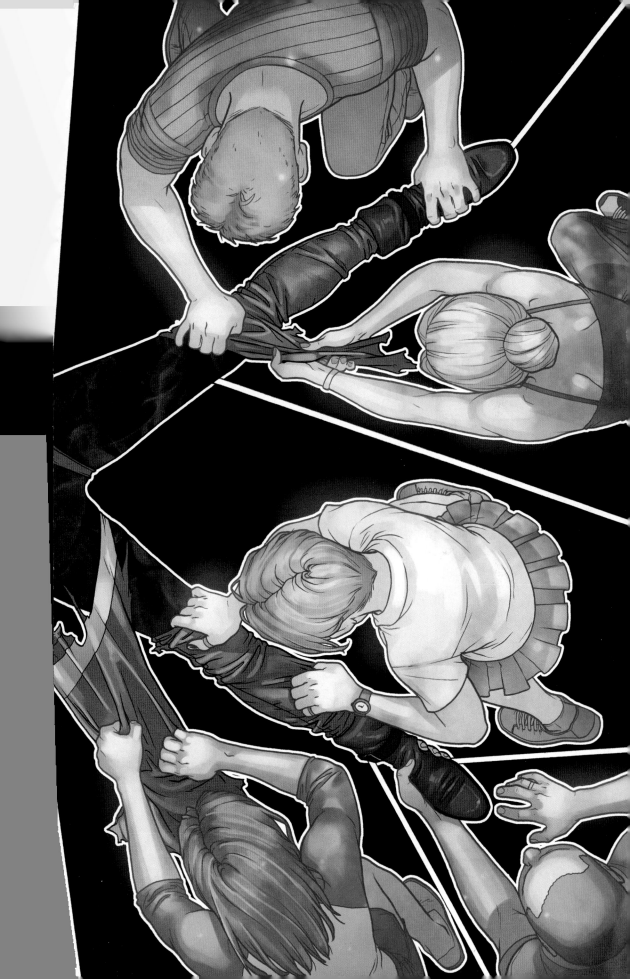

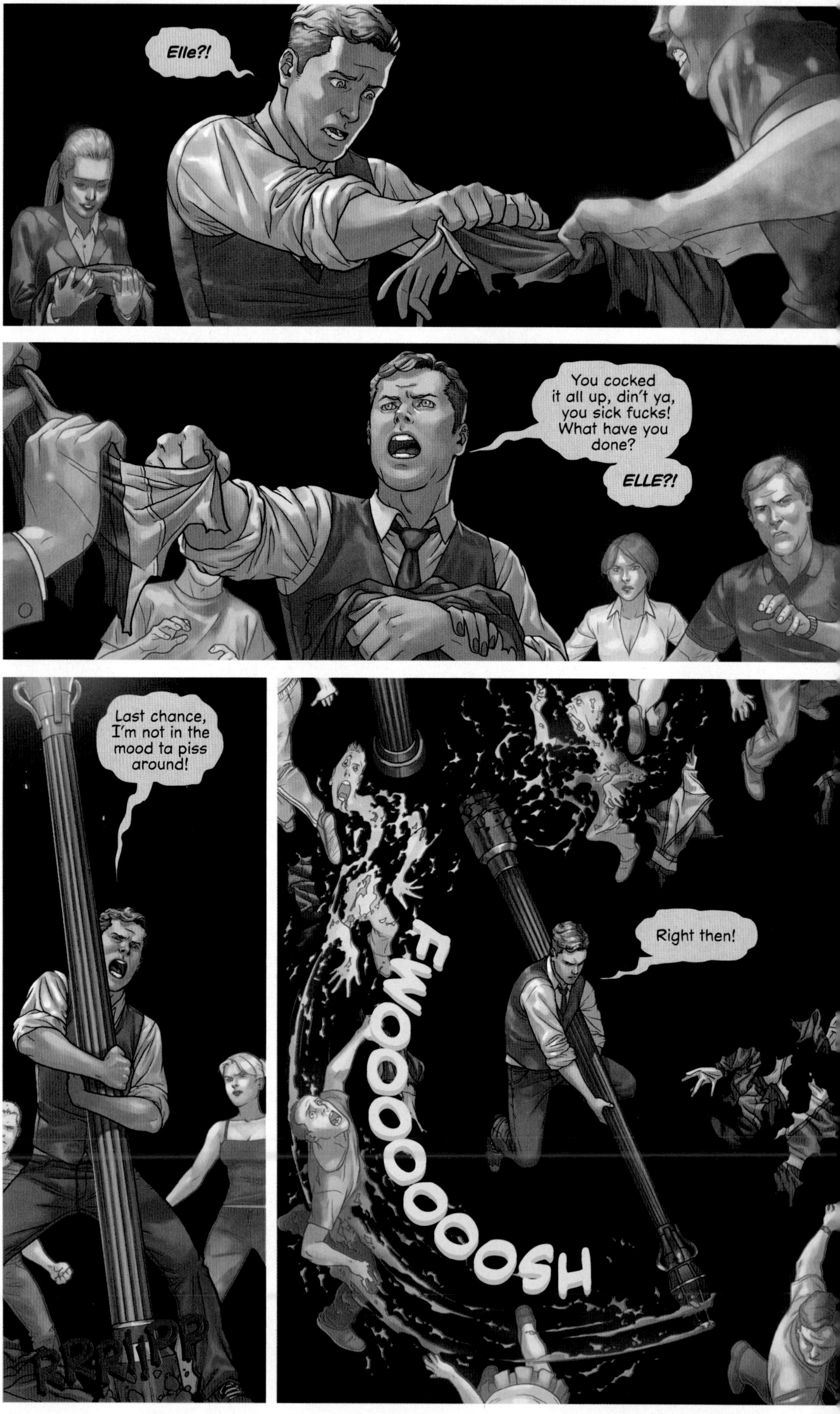
Elle?!
You cocked it all up, din't ya, you sick fucks! What have you done?
ELLE?!
Last chance, I'm not in the mood ta piss around!
Right then!
FWOOOOOOOSH

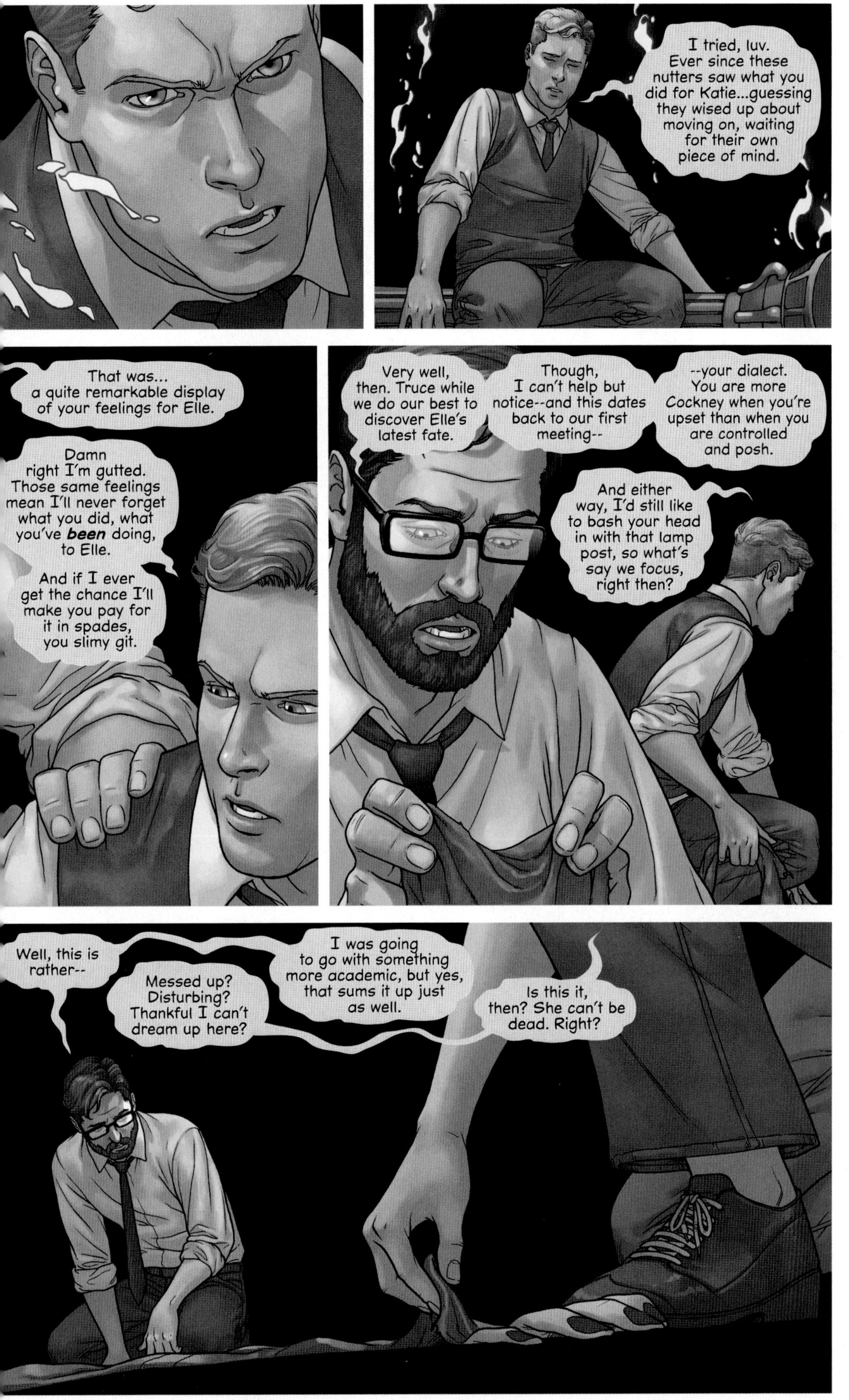
I tried, luv. Ever since these nutters saw what you did for Katie...guessing they wised up about moving on, waiting for their own piece of mind.
That was... a quite remarkable display of your feelings for Elle.
Damn right I'm gutted. Those same feelings mean I'll never forget what you did, what you've ***been*** doing, to Elle.
And if I ever get the chance I'll make you pay for it in spades, you slimy git.
Very well, then. Truce while we do our best to discover Elle's latest fate.
Though, I can't help but notice--and this dates back to our first meeting--
--your dialect. You are more Cockney when you're upset than when you are controlled and posh.
And either way, I'd still like to bash your head in with that lamp post, so what's say we focus, right then?
Well, this is rather--
Messed up? Disturbing? Thankful I can't dream up here?
I was going to go with something more academic, but yes, that sums it up just as well.
Is this it, then? She can't be dead. Right?

Based on what we witnessed, Ellis is not so much "dead" as she is...scattered. She'll have to find her own way back together piece by piece.
All the King's horses and all the King's men...
Of everything I may have held from her, from you both, over the many years I've worked with her there is one thing I would never lie about. She is no fragile creature.
Ellis Peterssen is the strongest woman I know. Now we can only hope she remembers that.

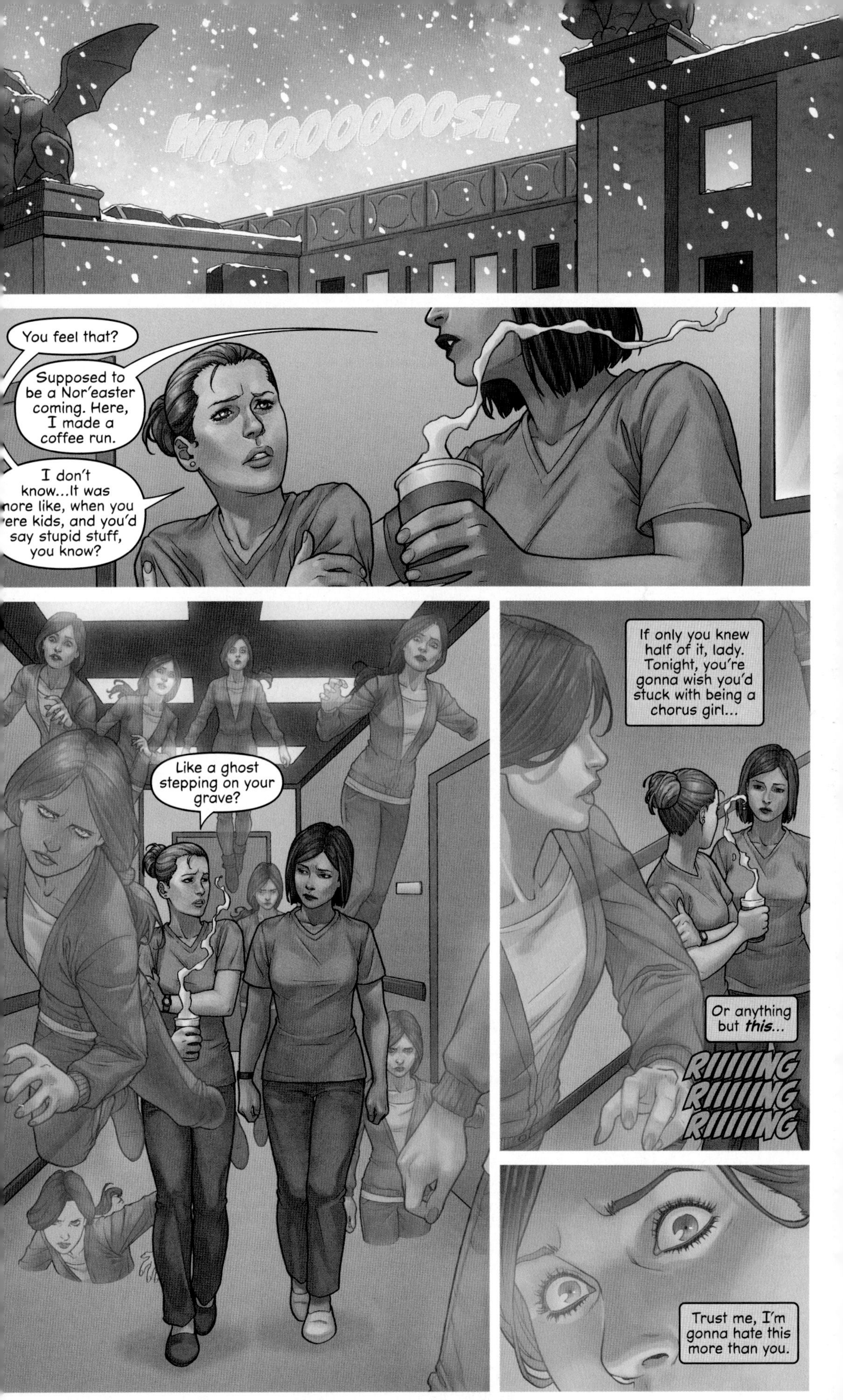
WHOOOOOOOOSH
You feel that?
Supposed to be a Nor'easter coming. Here, I made a coffee run.
I don't know...It was nore like, when you ere kids, and you'd say stupid stuff, you know?
Like a ghost stepping on your grave?
If only you knew half of it, lady. Tonight, you're gonna wish you'd stuck with being a chorus girl...
Or anything but *this*...
RIIIING RIIIING RIIIING
Trust me, I'm gonna hate this more than you.

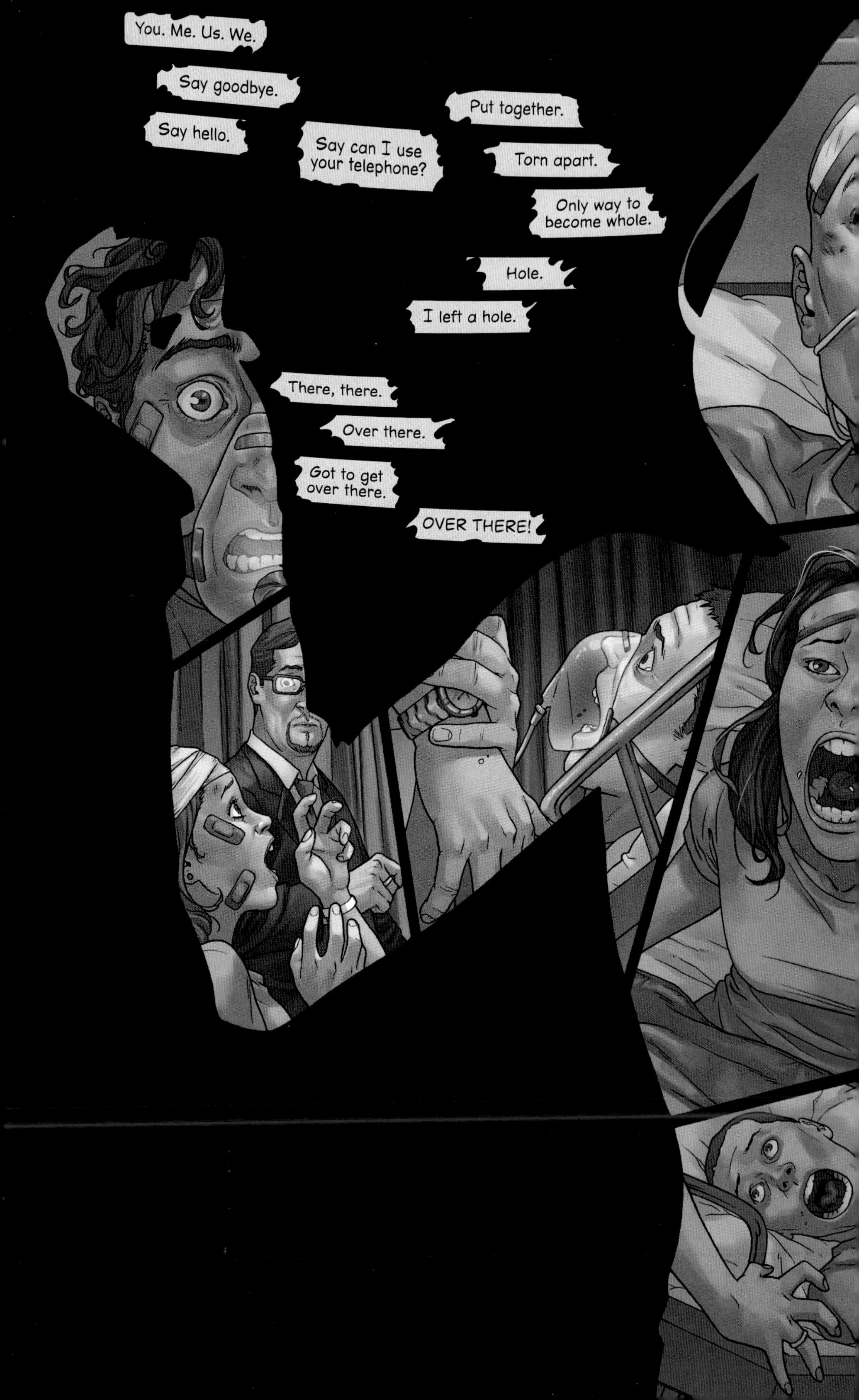
You. Me. Us. We.
Say goodbye.
Say hello.
Say can I use your telephone?
Put together.
Torn apart.
Only way to become whole.
Hole.
I left a hole.
There, there.
Over there.
Got to get over there.
OVER THERE!

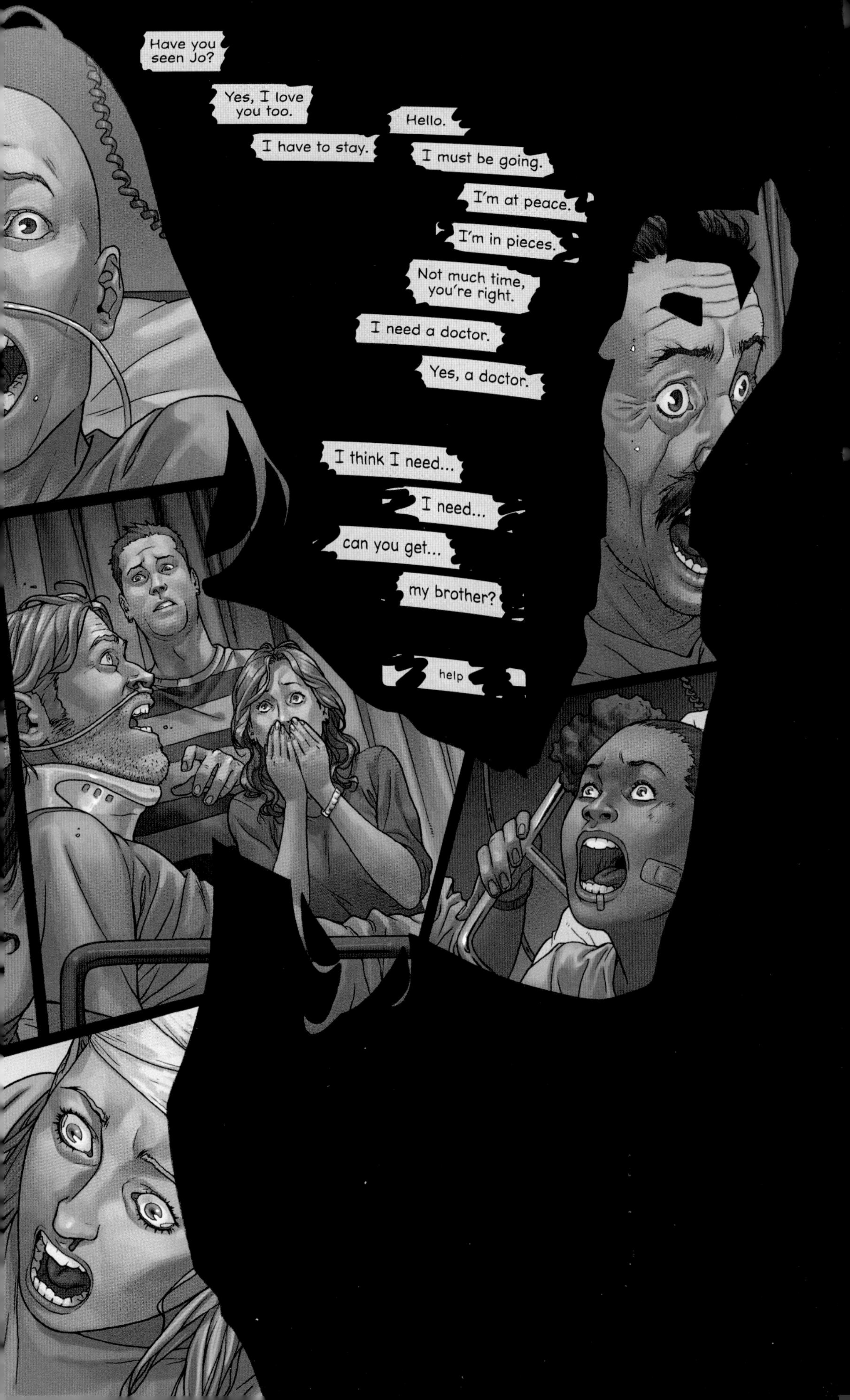
Have you seen Jo?
Yes, I love you too.
Hello.
I have to stay.
I must be going.
I'm at peace.
I'm in pieces.
Not much time, you're right.
I need a doctor.
Yes, a doctor.
I think I need...
I need...
can you get...
my brother?
help

OUT OF BODIES
PART I
"THE GOOD-BYE GIRL"

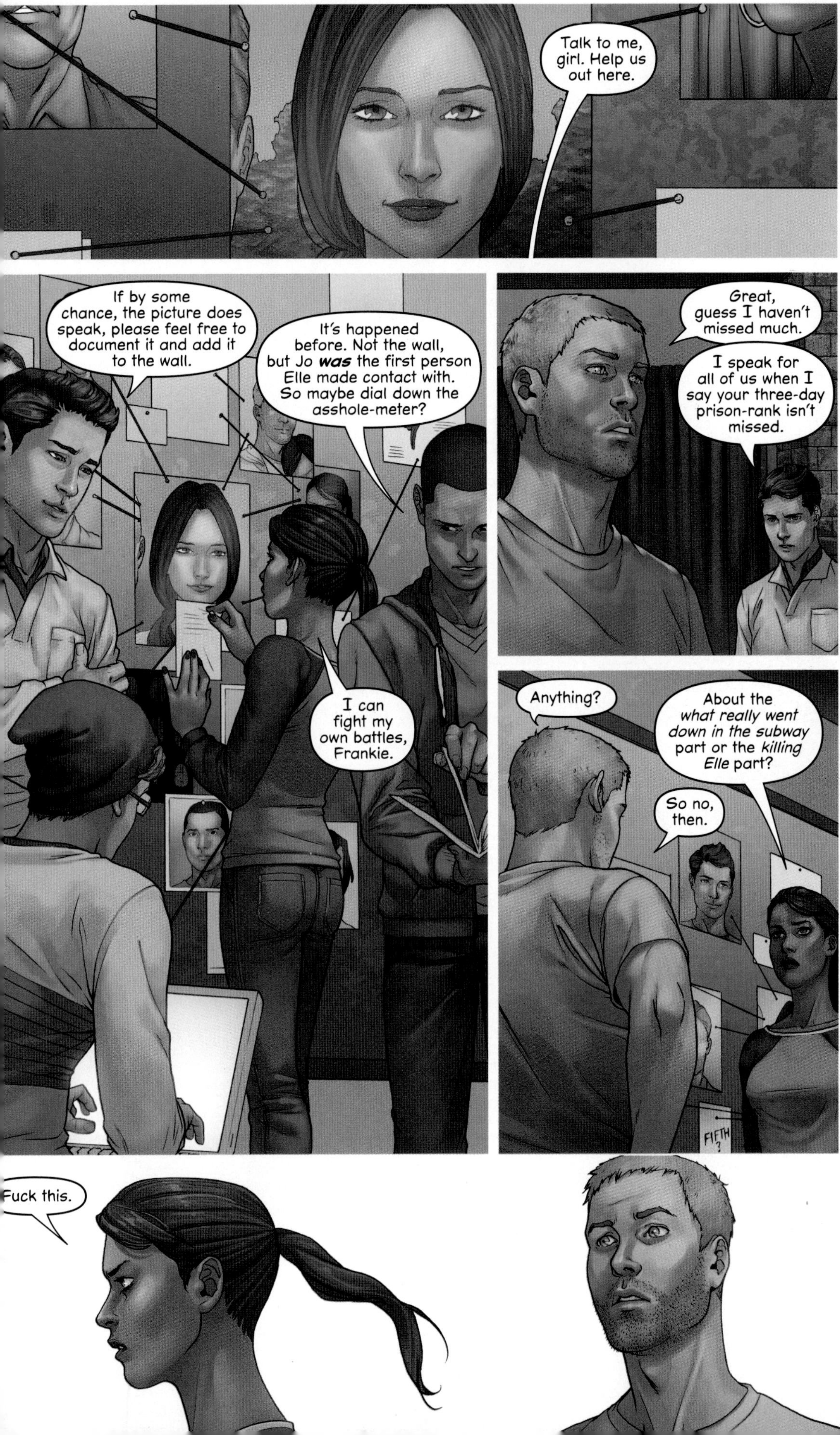

Talk to me, girl. Help us out here.
If by some chance, the picture does speak, please feel free to document it and add it to the wall.
It's happened before. Not the wall, but Jo *was* the first person Elle made contact with. So maybe dial down the asshole-meter?
I can fight my own battles, Frankie.
Great, guess I haven't missed much.
I speak for all of us when I say your three-day prison-rank isn't missed.
Anything?
About the *what really went down in the subway* part or the *killing Elle* part?
So no, then.
FIFTH ?
Fuck this.

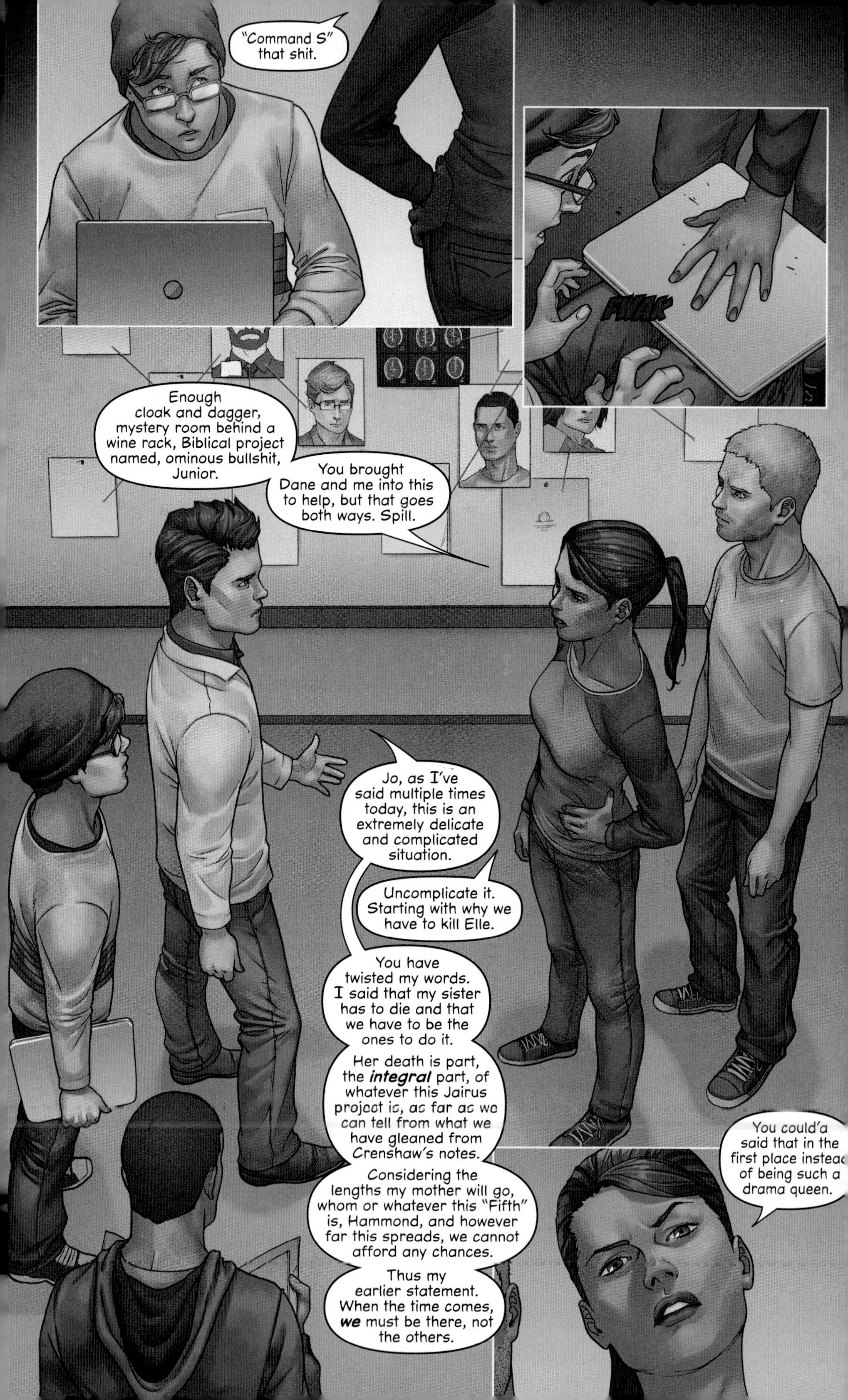
"Command S" that shit.
Enough cloak and dagger, mystery room behind a wine rack, Biblical project named, ominous bullshit, Junior.
You brought Dane and me into this to help, but that goes both ways. Spill.
Jo, as I've said multiple times today, this is an extremely delicate and complicated situation.
Uncomplicate it. Starting with why we have to kill Elle.
You have twisted my words. I said that my sister has to die and that we have to be the ones to do it.
Her death is part, the ***integral*** part, of whatever this Jairus project is, as far as we can tell from what we have gleaned from Crenshaw's notes.
Considering the lengths my mother will go, whom or whatever this "Fifth" is, Hammond, and however far this spreads, we cannot afford any chances.
Thus my earlier statement. When the time comes, ***we*** must be there, not the others.
You could'a said that in the first place instea of being such a drama queen.

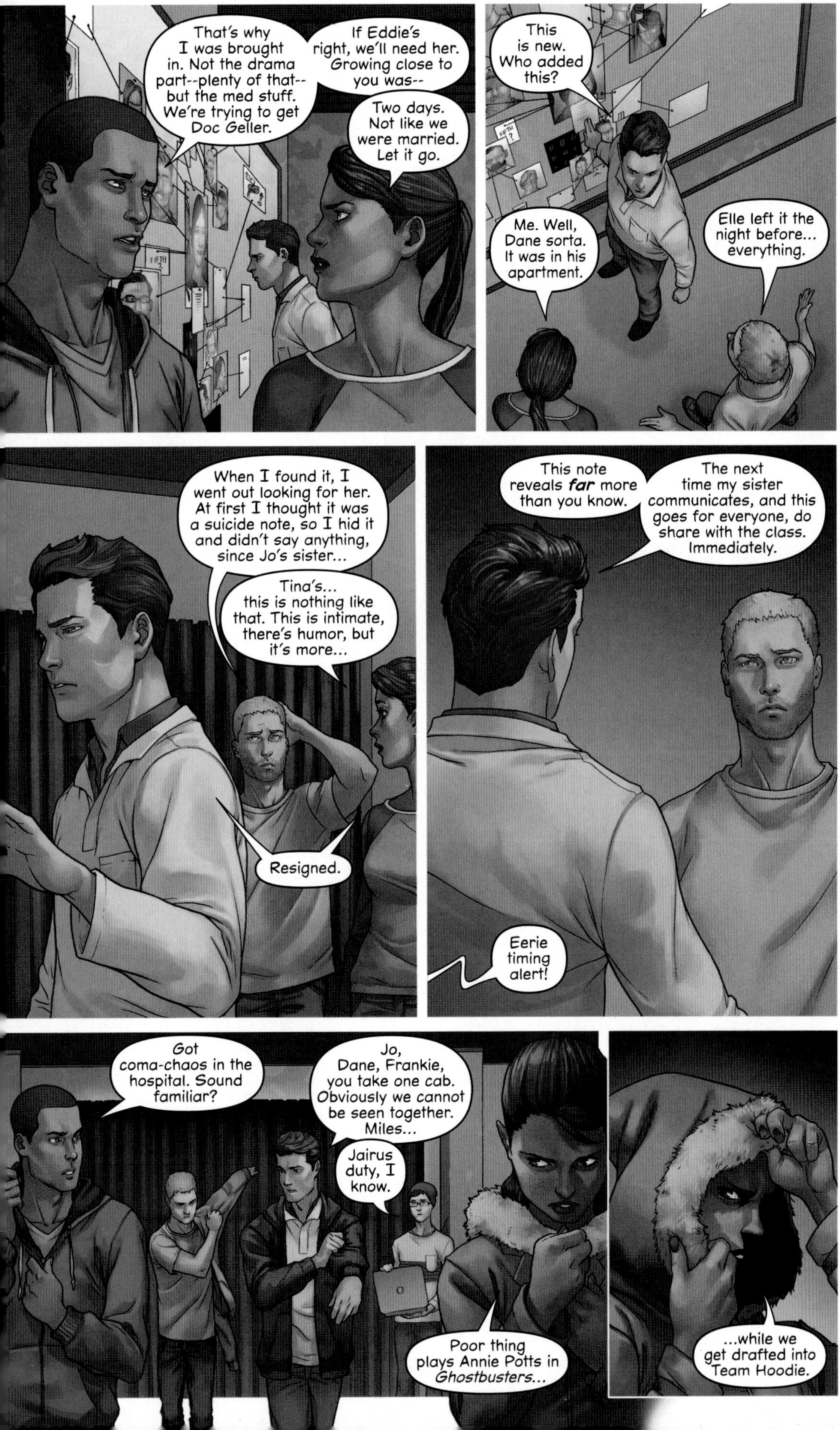
That's why I was brought in. Not the drama part--plenty of that--but the med stuff. We're trying to get Doc Geller.
If Eddie's right, we'll need her. Growing close to you was--
Two days. Not like we were married. Let it go.
This is new. Who added this?
Me. Well, Dane sorta. It was in his apartment.
Elle left it the night before... everything.
When I found it, I went out looking for her. At first I thought it was a suicide note, so I hid it and didn't say anything, since Jo's sister...
Tina's... this is nothing like that. This is intimate, there's humor, but it's more...
Resigned.
This note reveals ***far*** more than you know.
The next time my sister communicates, and this goes for everyone, do share with the class. Immediately.
Eerie timing alert!
Got coma-chaos in the hospital. Sound familiar?
Jo, Dane, Frankie, you take one cab. Obviously we cannot be seen together. Miles...
Jairus duty, I know.
Poor thing plays Annie Potts in *Ghostbusters*...
...while we get drafted into Team Hoodie.

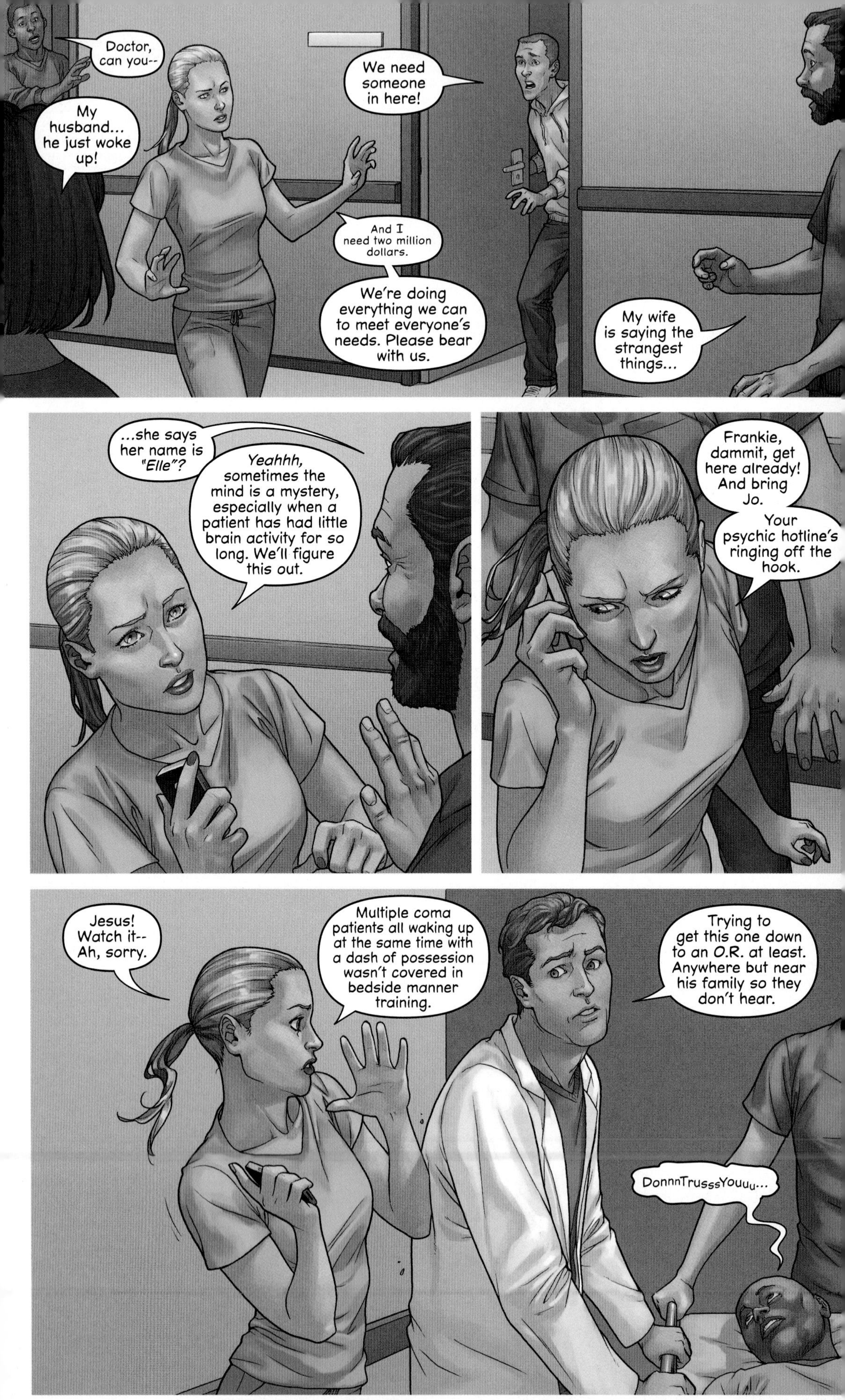
Doctor, can you--
My husband... he just woke up!
We need someone in here!
And I need two million dollars.
We're doing everything we can to meet everyone's needs. Please bear with us.
My wife is saying the strangest things...
...she says her name is "Elle"?
Yeahhh, sometimes the mind is a mystery, especially when a patient has had little brain activity for so long. We'll figure this out.
Frankie, dammit, get here already! And bring Jo.
Your psychic hotline's ringing off the hook.
Jesus! Watch it-- Ah, sorry.
Multiple coma patients all waking up at the same time with a dash of possession wasn't covered in bedside manner training.
Trying to get this one down to an O.R. at least. Anywhere but near his family so they don't hear.
DonnnTrusssYouuu...

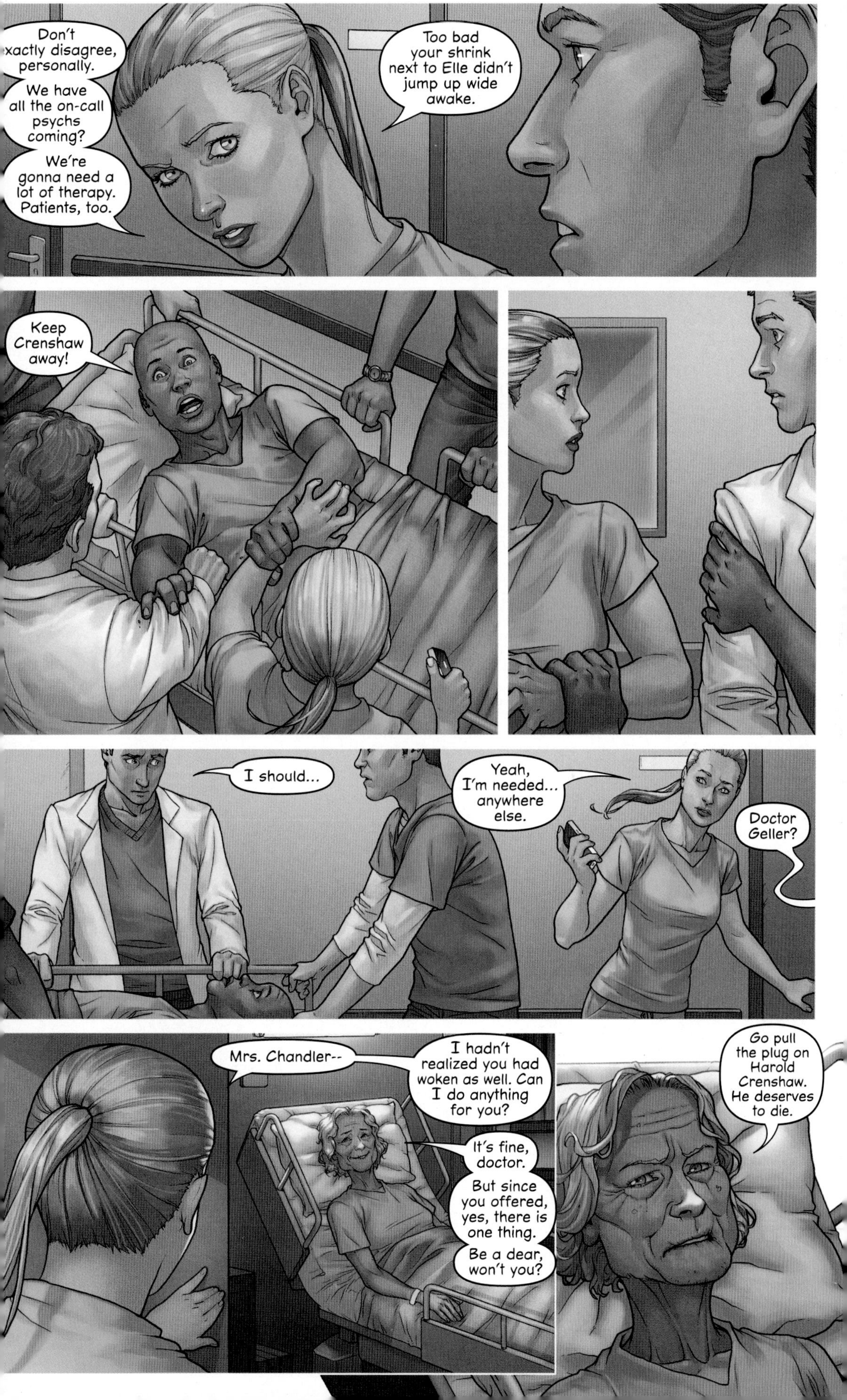

Don't xactly disagree, personally.
We have all the on-call psychs coming?
We're gonna need a lot of therapy. Patients, too.
Too bad your shrink next to Elle didn't jump up wide awake.
Keep Crenshaw away!
I should...
Yeah, I'm needed... anywhere else.
Doctor Geller?
Mrs. Chandler--
I hadn't realized you had woken as well. Can I do anything for you?
It's fine, doctor.
But since you offered, yes, there is one thing.
Be a dear, won't you?
Go pull the plug on Harold Crenshaw. He deserves to die.

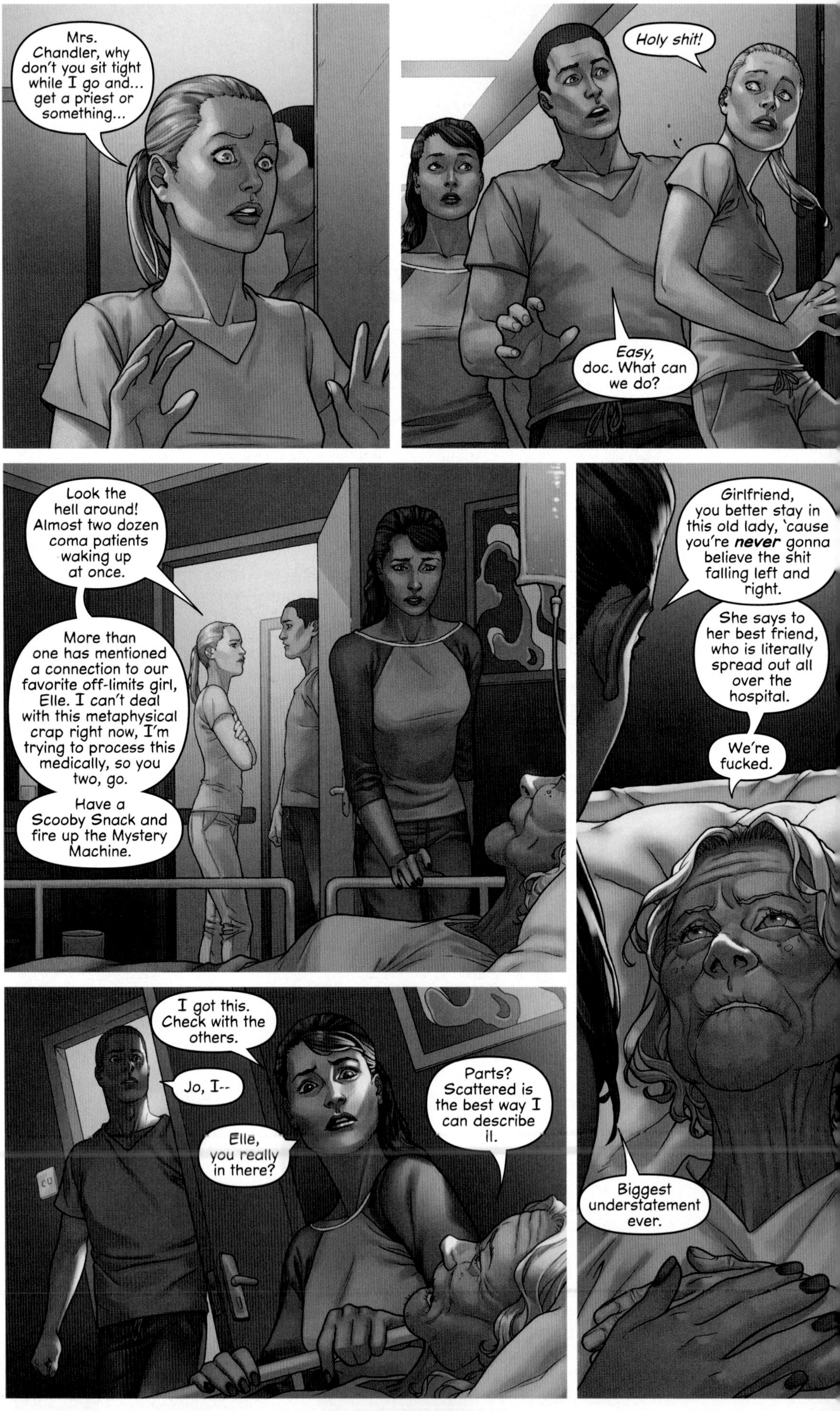
Mrs. Chandler, why don't you sit tight while I go and... get a priest or something...
Holy shit!
Easy, doc. What can we do?
Look the hell around! Almost two dozen coma patients waking up at once.
More than one has mentioned a connection to our favorite off-limits girl, Elle. I can't deal with this metaphysical crap right now, I'm trying to process this medically, so you two, go.
Have a Scooby Snack and fire up the Mystery Machine.
Girlfriend, you better stay in this old lady, 'cause you're ***never*** gonna believe the shit falling left and right.
She says to her best friend, who is literally spread out all over the hospital.
We're fucked.
I got this. Check with the others.
Jo, I--
Elle, you really in there?
Parts? Scattered is the best way I can describe il.
Biggest understatement ever.

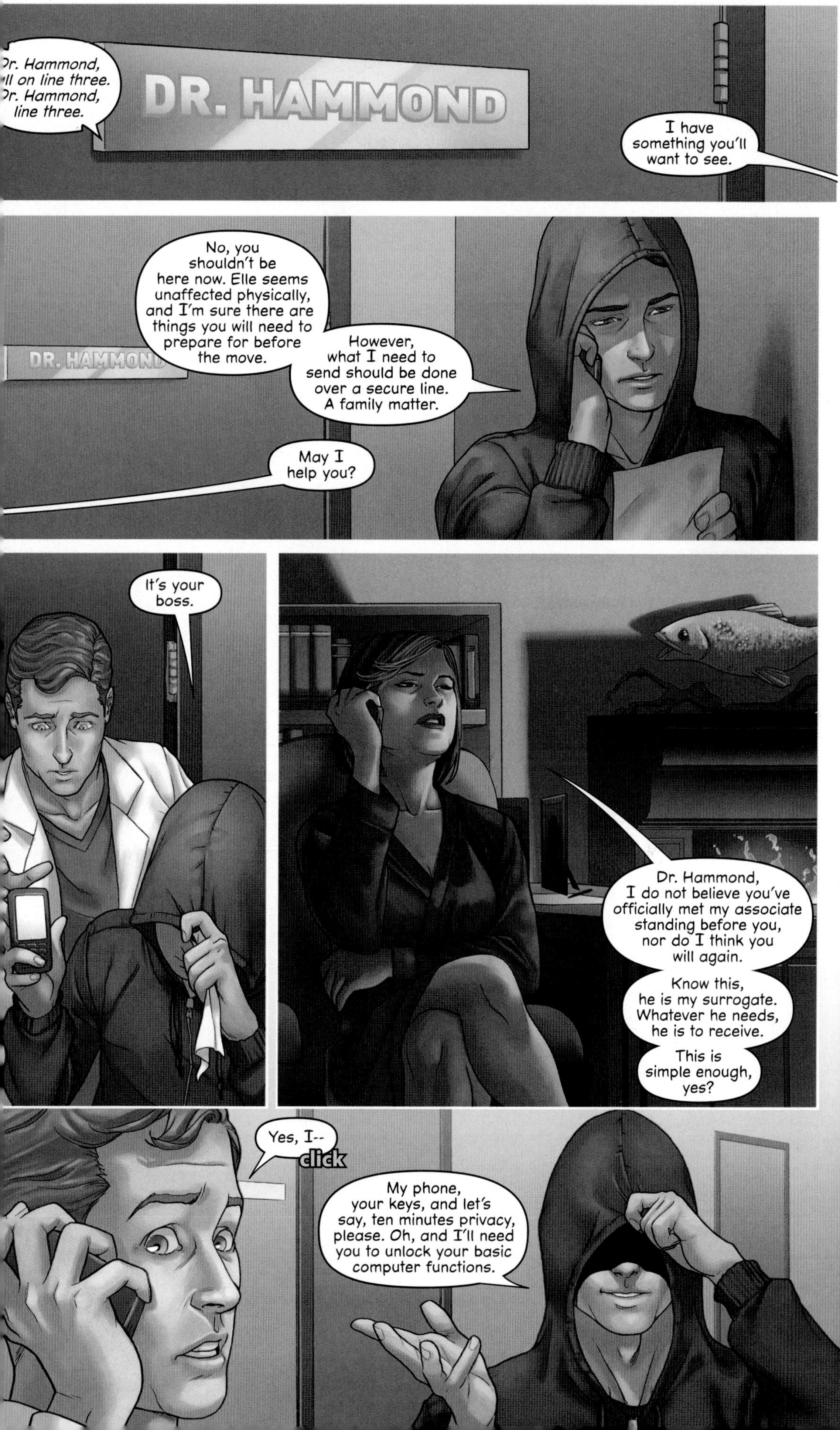

Dr. Hammond, call on line three. Dr. Hammond, line three.
DR. HAMMOND
I have something you'll want to see.
No, you shouldn't be here now. Elle seems unaffected physically, and I'm sure there are things you will need to prepare for before the move.
DR. HAMMOND
However, what I need to send should be done over a secure line. A family matter.
May I help you?
It's your boss.
Dr. Hammond, I do not believe you've officially met my associate standing before you, nor do I think you will again.
Know this, he is my surrogate. Whatever he needs, he is to receive.
This is simple enough, yes?
Yes, I--
click
My phone, your keys, and let's say, ten minutes privacy, please. Oh, and I'll need you to unlock your basic computer functions.

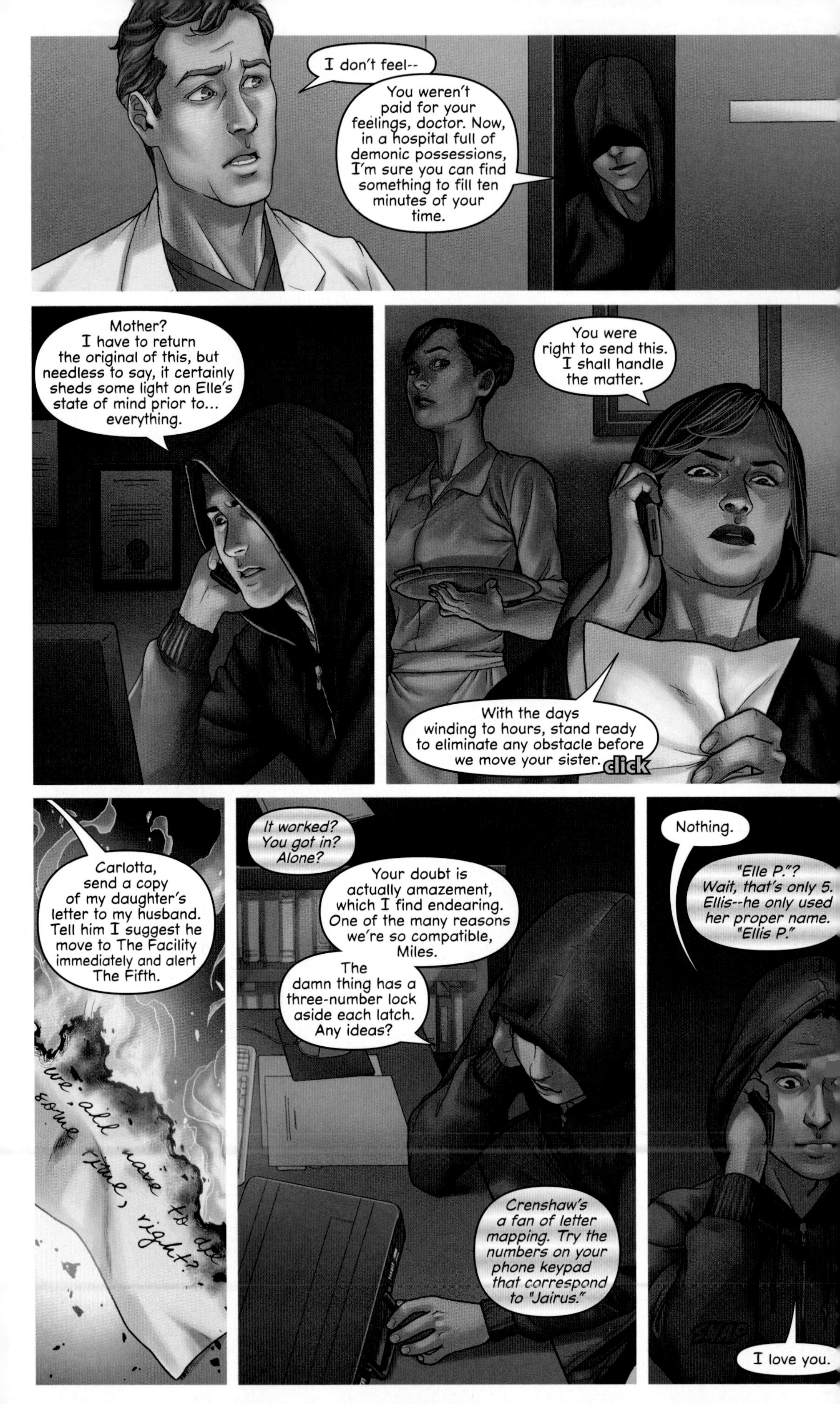

I don't feel--
You weren't paid for your feelings, doctor. Now, in a hospital full of demonic possessions, I'm sure you can find something to fill ten minutes of your time.
Mother? I have to return the original of this, but needless to say, it certainly sheds some light on Elle's state of mind prior to... everything.
You were right to send this. I shall handle the matter.
With the days winding to hours, stand ready to eliminate any obstacle before we move your sister.
click
Carlotta, send a copy of my daughter's letter to my husband. Tell him I suggest he move to The Facility immediately and alert The Fifth.
we all have to die some time, right?
It worked? You got in? Alone?
Your doubt is actually amazement, which I find endearing. One of the many reasons we're so compatible, Miles.
The damn thing has a three-number lock aside each latch. Any ideas?
Crenshaw's a fan of letter mapping. Try the numbers on your phone keypad that correspond to "Jairus."
Nothing.
"Elle P."? Wait, that's only 5. Ellis--he only used her proper name. "Ellis P."
I love you.

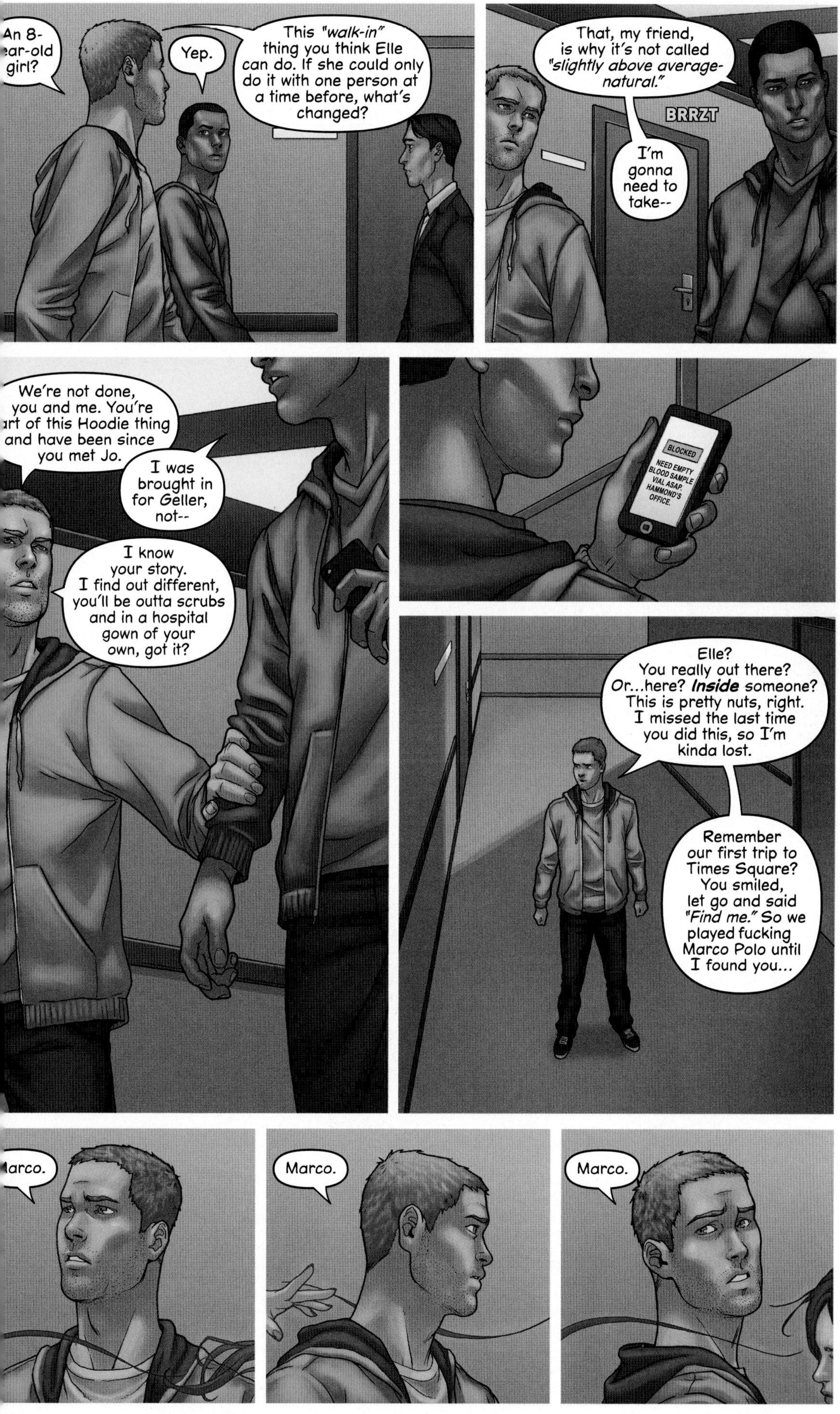
An 8-
ear-old
girl?
Yep.
This "walk-in" thing you think Elle can do. If she could only do it with one person at a time before, what's changed?
That, my friend, is why it's not called "slightly above average-natural."
BRRZT
I'm gonna need to take--
We're not done, you and me. You're art of this Hoodie thing and have been since you met Jo.
I was brought in for Geller, not--
I know your story. I find out different, you'll be outta scrubs and in a hospital gown of your own, got it?
BLOCKED
NEED EMPTY BLOOD SAMPLE VIAL ASAP. HAMMOND'S OFFICE.
Elle? You really out there? Or...here? *Inside* someone? This is pretty nuts, right. I missed the last time you did this, so I'm kinda lost.
Remember our first trip to Times Square? You smiled, let go and said "Find me." So we played fucking Marco Polo until I found you...
arco.
Marco.
Marco.

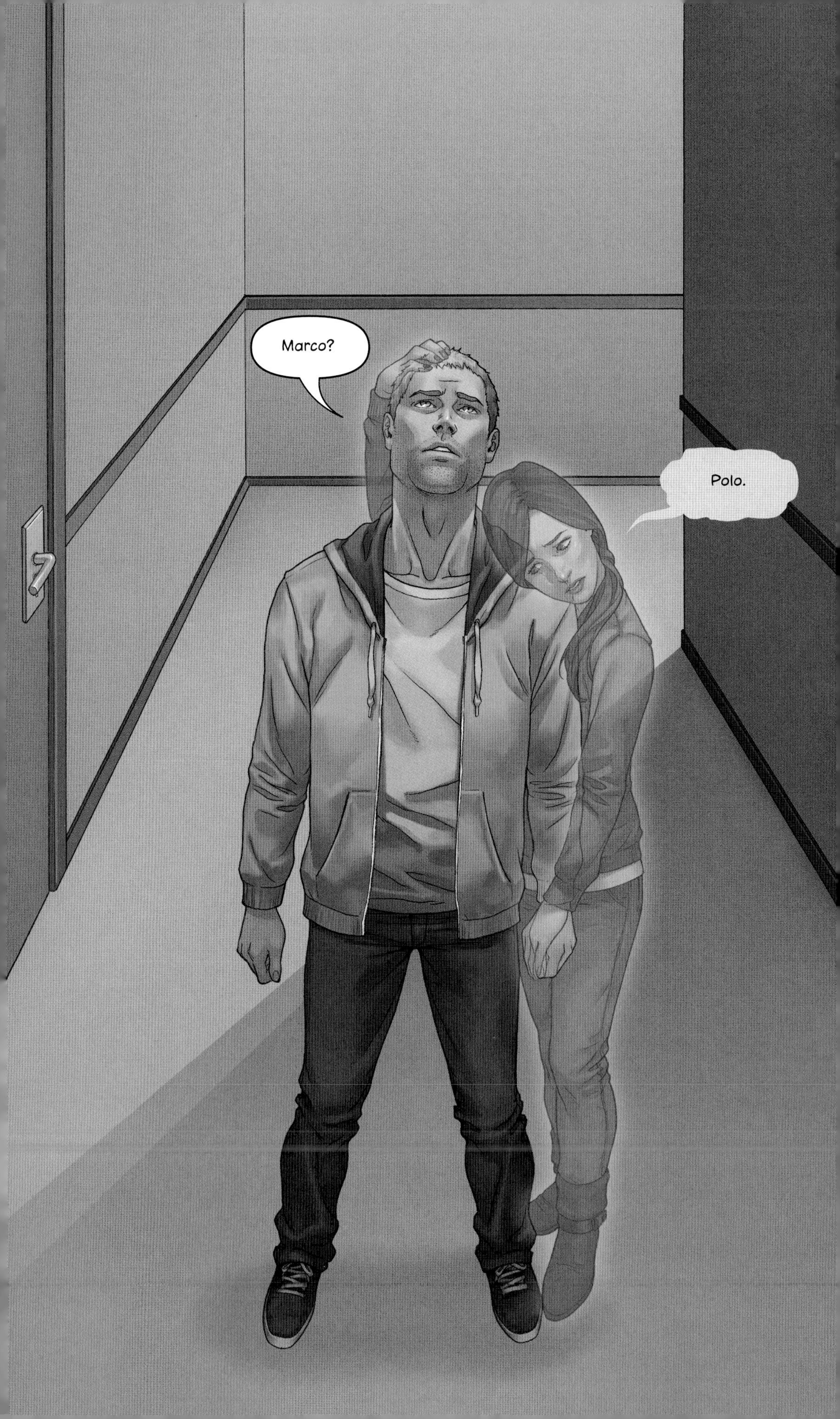
Marco?
Polo.

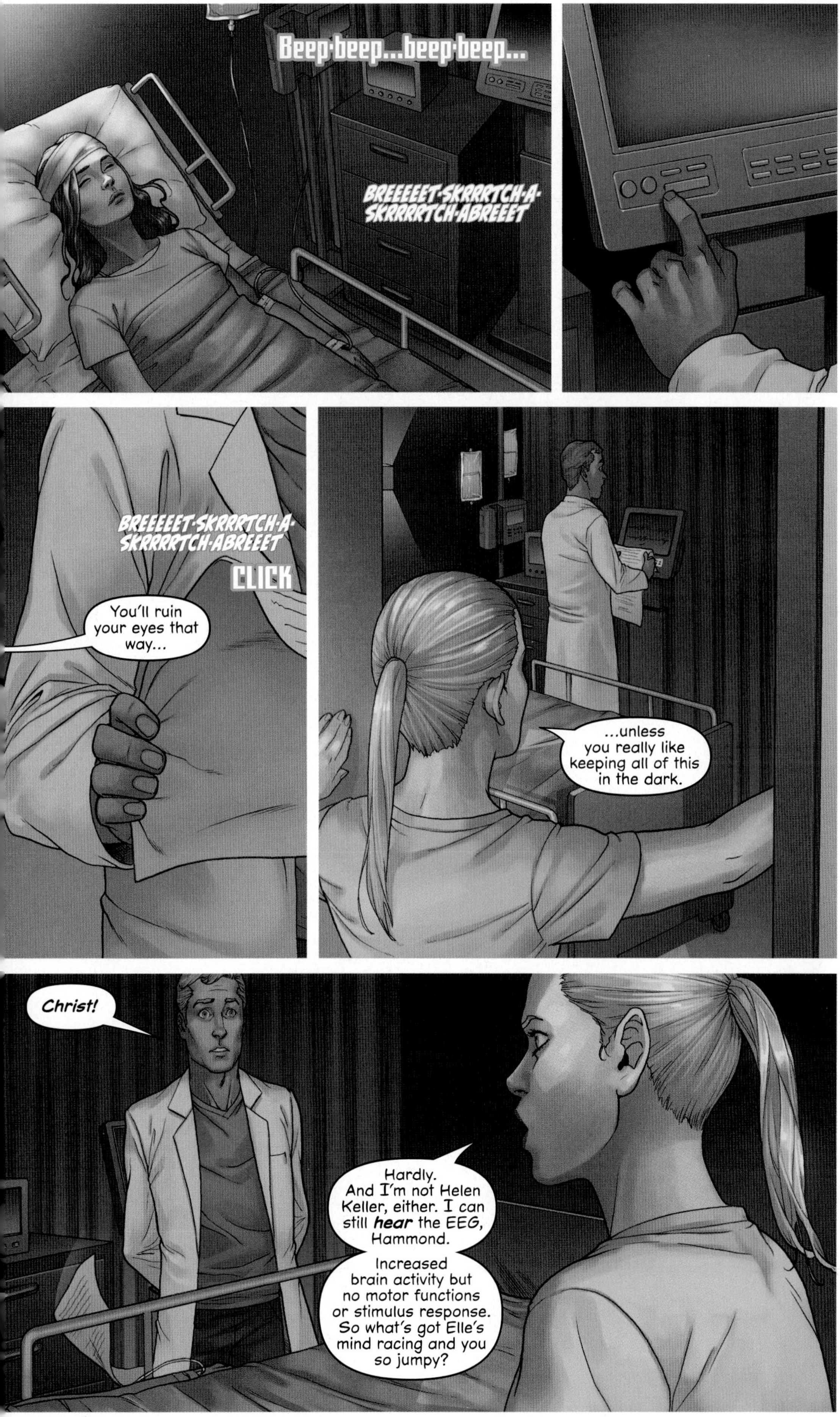
Beep·beep...beep·beep...
BREEEEET·SKRRRTCH·A·SKRRRRTCH·ABREEET
BREEEEET·SKRRRTCH·A·SKRRRRTCH·ABREEET
CLICK
You'll ruin your eyes that way...
...unless you really like keeping all of this in the dark.
Christ!
Hardly. And I'm not Helen Keller, either. I can still *hear* the EEG, Hammond.
Increased brain activity but no motor functions or stimulus response. So what's got Elle's mind racing and you so jumpy?

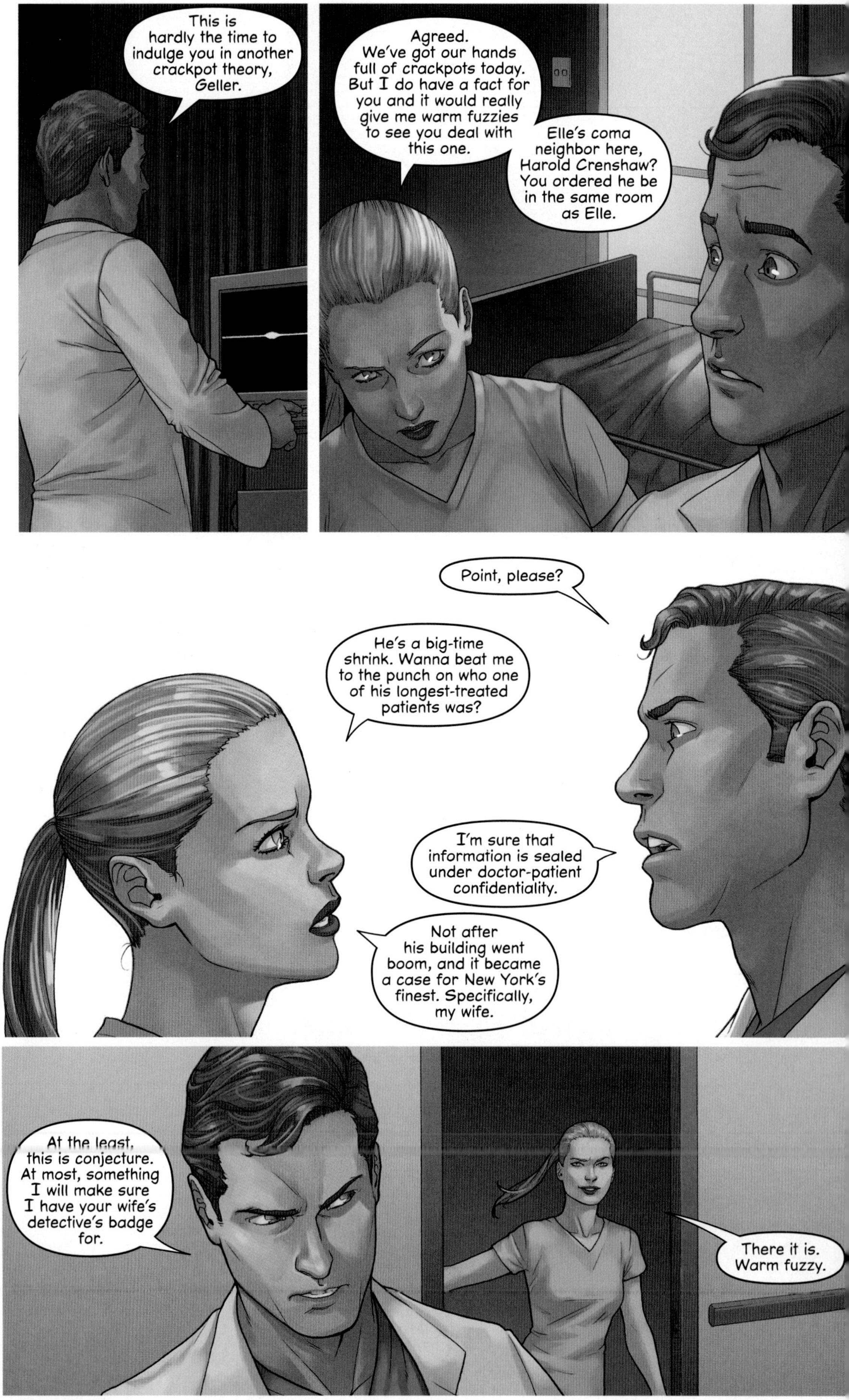
This is hardly the time to indulge you in another crackpot theory, Geller.
Agreed. We've got our hands full of crackpots today. But I do have a fact for you and it would really give me warm fuzzies to see you deal with this one.
Elle's coma neighbor here, Harold Crenshaw? You ordered he be in the same room as Elle.
Point, please?
He's a big-time shrink. Wanna beat me to the punch on who one of his longest-treated patients was?
I'm sure that information is sealed under doctor-patient confidentiality.
Not after his building went boom, and it became a case for New York's finest. Specifically, my wife.
At the least, this is conjecture. At most, something I will make sure I have your wife's detective's badge for.
There it is. Warm fuzzy.

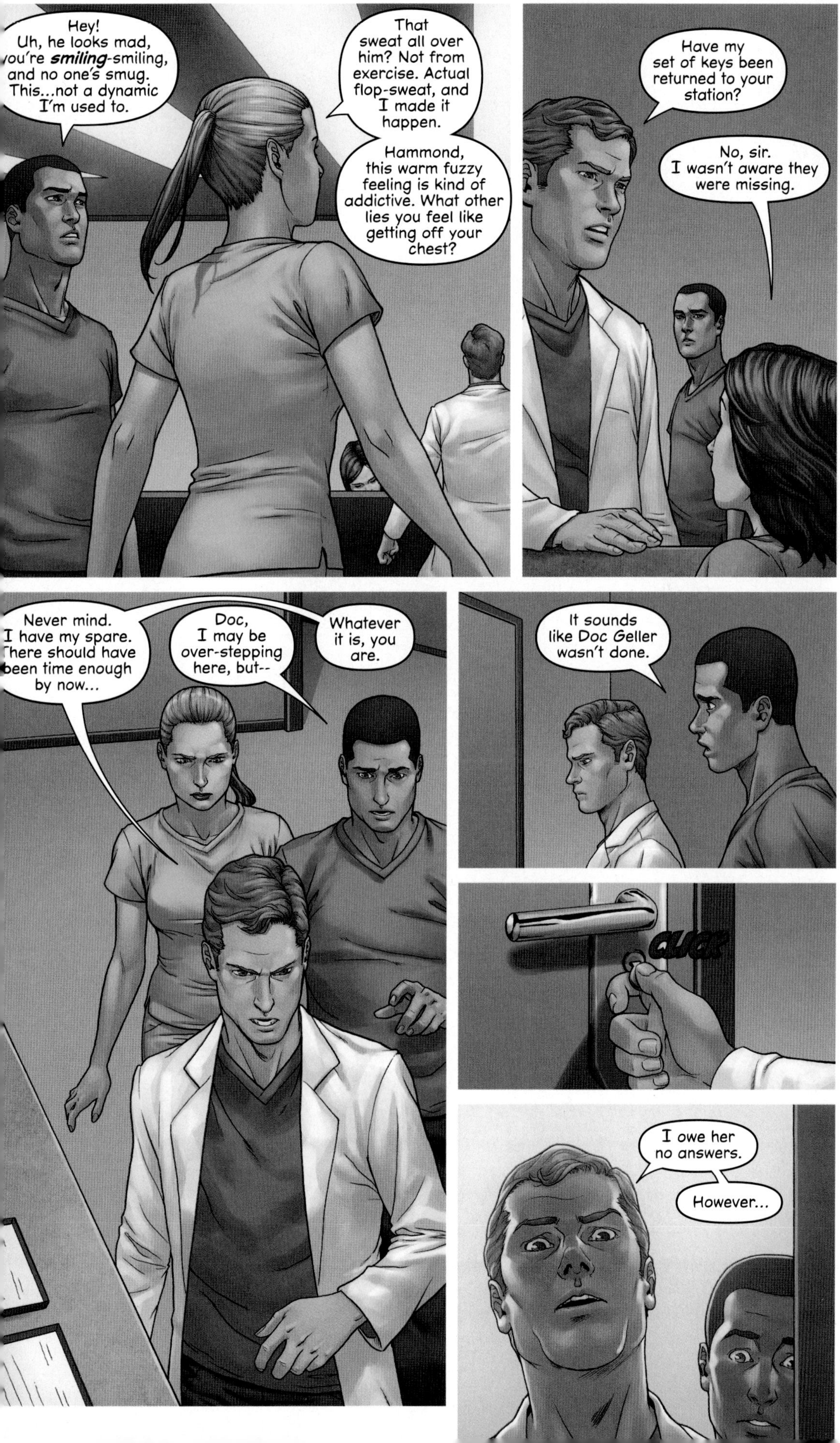

Hey! Uh, he looks mad, you're ***smiling***-smiling, and no one's smug. This...not a dynamic I'm used to.
That sweat all over him? Not from exercise. Actual flop-sweat, and I made it happen.
Hammond, this warm fuzzy feeling is kind of addictive. What other lies you feel like getting off your chest?
Have my set of keys been returned to your station?
No, sir. I wasn't aware they were missing.
Never mind. I have my spare. There should have been time enough by now...
Doc, I may be over-stepping here, but--
Whatever it is, you are.
It sounds like Doc Geller wasn't done.
CLICK
I owe her no answers.
However...

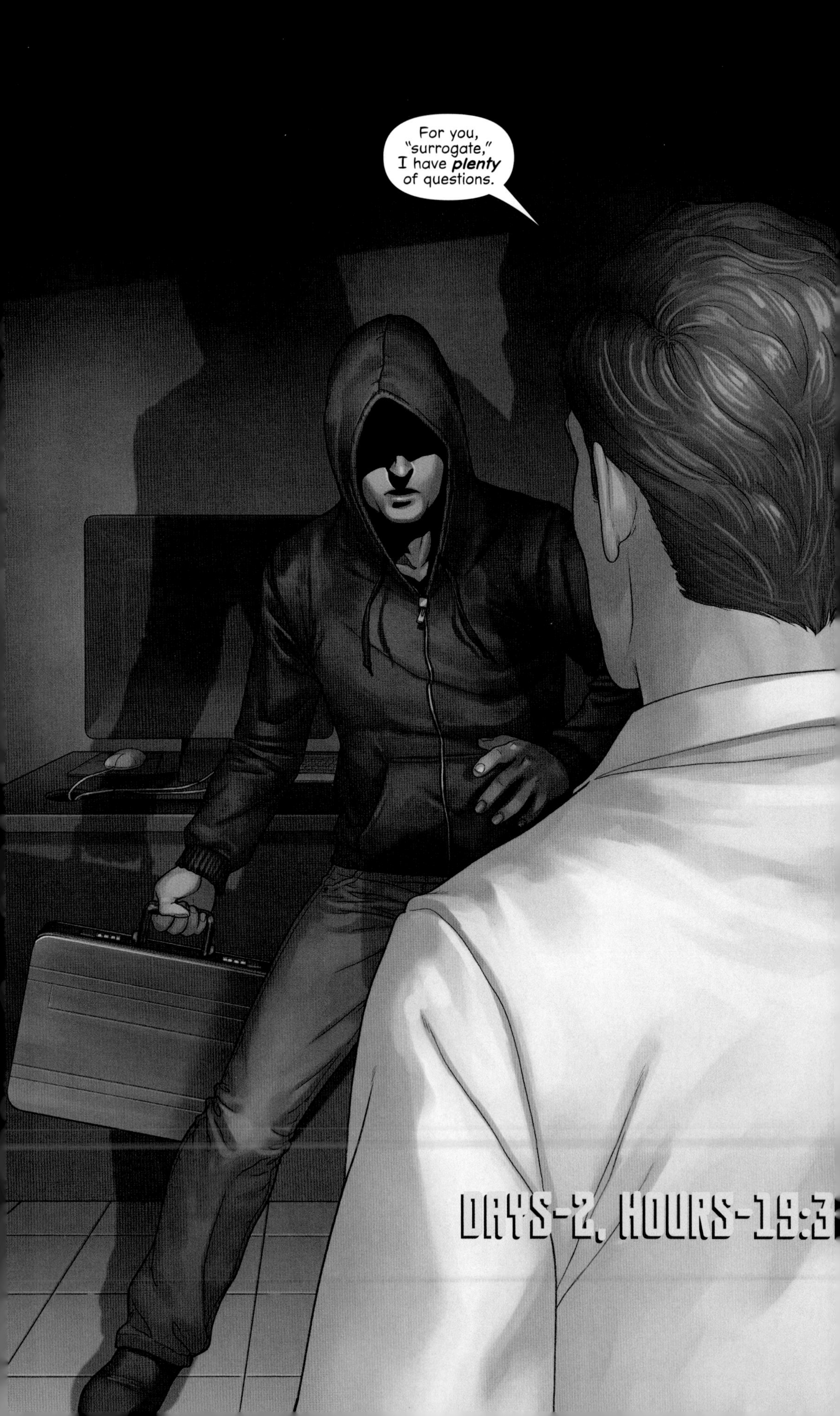
For you, "surrogate," I have ***plenty*** of questions.
DAYS-2, HOURS-19:3

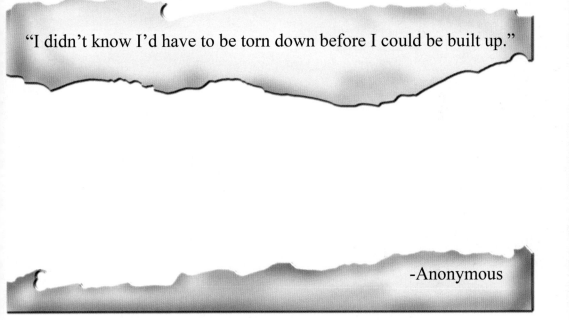

"I didn't know I'd have to be torn down before I could be built up."

-Anonymous

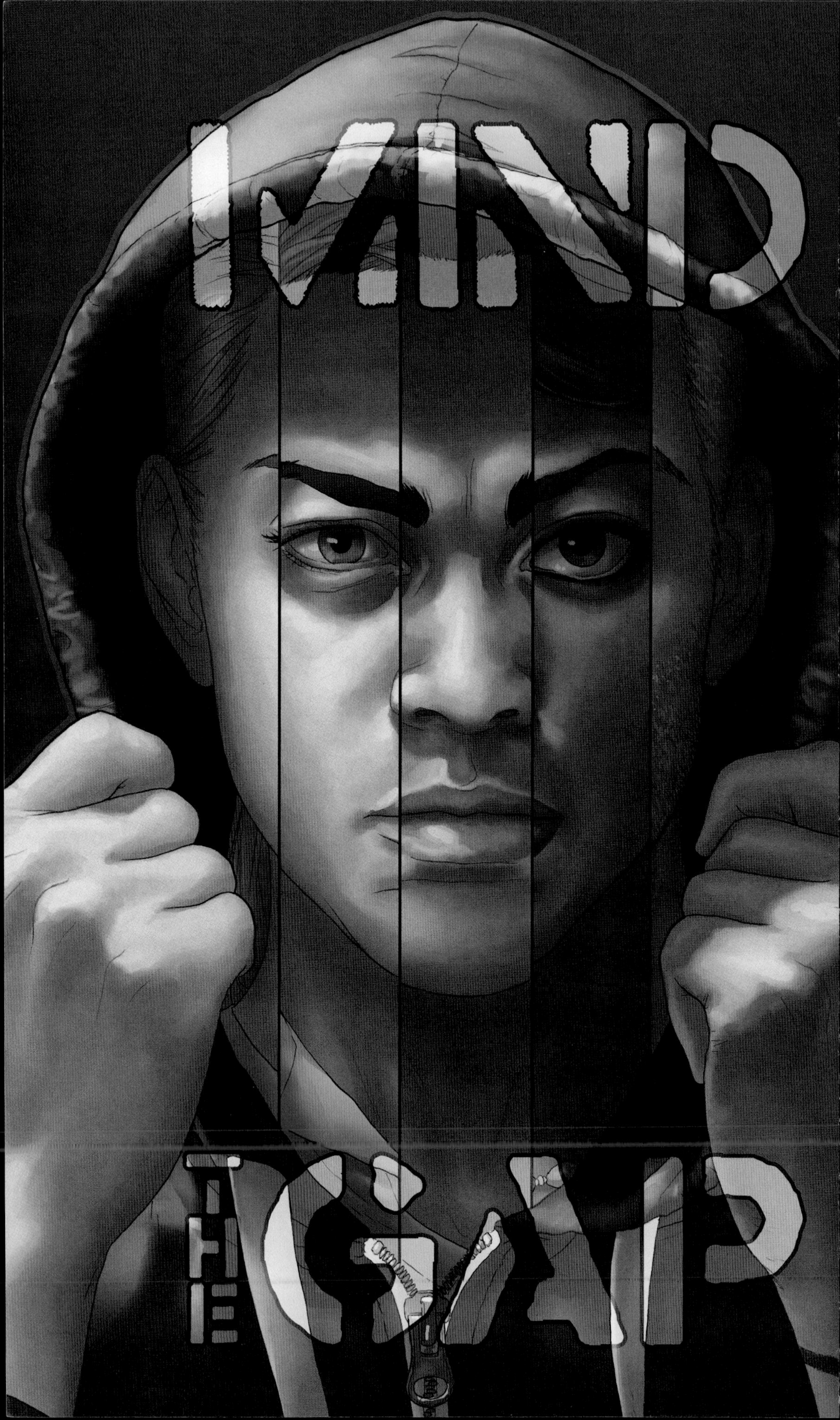
MIND
THE
GAP

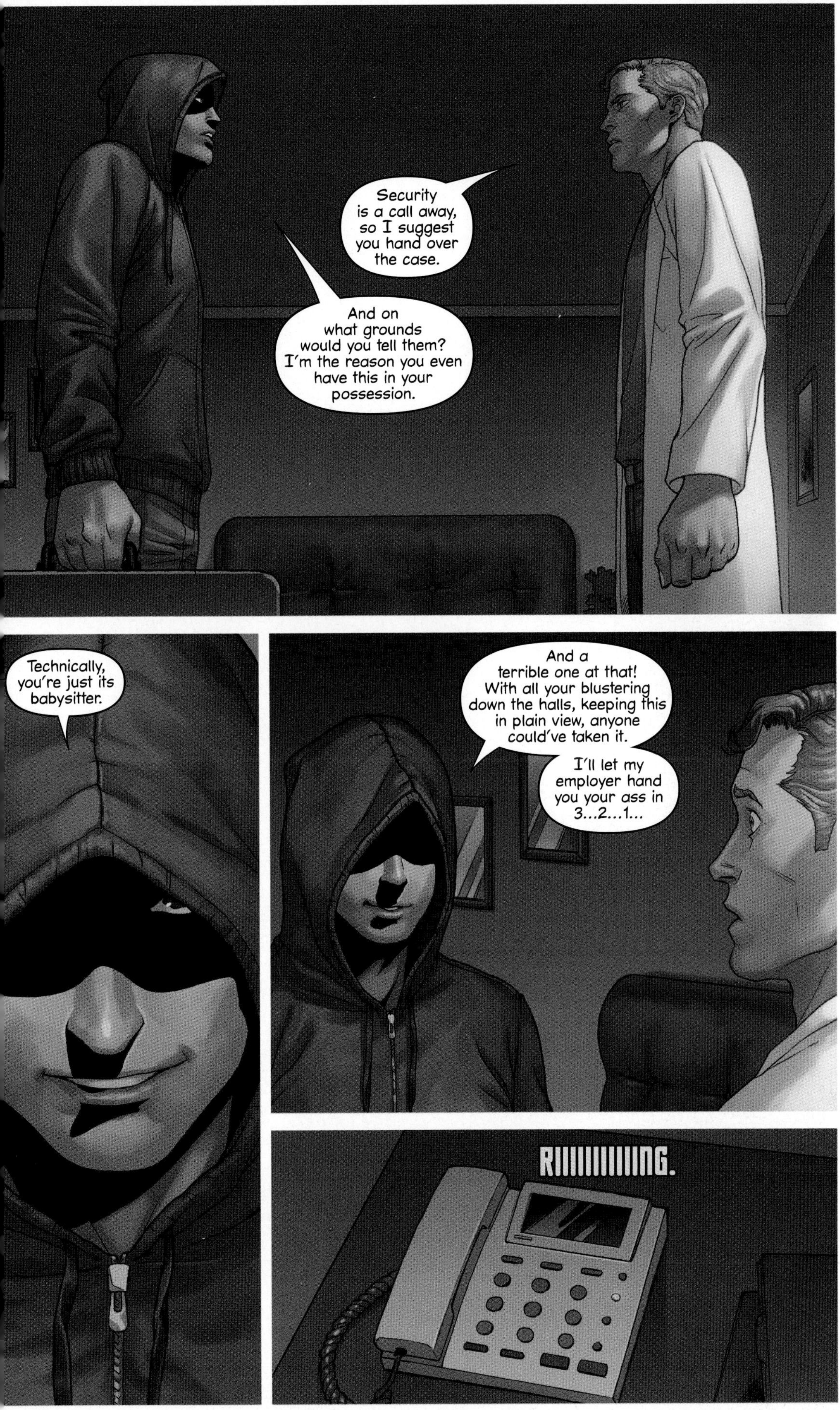
Security is a call away, so I suggest you hand over the case.
And on what grounds would you tell them? I'm the reason you even have this in your possession.
Technically, you're just its babysitter.
And a terrible one at that! With all your blustering down the halls, keeping this in plain view, anyone could've taken it.
I'll let my employer hand you your ass in 3...2...1...
RIIIIIIIIIIING.

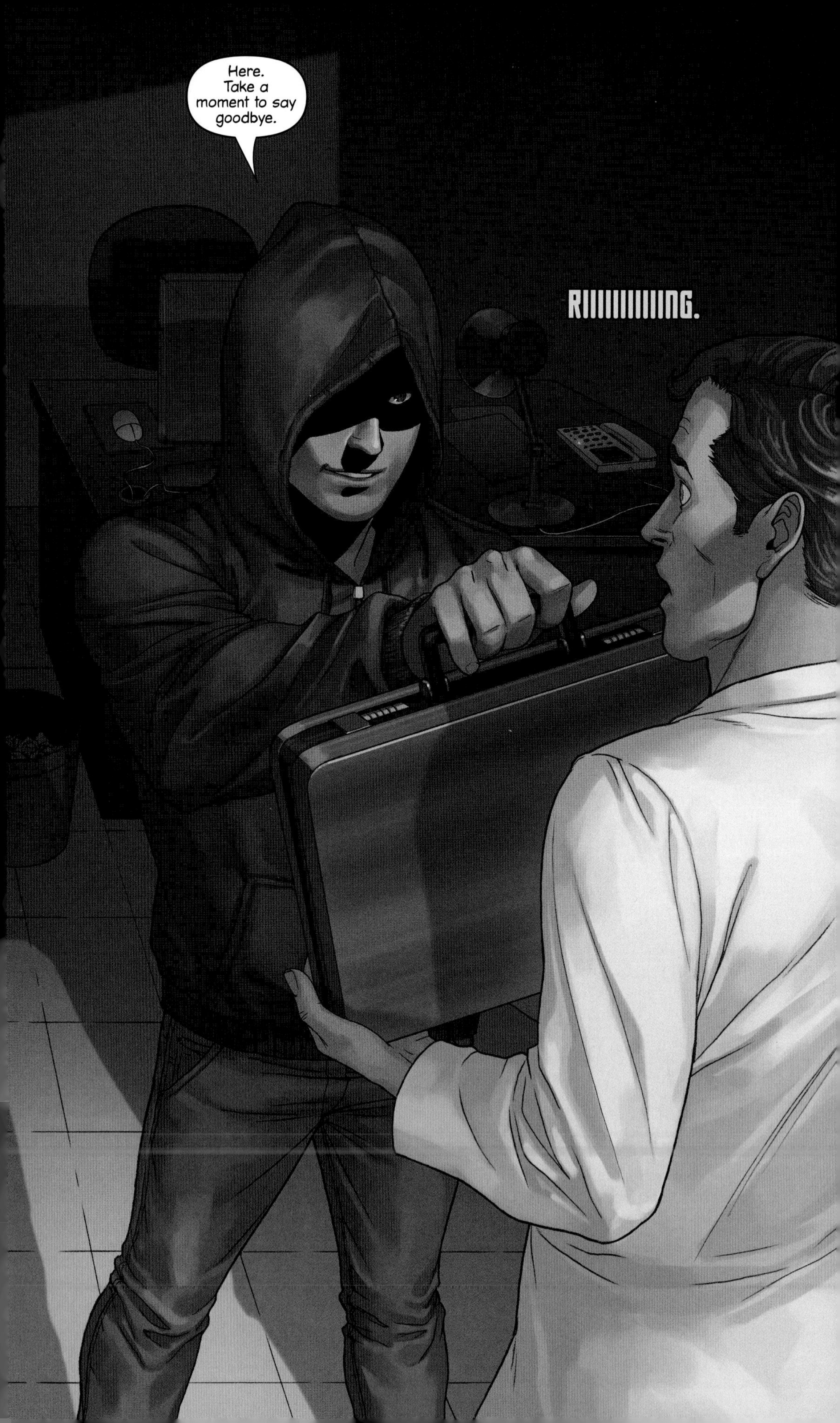
Here. Take a moment to say goodbye.
RIIIIIIIIIING.

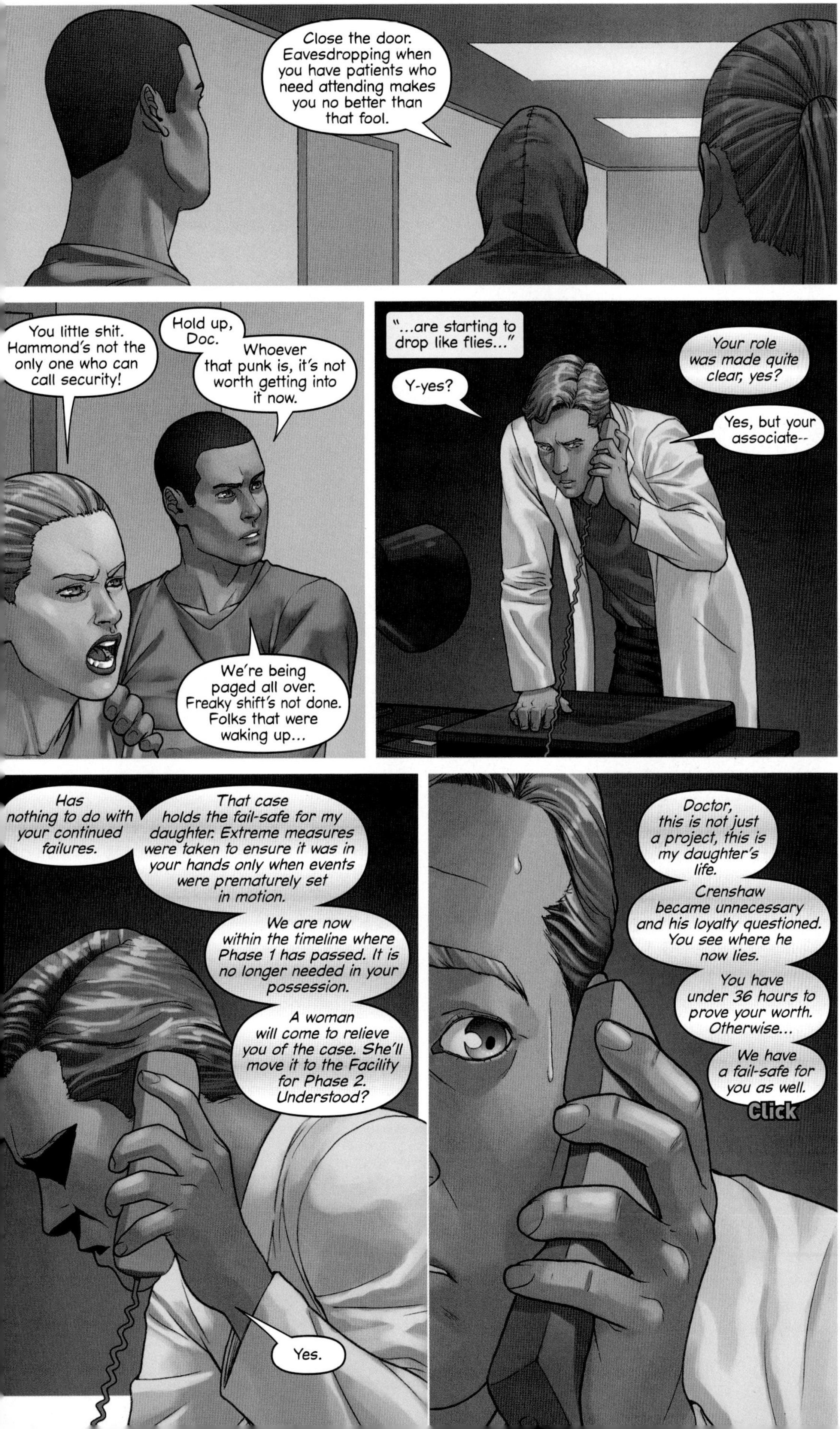
Close the door. Eavesdropping when you have patients who need attending makes you no better than that fool.
You little shit. Hammond's not the only one who can call security!
Hold up, Doc.
Whoever that punk is, it's not worth getting into it now.
We're being paged all over. Freaky shift's not done. Folks that were waking up...
"...are starting to drop like flies..."
Y-yes?
Your role was made quite clear, yes?
Yes, but your associate--
Has nothing to do with your continued failures.
That case holds the fail-safe for my daughter. Extreme measures were taken to ensure it was in your hands only when events were prematurely set in motion.
We are now within the timeline where Phase 1 has passed. It is no longer needed in your possession.
A woman will come to relieve you of the case. She'll move it to the Facility for Phase 2. Understood?
Yes.
Doctor, this is not just a project, this is my daughter's life.
Crenshaw became unnecessary and his loyalty questioned. You see where he now lies.
You have under 36 hours to prove your worth. Otherwise...
We have a fail-safe for you as well.
Click

OUT OF BODIES
PART 2
"SOME OF ITS PARTS"

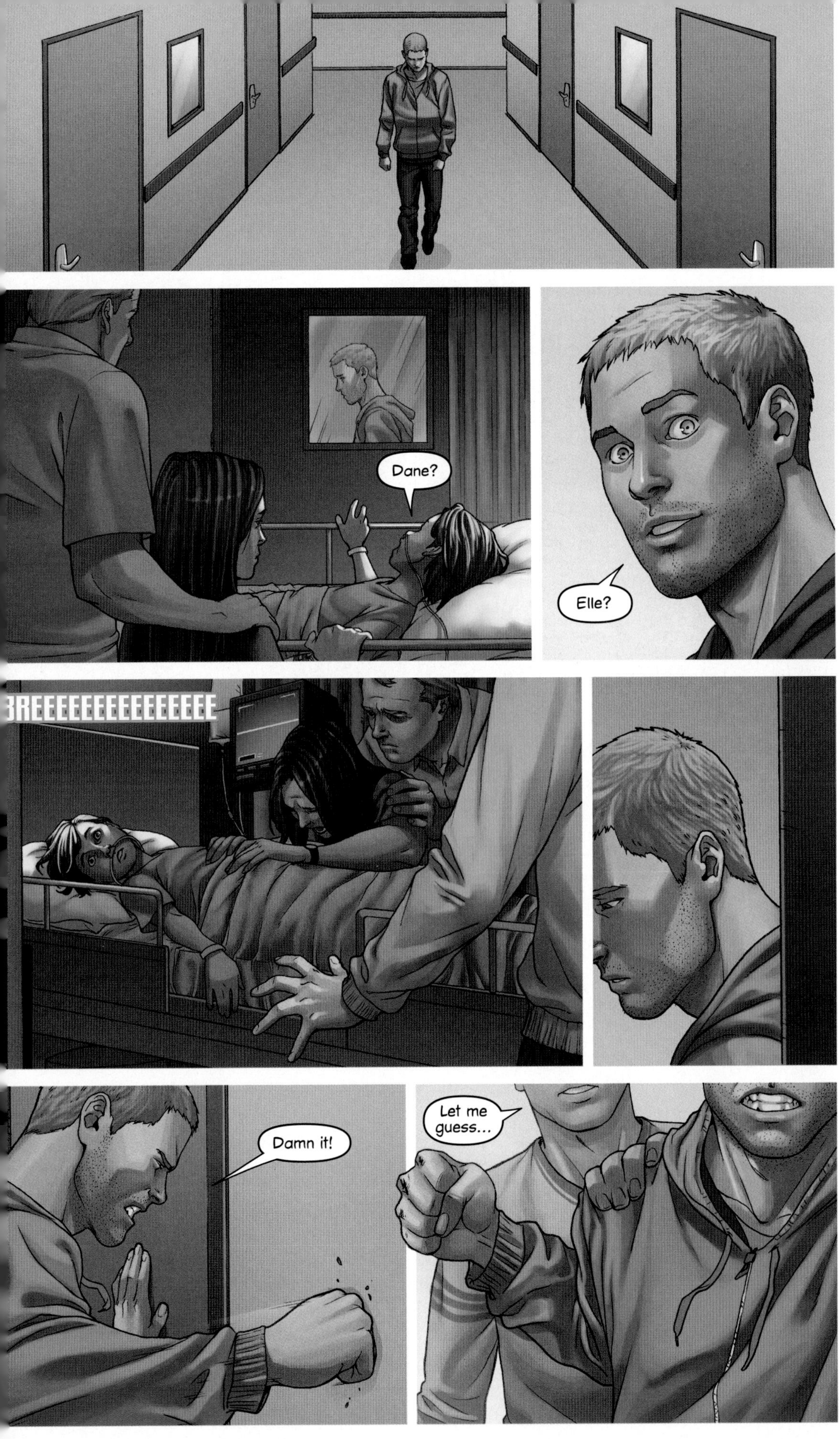

Dane?
Elle?
BREEEEEEEEEEEEEEE
Damn it!
Let me guess...

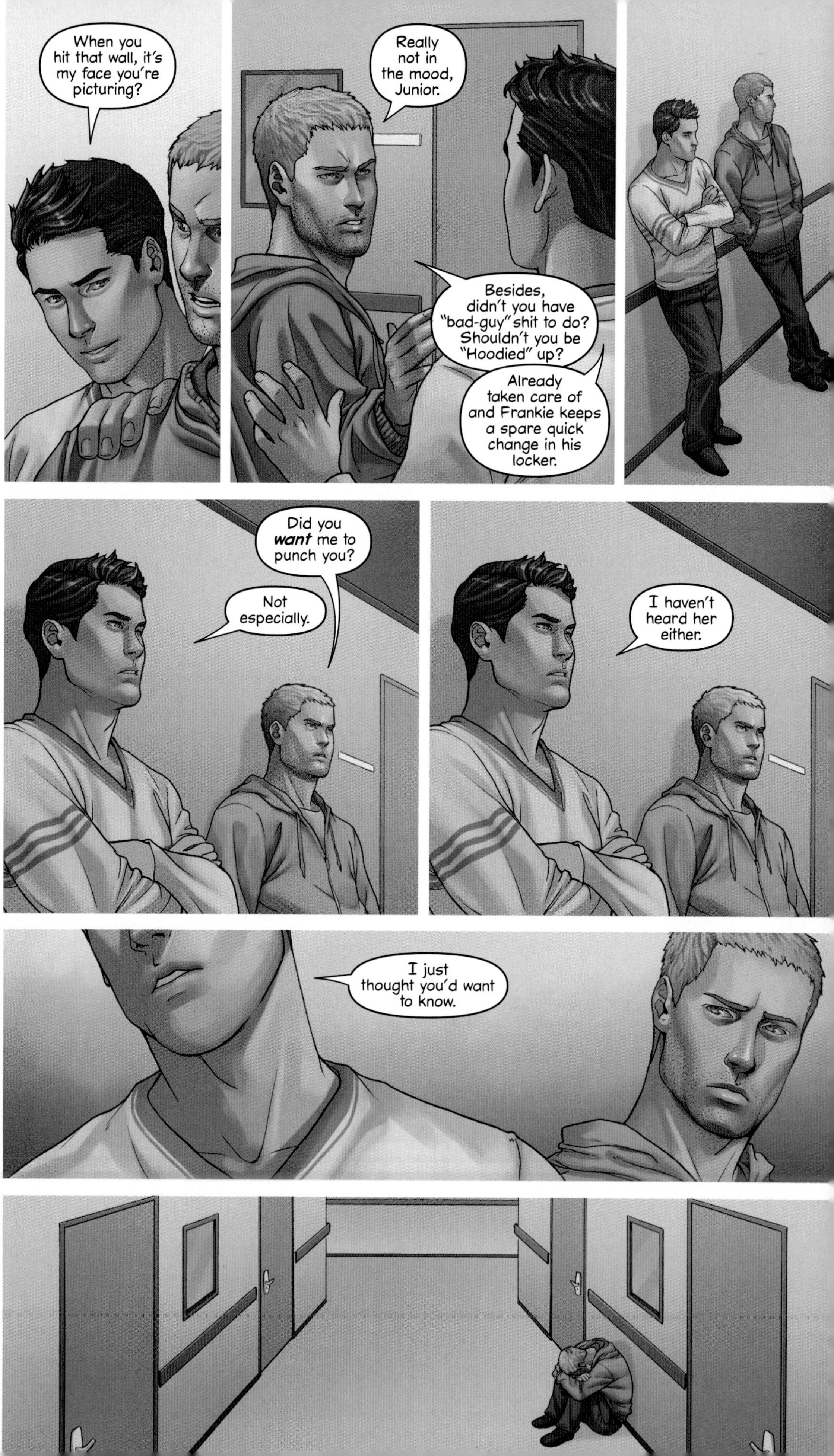

When you hit that wall, it's my face you're picturing?
Really not in the mood, Junior.
Besides, didn't you have "bad-guy" shit to do? Shouldn't you be "Hoodied" up?
Already taken care of and Frankie keeps a spare quick change in his locker.
Did you *want* me to punch you?
Not especially.
I haven't heard her either.
I just thought you'd want to know.

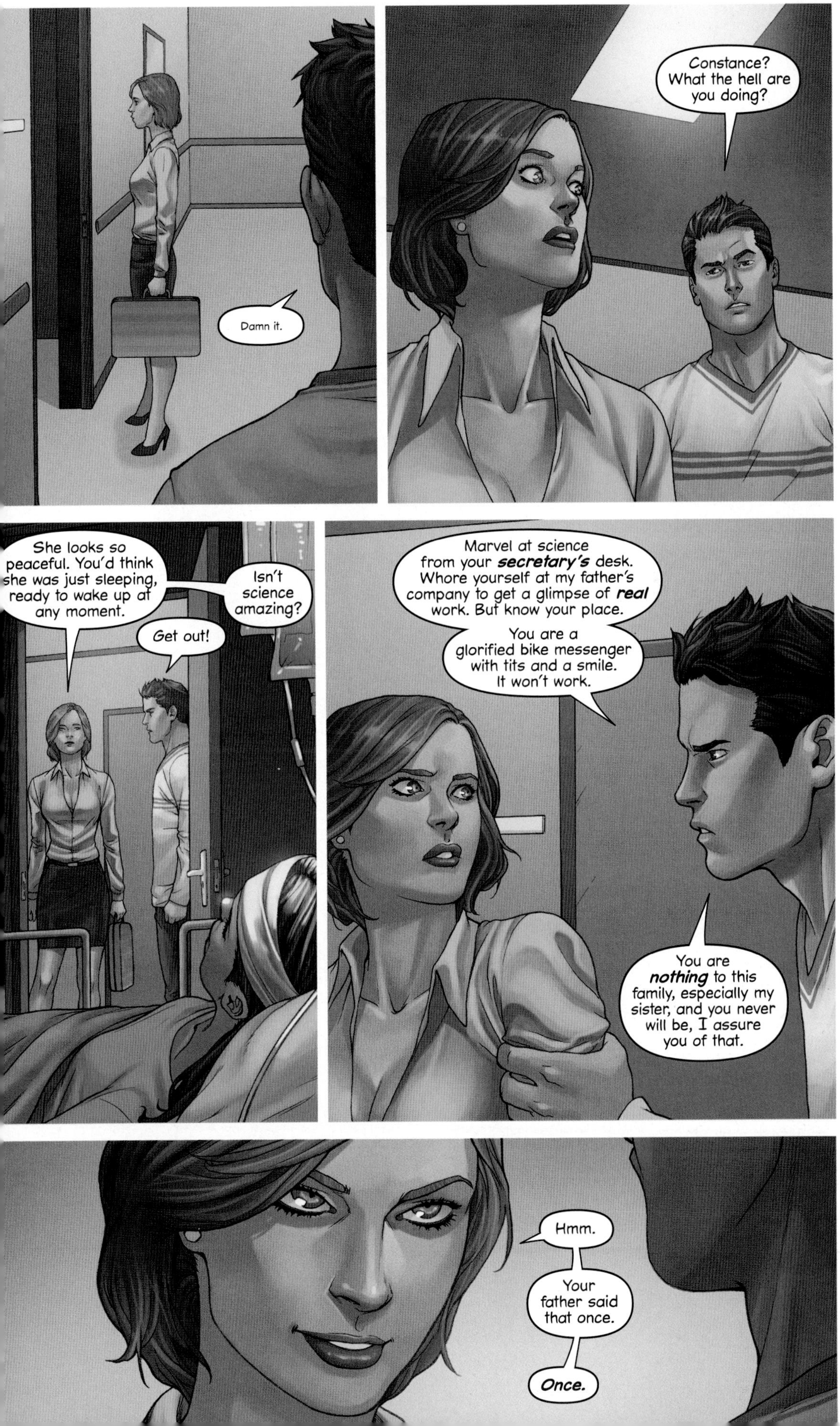
Damn it.
Constance? What the hell are you doing?
She looks so peaceful. You'd think she was just sleeping, ready to wake up at any moment.
Isn't science amazing?
Get out!
Marvel at science from your ***secretary's*** desk. Whore yourself at my father's company to get a glimpse of ***real*** work. But know your place.
You are a glorified bike messenger with tits and a smile. It won't work.
You are ***nothing*** to this family, especially my sister, and you never will be, I assure you of that.
Hmm.
Your father said that once.
Once.

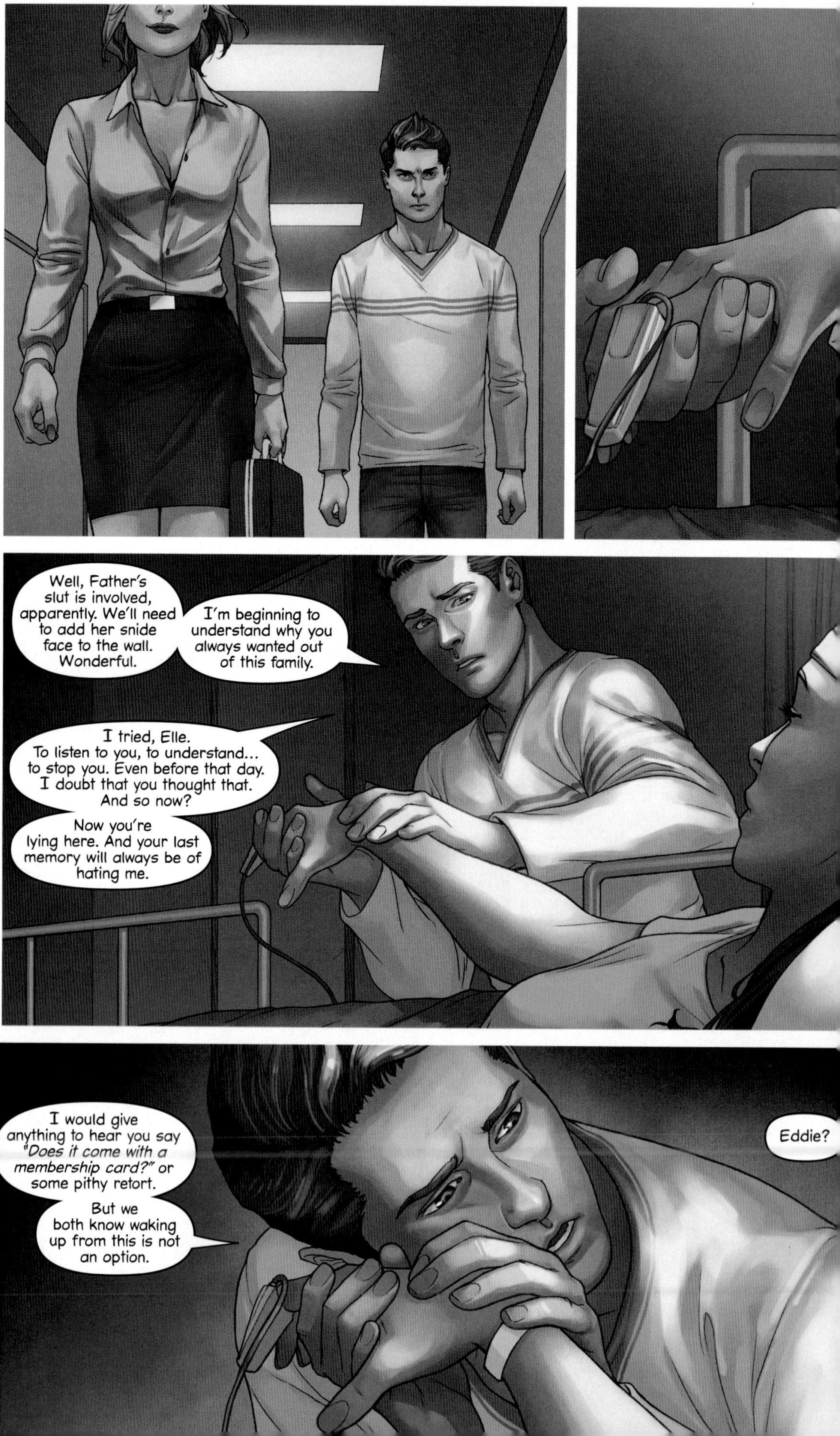
Well, Father's slut is involved, apparently. We'll need to add her snide face to the wall. Wonderful.
I'm beginning to understand why you always wanted out of this family.
I tried, Elle. To listen to you, to understand... to stop you. Even before that day. I doubt that you thought that. And so now?
Now you're lying here. And your last memory will always be of hating me.
I would give anything to hear you say *"Does it come with a membership card?"* or some pithy retort.
But we both know waking up from this is not an option.
Eddie?

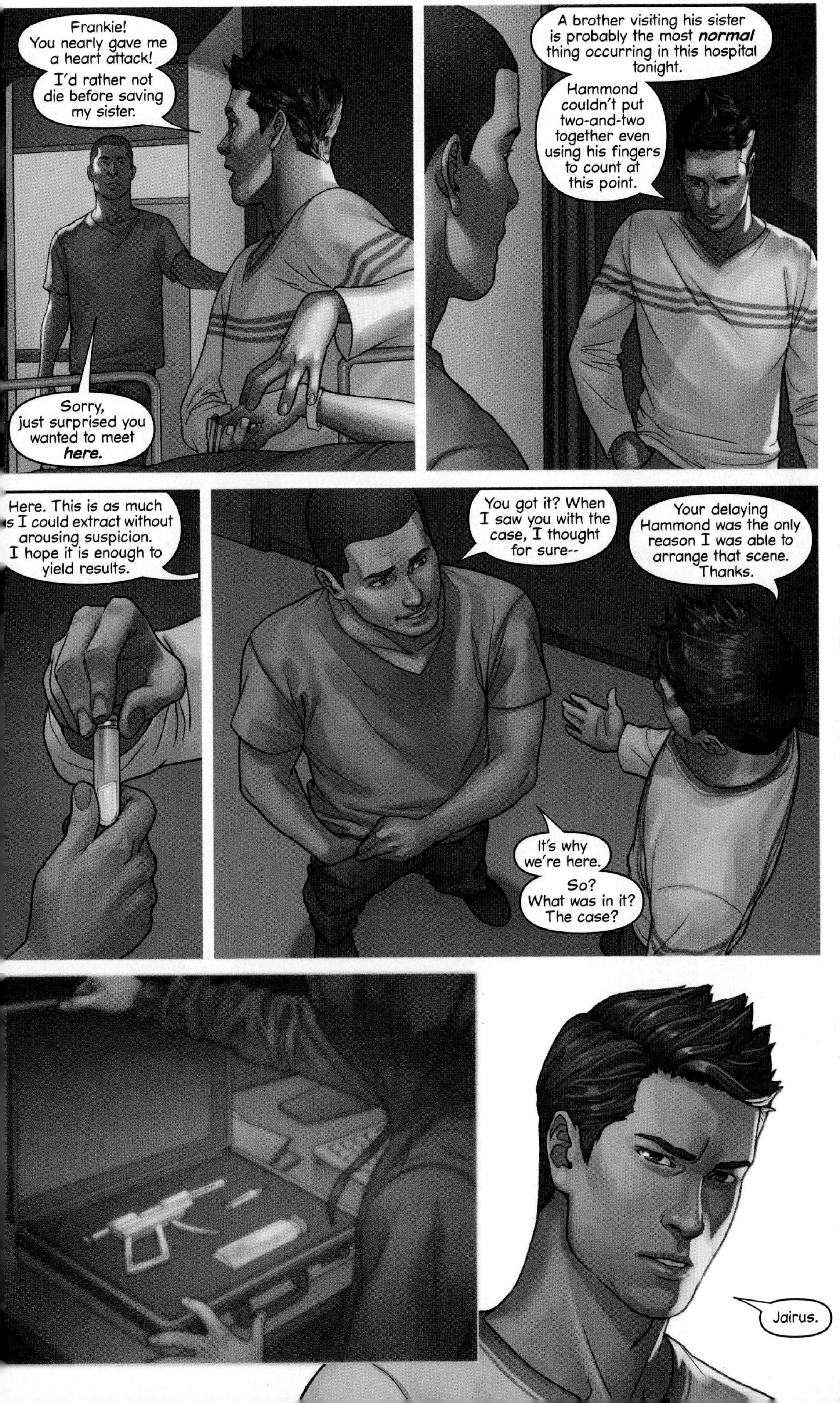
Frankie! You nearly gave me a heart attack!
I'd rather not die before saving my sister.
Sorry, just surprised you wanted to meet **here.**
A brother visiting his sister is probably the most **normal** thing occurring in this hospital tonight.
Hammond couldn't put two-and-two together even using his fingers to count at this point.
Here. This is as much as I could extract without arousing suspicion. I hope it is enough to yield results.
You got it? When I saw you with the case, I thought for sure--
Your delaying Hammond was the only reason I was able to arrange that scene. Thanks.
It's why we're here.
So? What was in it? The case?
Jairus.

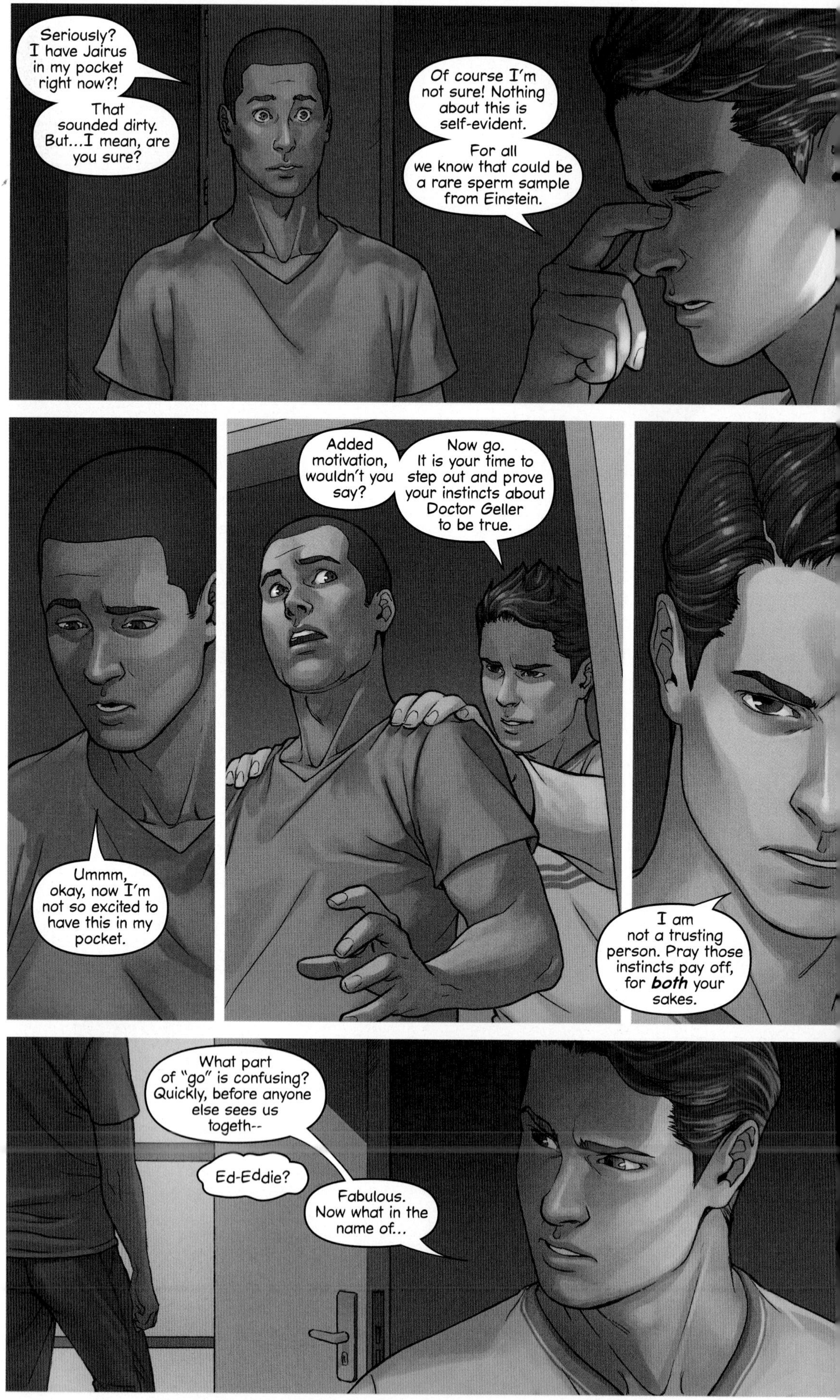
Seriously? I have Jairus in my pocket right now?!
That sounded dirty. But...I mean, are you sure?
Of course I'm not sure! Nothing about this is self-evident.
For all we know that could be a rare sperm sample from Einstein.
Ummm, okay, now I'm not so excited to have this in my pocket.
Added motivation, wouldn't you say?
Now go. It is your time to step out and prove your instincts about Doctor Geller to be true.
I am not a trusting person. Pray those instincts pay off, for ***both*** your sakes.
What part of "go" is confusing? Quickly, before anyone else sees us togeth--
Ed-Eddie?
Fabulous. Now what in the name of...

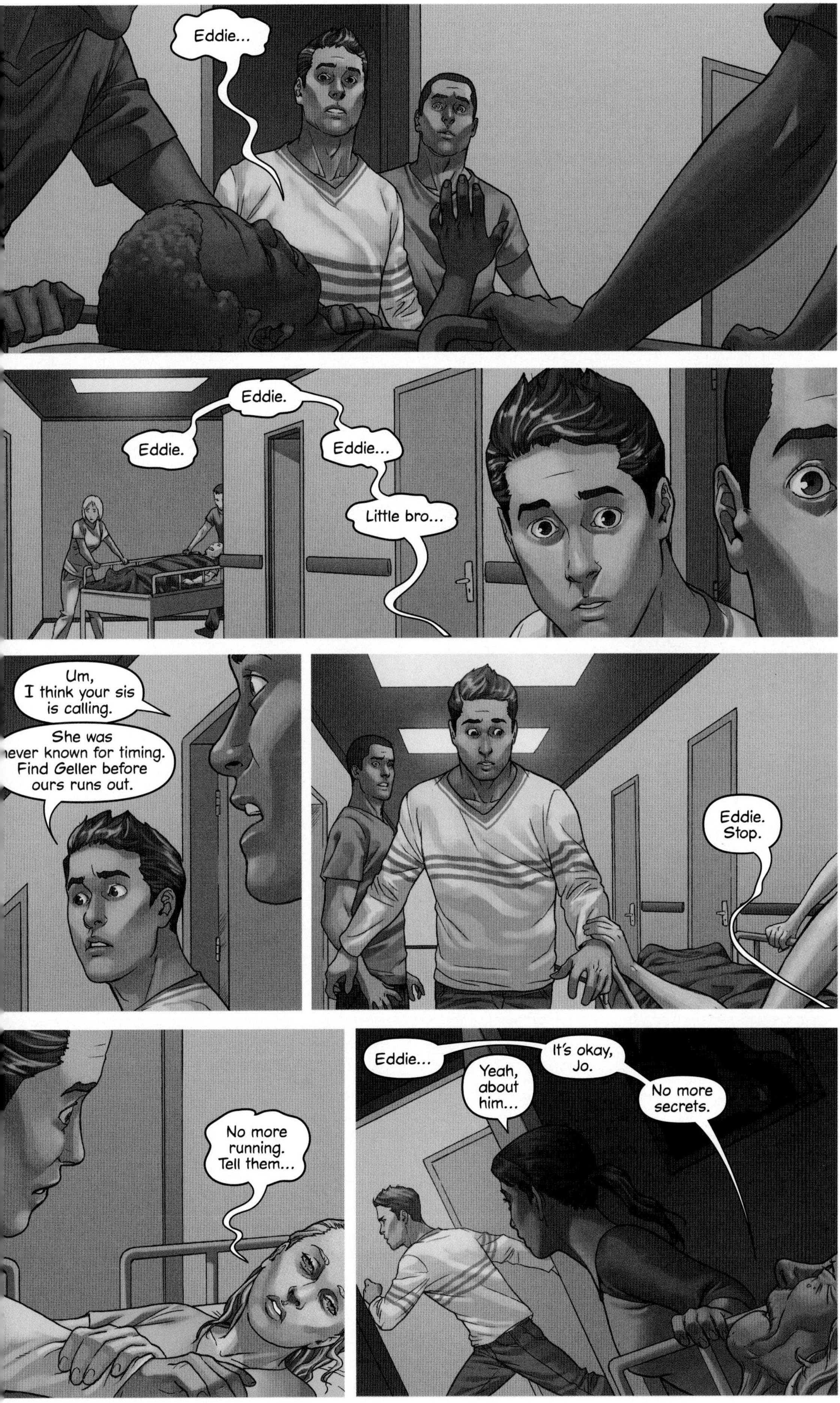
Eddie...
Eddie.
Eddie.
Eddie...
Little bro...
Um, I think your sis is calling.
She was ever known for timing. Find Geller before ours runs out.
Eddie. Stop.
No more running. Tell them...
Eddie...
It's okay, Jo.
Yeah, about him...
No more secrets.

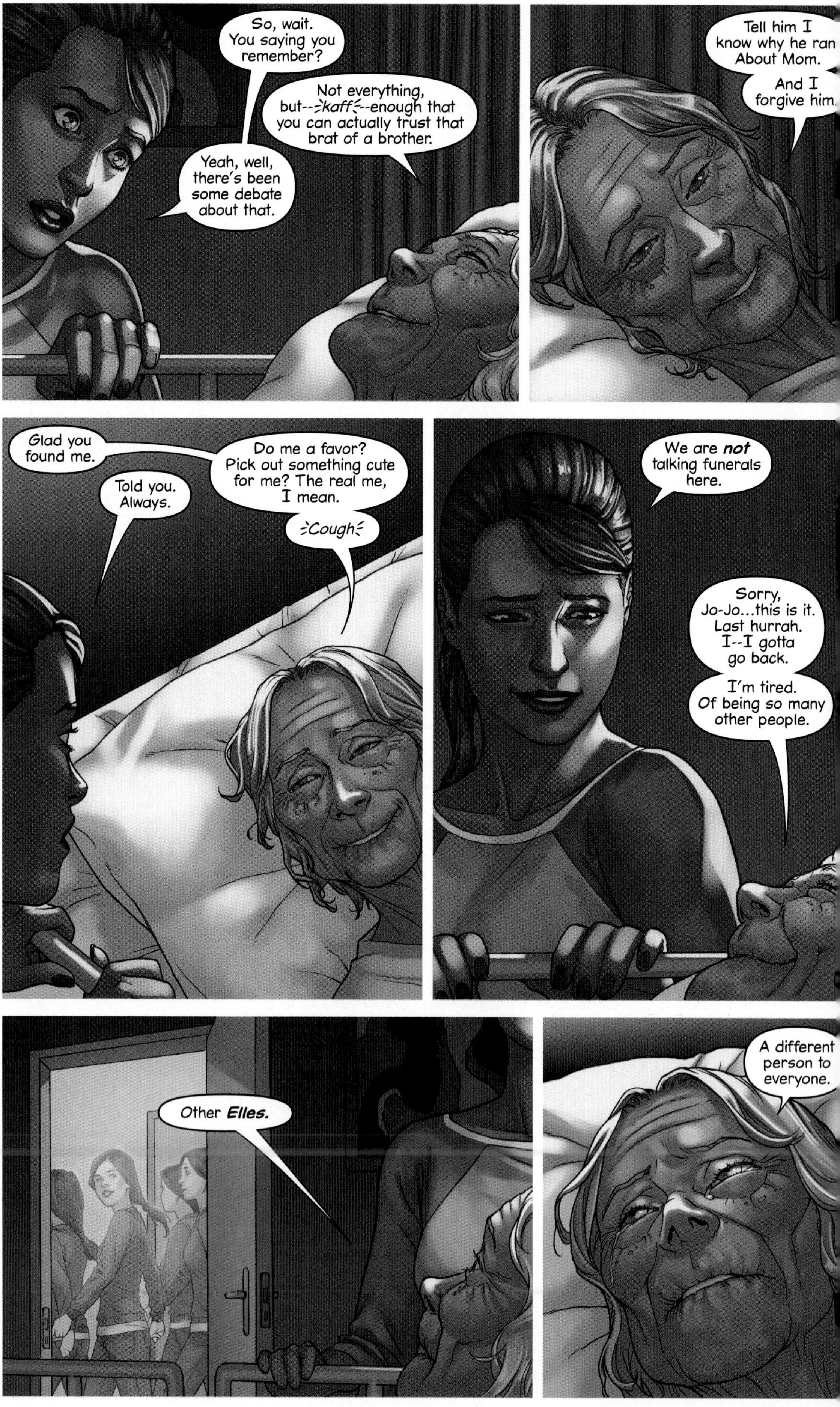
So, wait. You saying you remember?
Not everything, but--kaff--enough that you can actually trust that brat of a brother.
Yeah, well, there's been some debate about that.
Tell him I know why he ran About Mom.
And I forgive him.
Glad you found me.
Do me a favor? Pick out something cute for me? The real me, I mean.
Told you. Always.
Cough
We are *not* talking funerals here.
Sorry, Jo-Jo...this is it. Last hurrah. I--I gotta go back.
I'm tired. Of being so many other people.
Other *Elles.*
A different person to everyone.

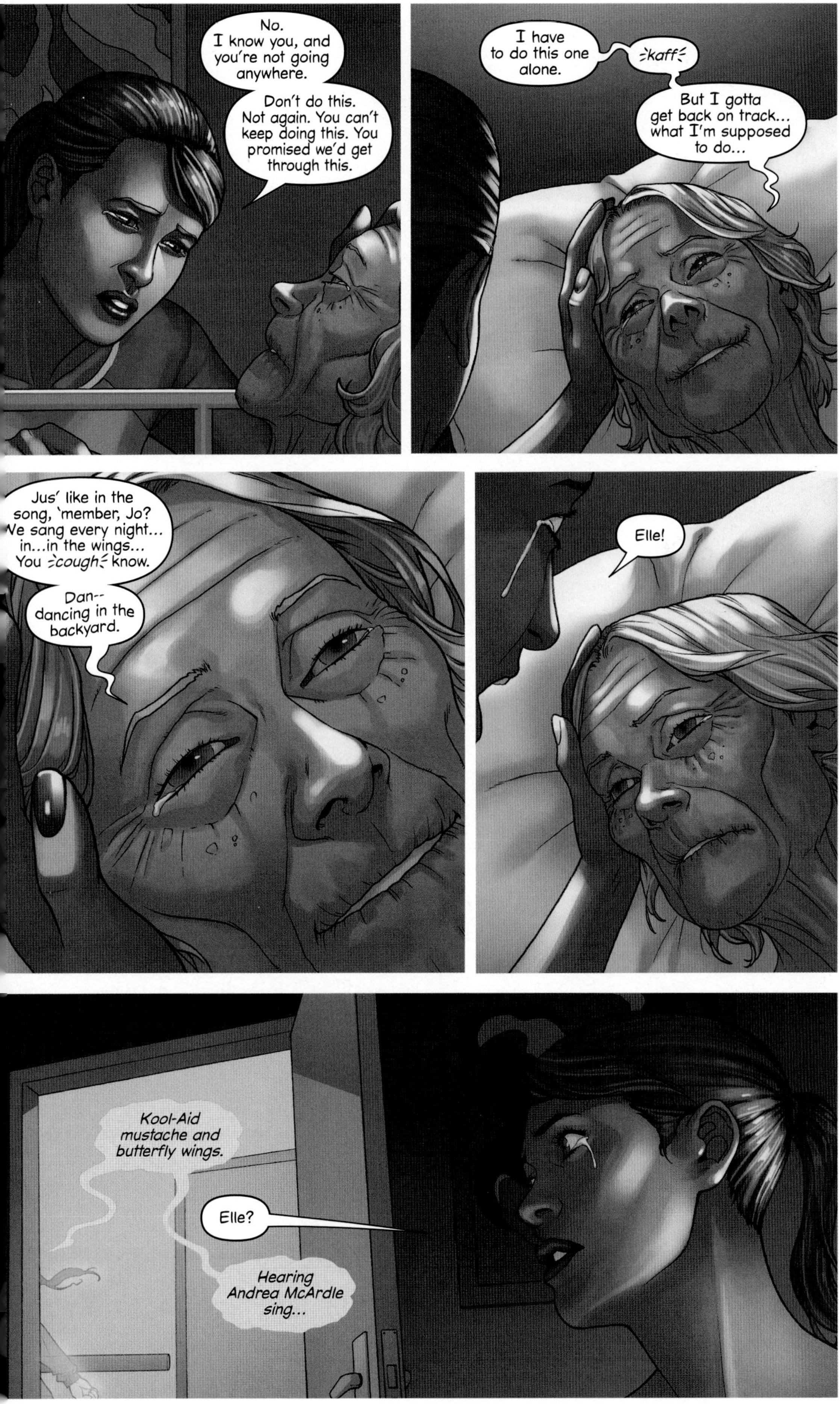
No. I know you, and you're not going anywhere.
Don't do this. Not again. You can't keep doing this. You promised we'd get through this.
I have to do this one alone.
kaff
But I gotta get back on track... what I'm supposed to do...
Jus' like in the song, 'member, Jo? We sang every night... in...in the wings... You cough know.
Dan-- dancing in the backyard.
Elle!
Kool-Aid mustache and butterfly wings.
Elle?
Hearing Andrea McArdle sing...

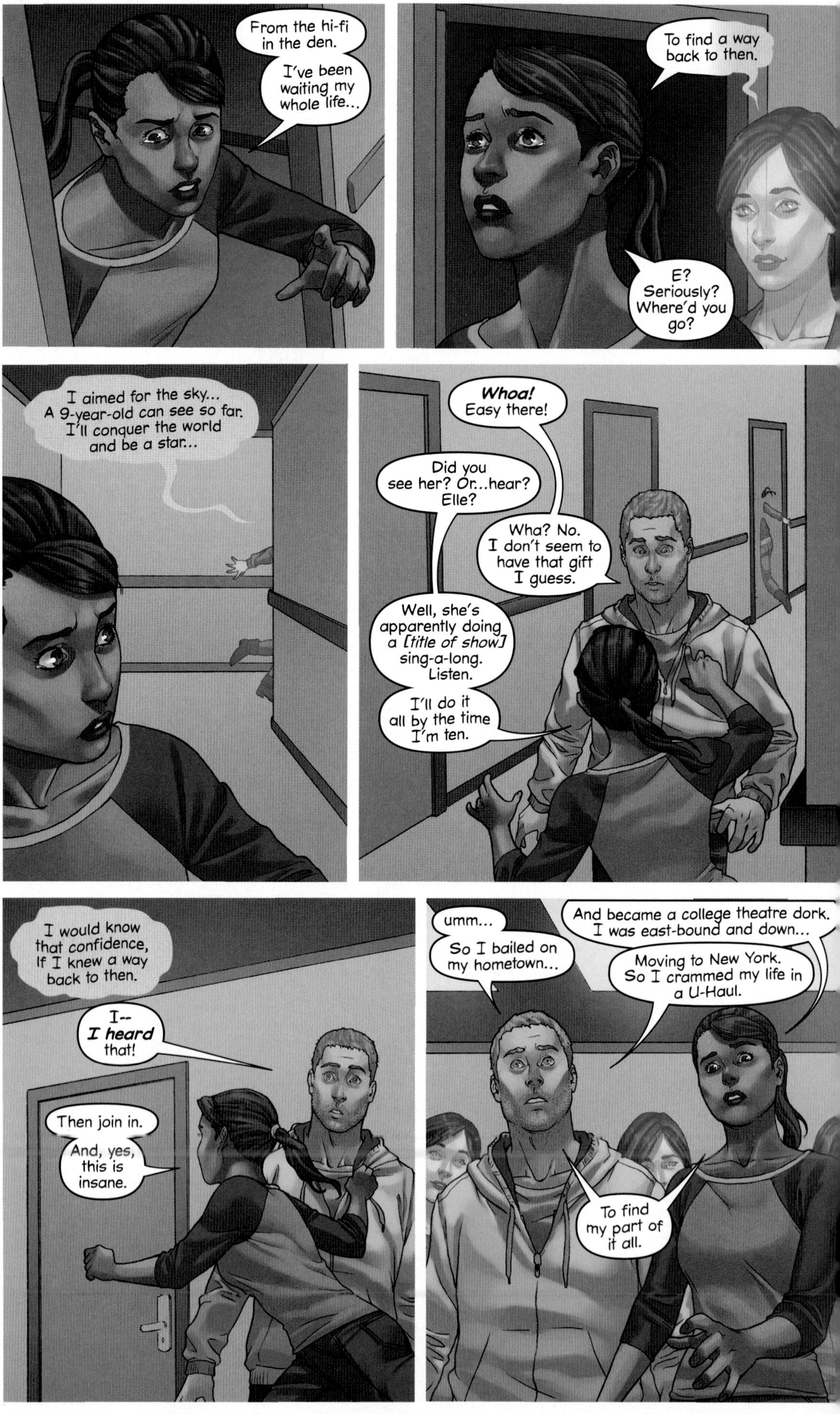
From the hi-fi in the den.
I've been waiting my whole life...
To find a way back to then.
E? Seriously? Where'd you go?
I aimed for the sky... A 9-year-old can see so far. I'll conquer the world and be a star...
Whoa! Easy there!
Did you see her? Or...hear? Elle?
Wha? No. I don't seem to have that gift I guess.
Well, she's apparently doing a [*title of show*] sing-a-long. Listen.
I'll do it all by the time I'm ten.
I would know that confidence, If I knew a way back to then.
I-- ***I heard*** that!
Then join in.
And, yes, this is insane.
umm...
So I bailed on my hometown...
And became a college theatre dork. I was east-bound and down...
Moving to New York. So I crammed my life in a U-Haul.
To find my part of it all.

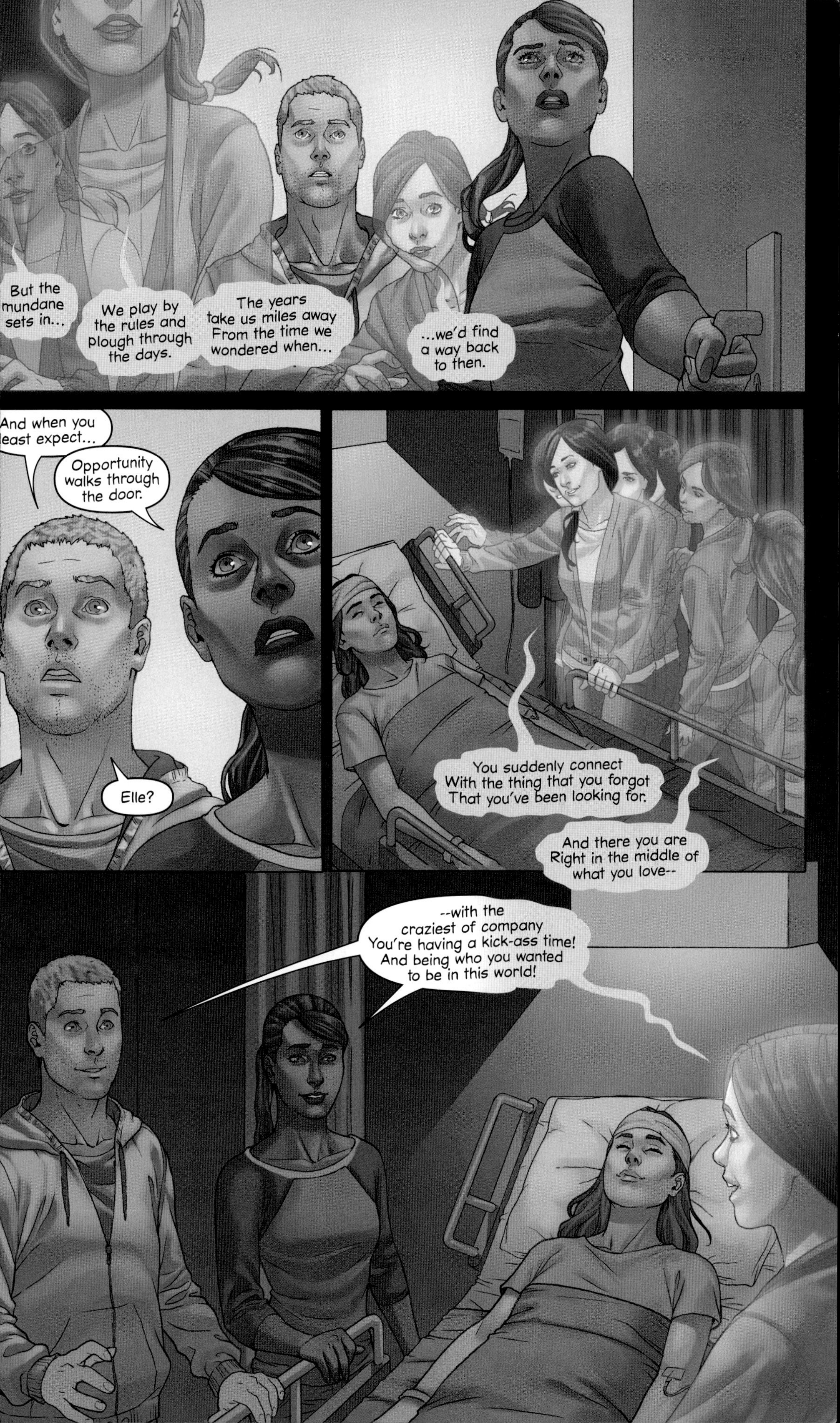

But the mundane sets in...
We play by the rules and plough through the days.
The years take us miles away From the time we wondered when...
...we'd find a way back to then.
And when you least expect...
Opportunity walks through the door.
Elle?
You suddenly connect With the thing that you forgot That you've been looking for.
And there you are Right in the middle of what you love--
--with the craziest of company You're having a kick-ass time! And being who you wanted to be in this world!

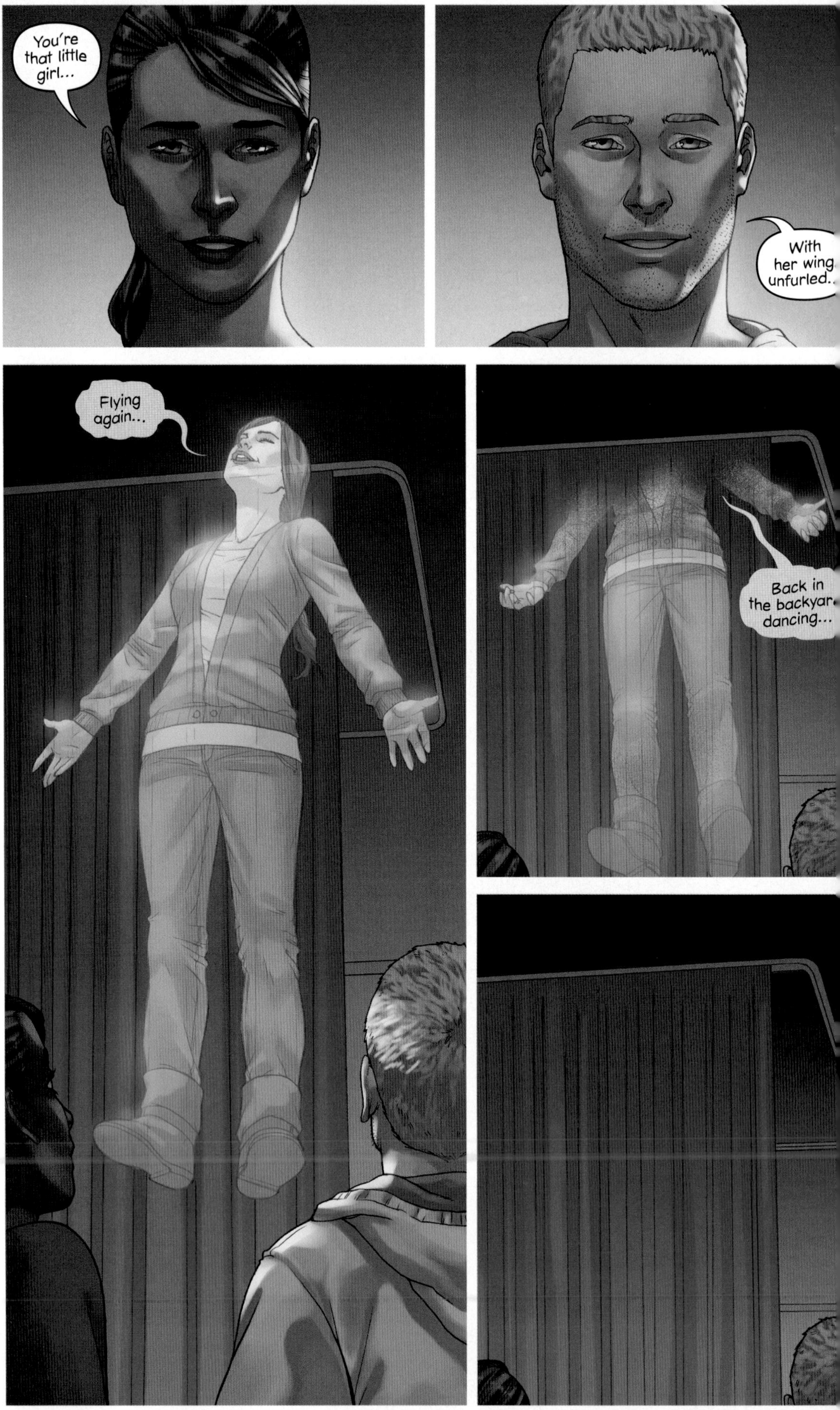
You're that little girl...
With her wing unfurled..
Flying again...
Back in the backyar dancing...

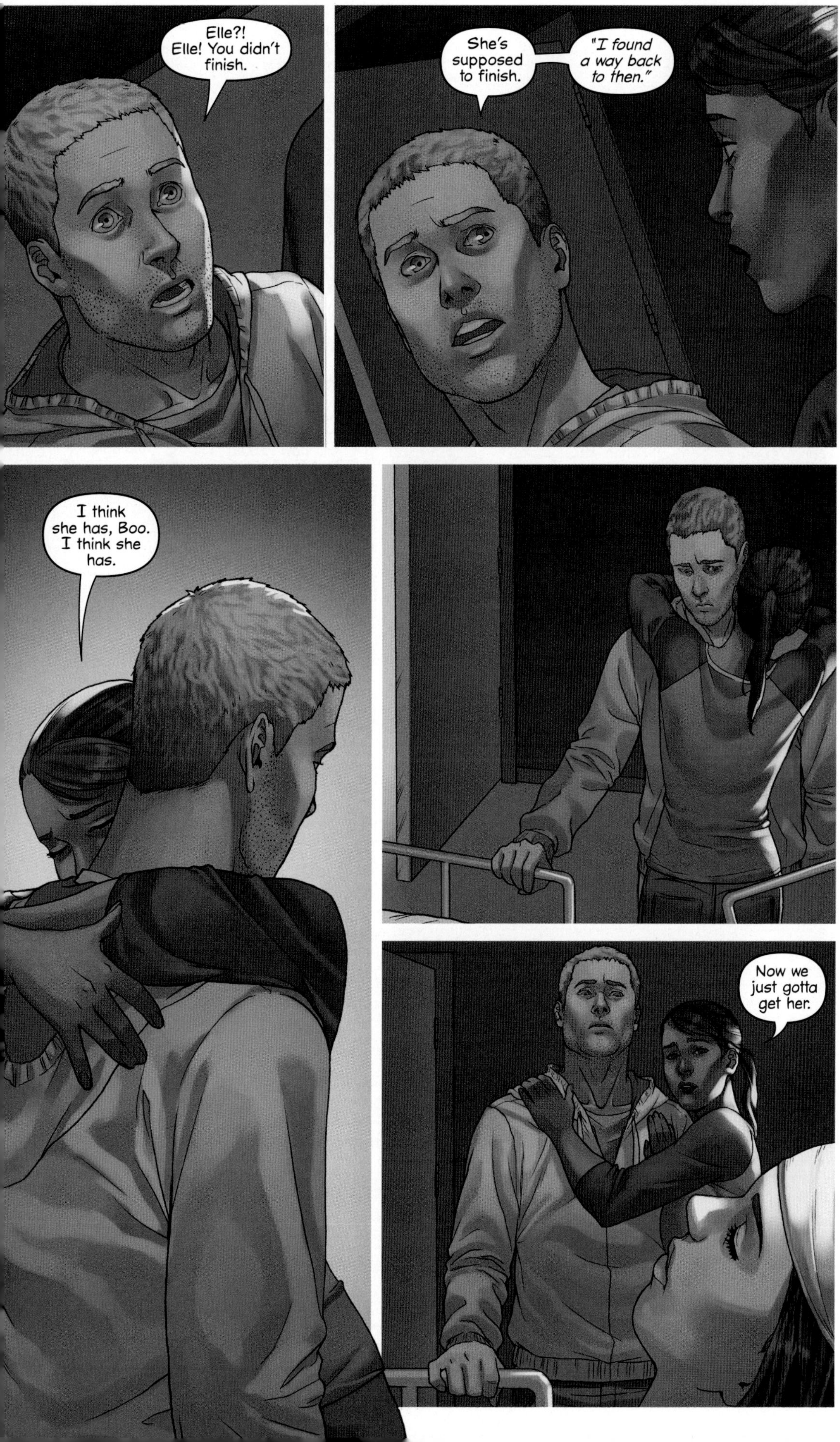
Elle?! Elle! You didn't finish.
She's supposed to finish.
"I found a way back to then."
I think she has, Boo. I think she has.
Now we just gotta get her.

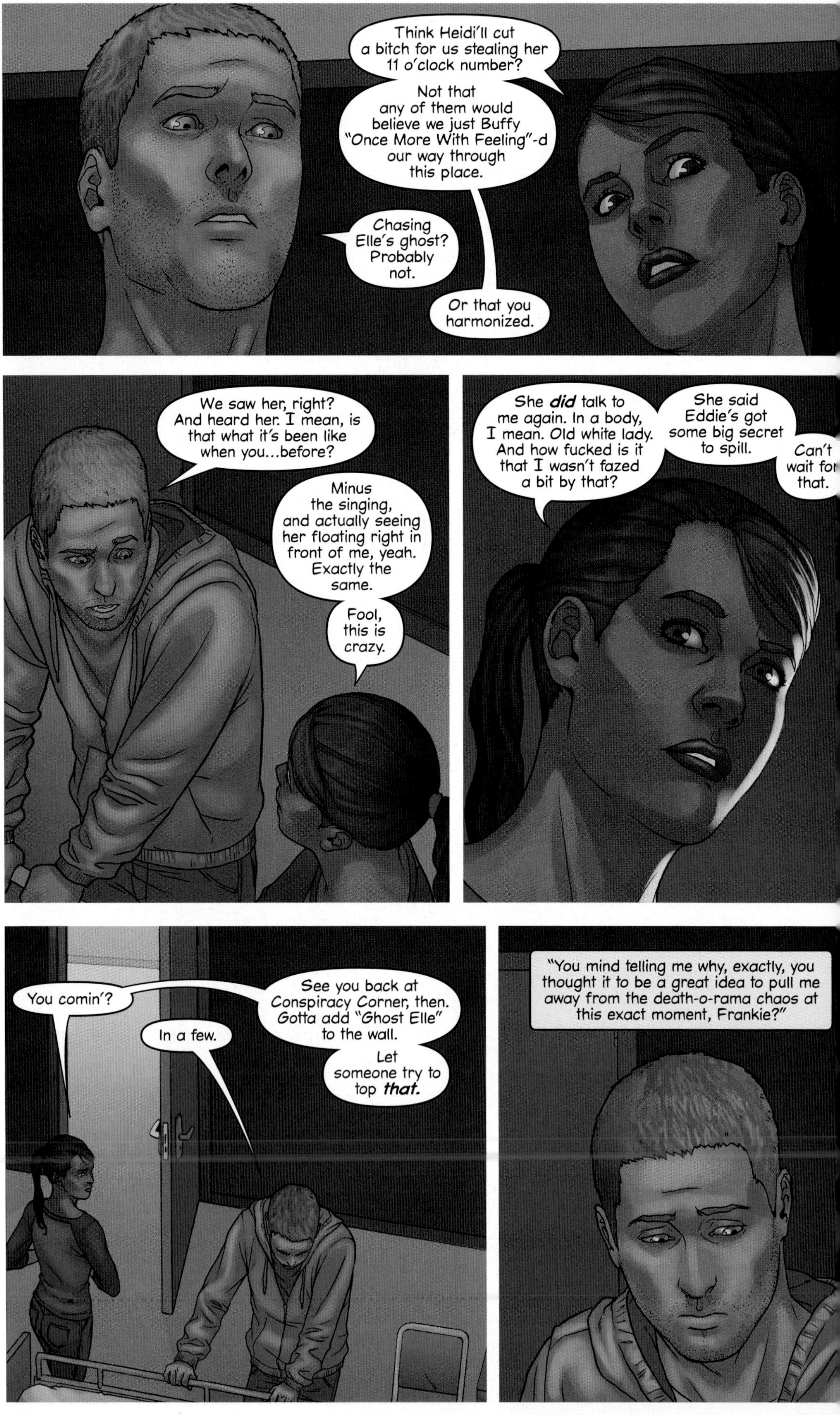
Think Heidi'll cut a bitch for us stealing her 11 o'clock number?
Not that any of them would believe we just Buffy "Once More With Feeling"-d our way through this place.
Chasing Elle's ghost? Probably not.
Or that you harmonized.
We saw her, right? And heard her. I mean, is that what it's been like when you...before?
Minus the singing, and actually seeing her floating right in front of me, yeah. Exactly the same.
Fool, this is crazy.
She *did* talk to me again. In a body, I mean. Old white lady. And how fucked is it that I wasn't fazed a bit by that?
She said Eddie's got some big secret to spill.
Can't wait fo that.
You comin'?
See you back at Conspiracy Corner, then. Gotta add "Ghost Elle" to the wall.
In a few.
Let someone try to top *that.*
"You mind telling me why, exactly, you thought it to be a great idea to pull me away from the death-o-rama chaos at this exact moment, Frankie?"

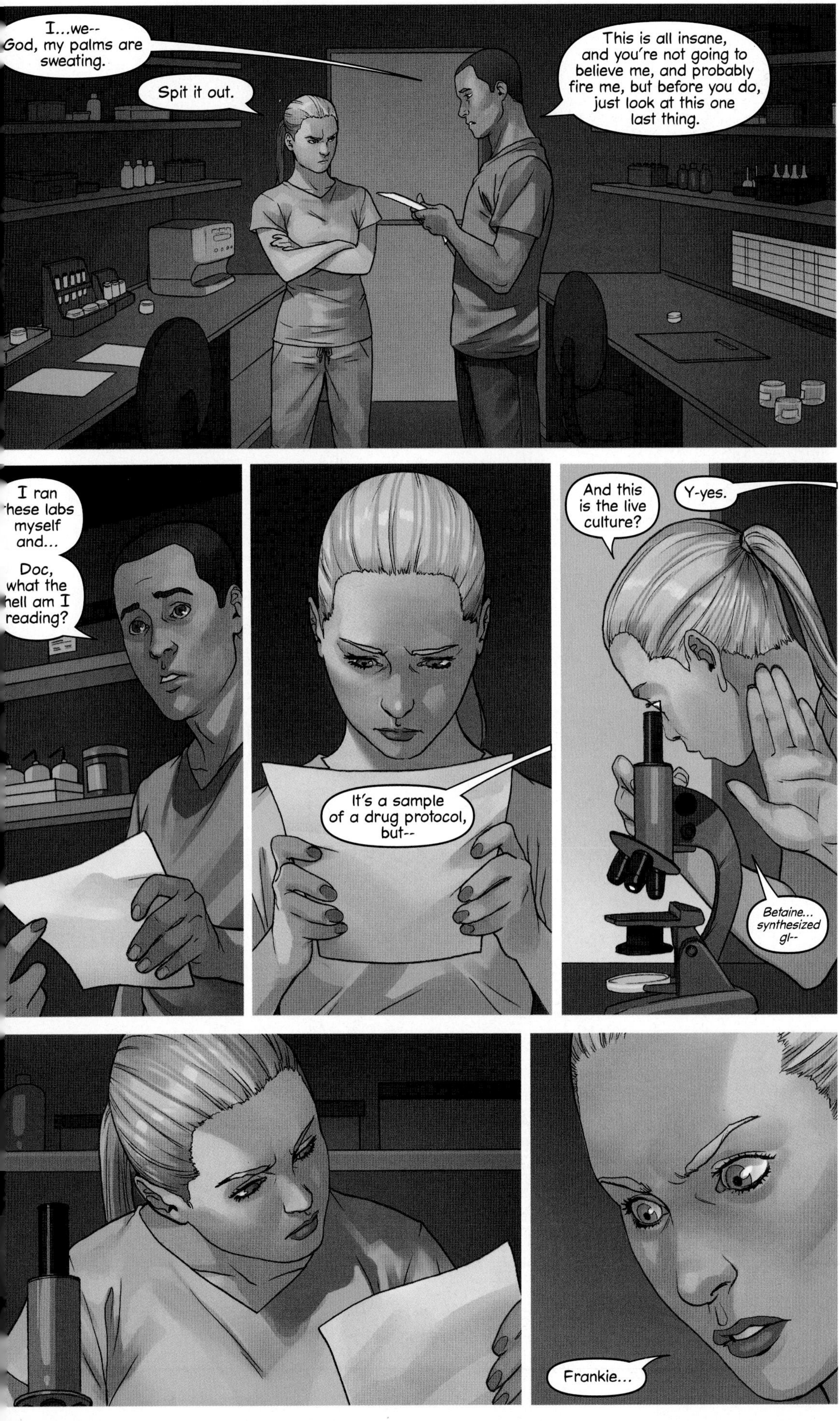
I...we--
God, my palms are sweating.
Spit it out.
This is all insane, and you're not going to believe me, and probably fire me, but before you do, just look at this one last thing.
I ran these labs myself and...
Doc, what the hell am I reading?
It's a sample of a drug protocol, but--
And this is the live culture?
Y-yes.
Betaine... synthesized gl--
Frankie...

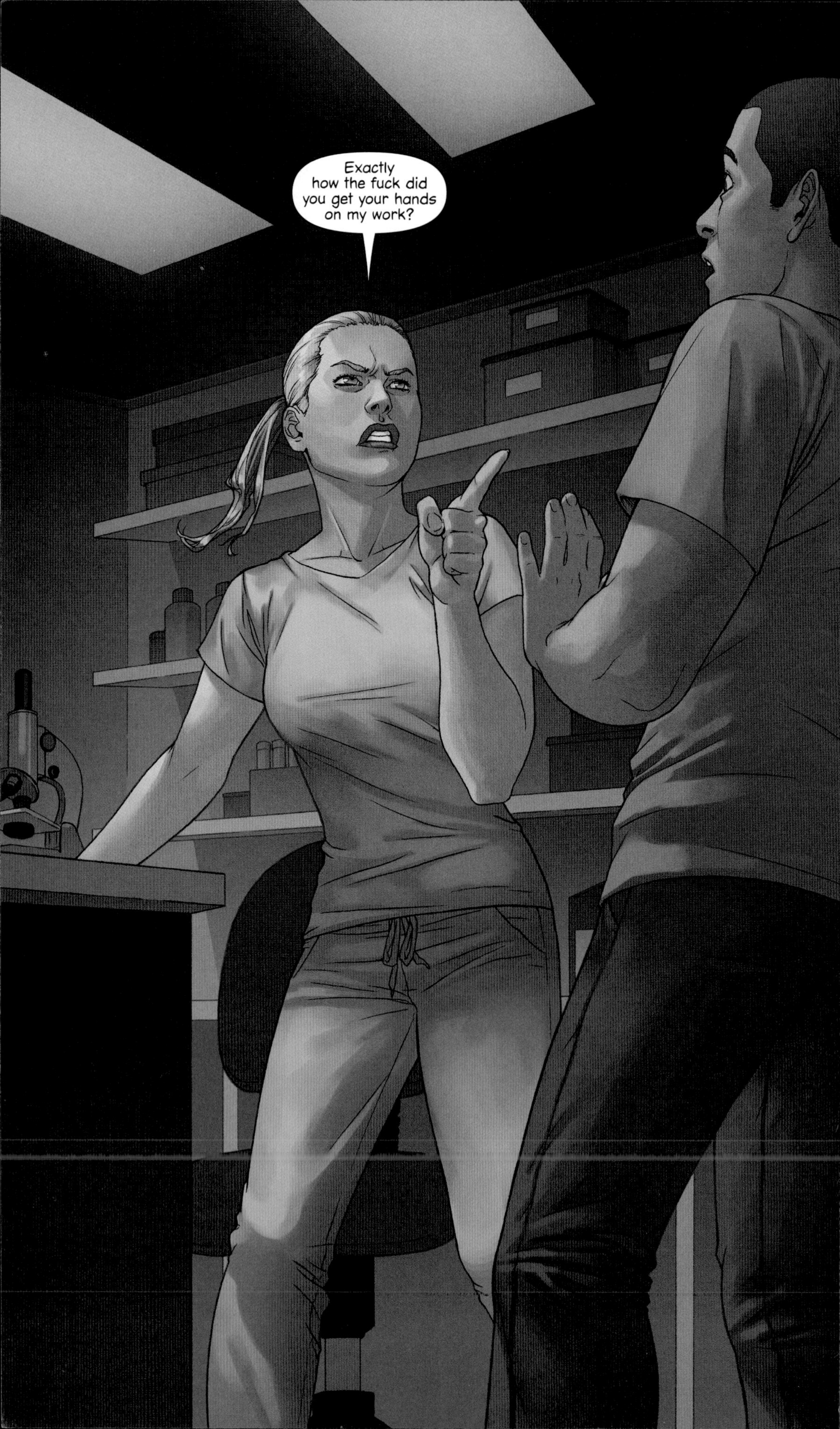
Exactly how the fuck did you get your hands on my work?

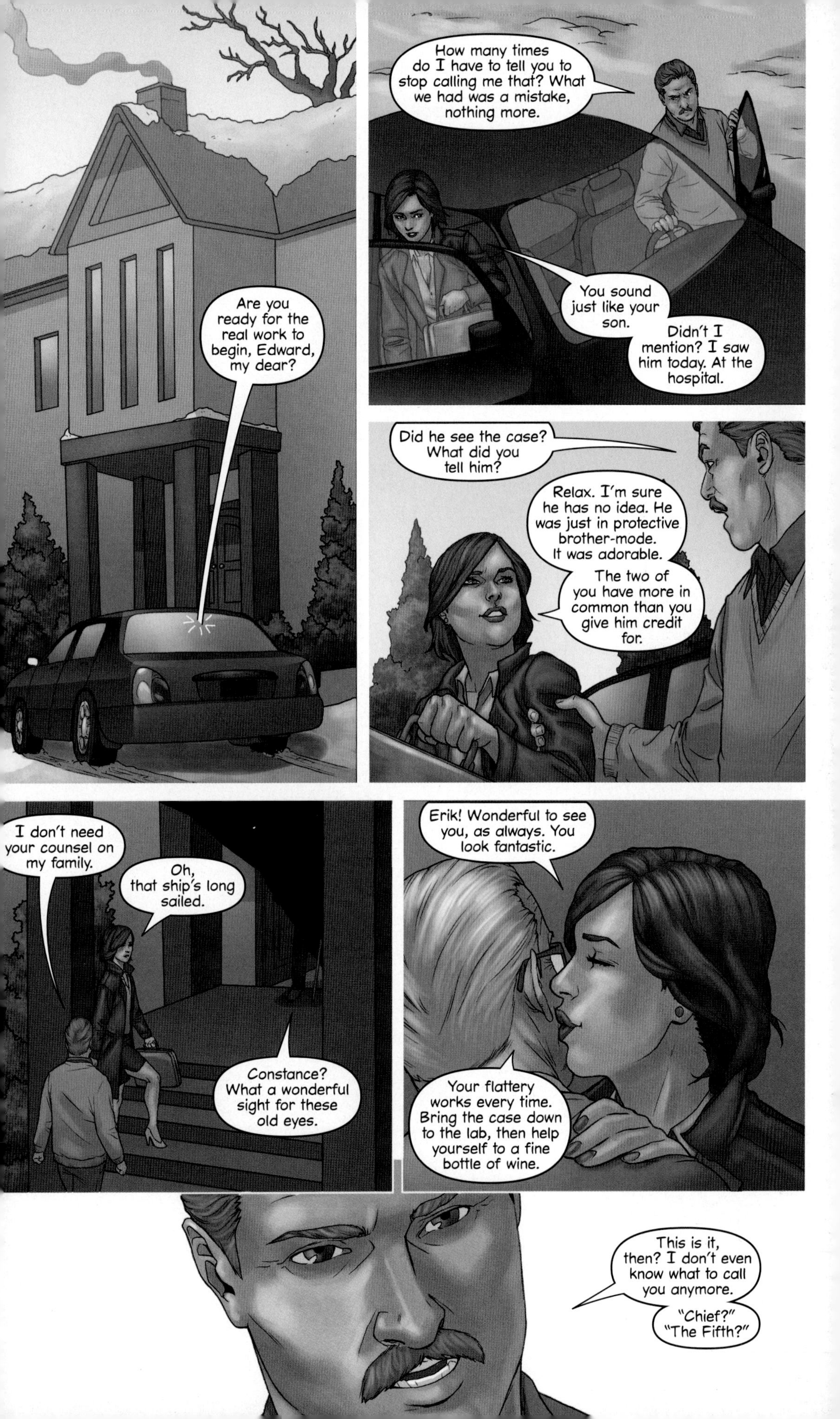
Are you ready for the real work to begin, Edward, my dear?
How many times do I have to tell you to stop calling me that? What we had was a mistake, nothing more.
You sound just like your son.
Didn't I mention? I saw him today. At the hospital.
Did he see the case? What did you tell him?
Relax. I'm sure he has no idea. He was just in protective brother-mode. It was adorable.
The two of you have more in common than you give him credit for.
I don't need your counsel on my family.
Oh, that ship's long sailed.
Constance? What a wonderful sight for these old eyes.
Erik! Wonderful to see you, as always. You look fantastic.
Your flattery works every time. Bring the case down to the lab, then help yourself to a fine bottle of wine.
This is it, then? I don't even know what to call you anymore.
"Chief?" "The Fifth?"

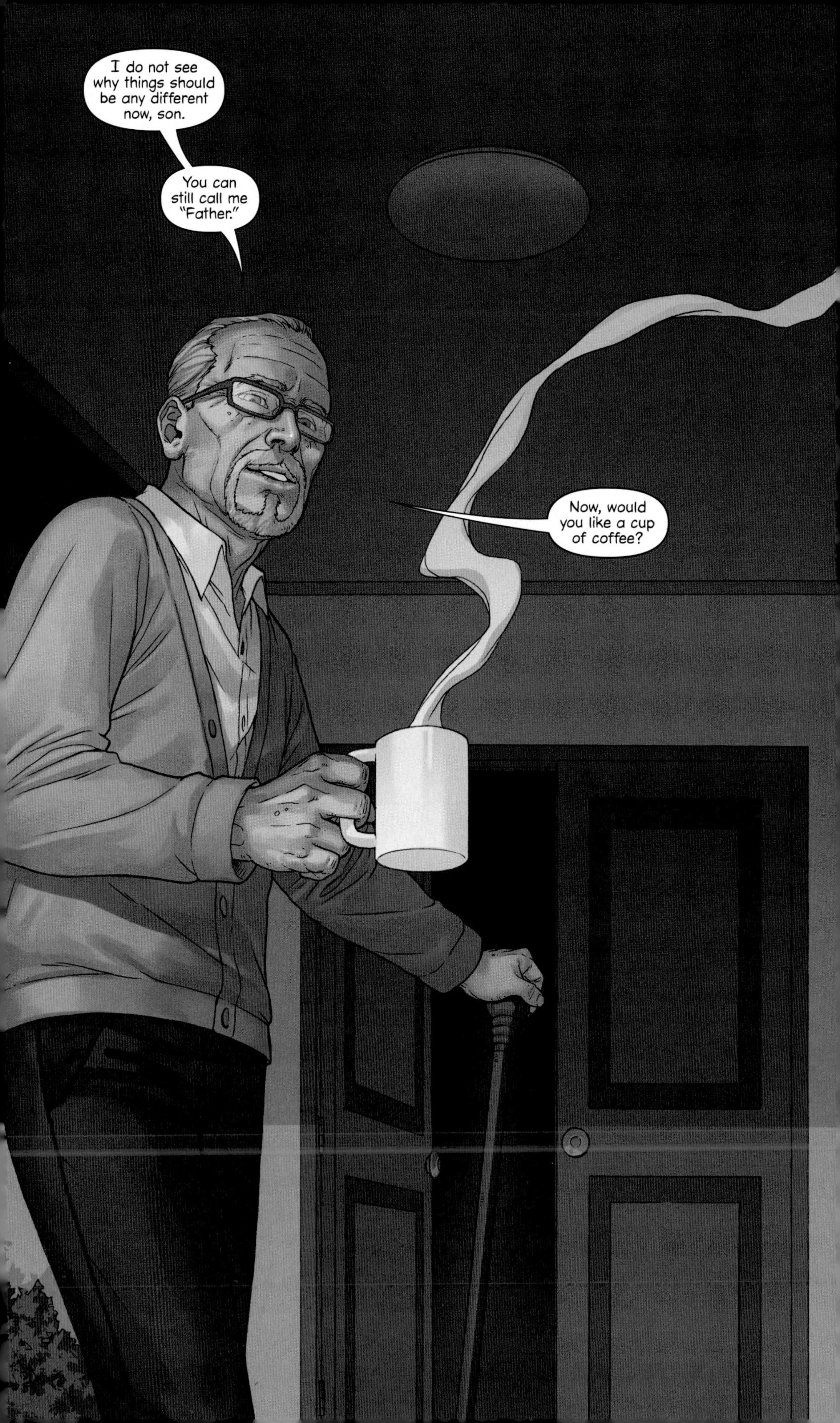

I do not see why things should be any different now, son.
You can still call me "Father."
Now, would you like a cup of coffee?

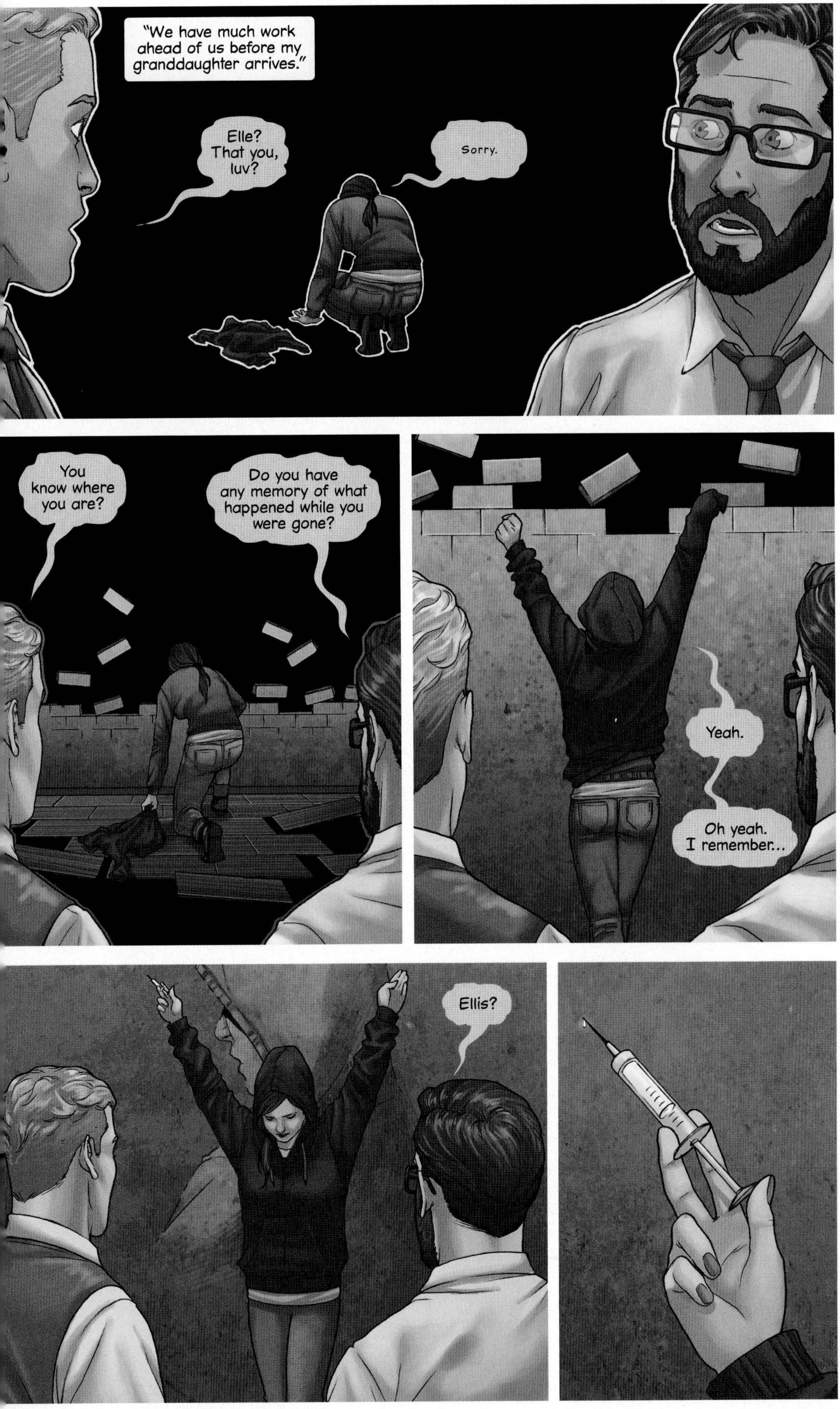
"We have much work ahead of us before my granddaughter arrives."
Elle? That you, luv?
Sorry.
You know where you are?
Do you have any memory of what happened while you were gone?
Yeah.
Oh yeah. I remember...
Ellis?

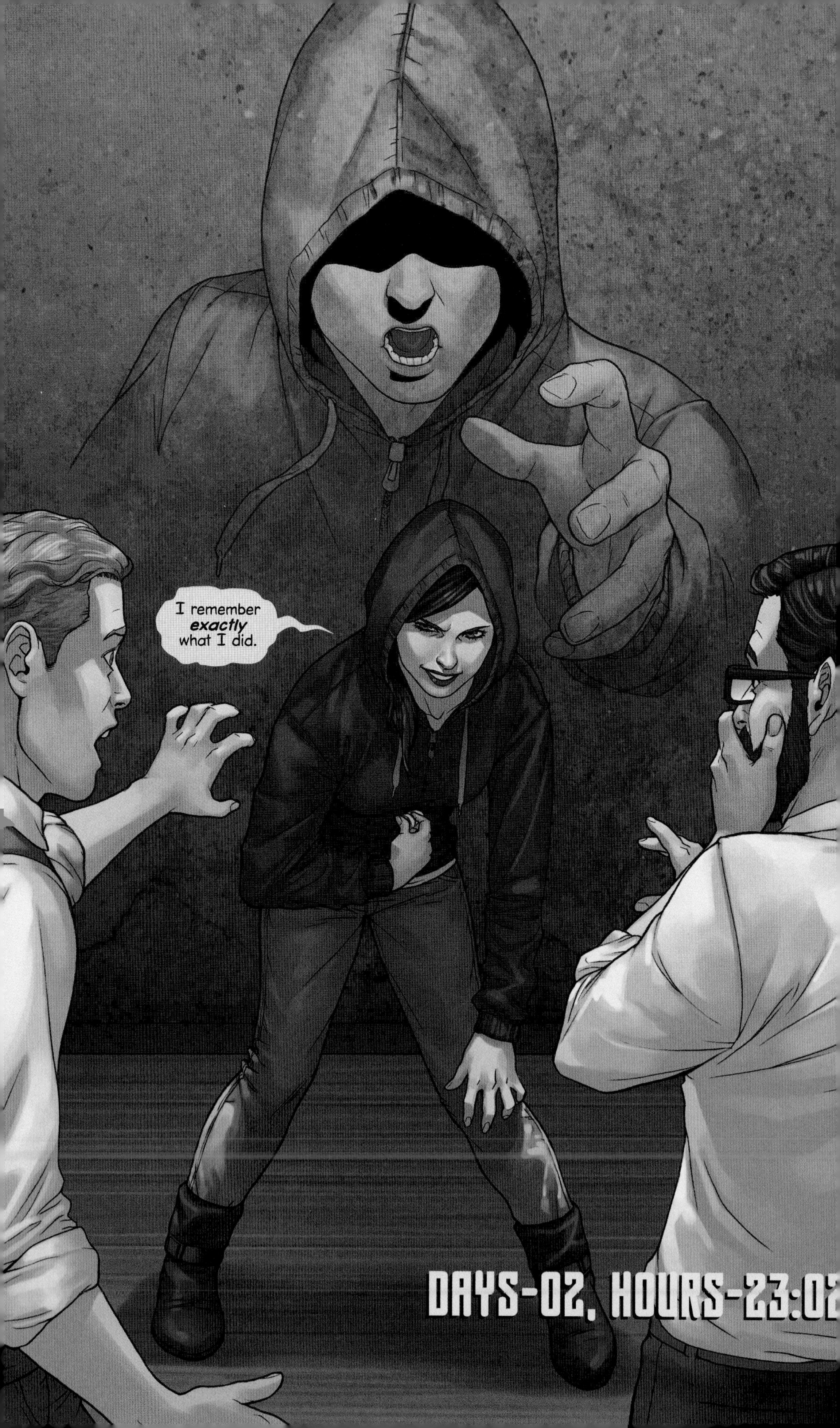
I remember *exactly* what I did.
DAYS-02, HOURS-23:02

"A purpose of human life, no matter who is controlling it, is to love whoever is around to be loved."

-Kurt Vonnegut, *The Sirens of Titan*

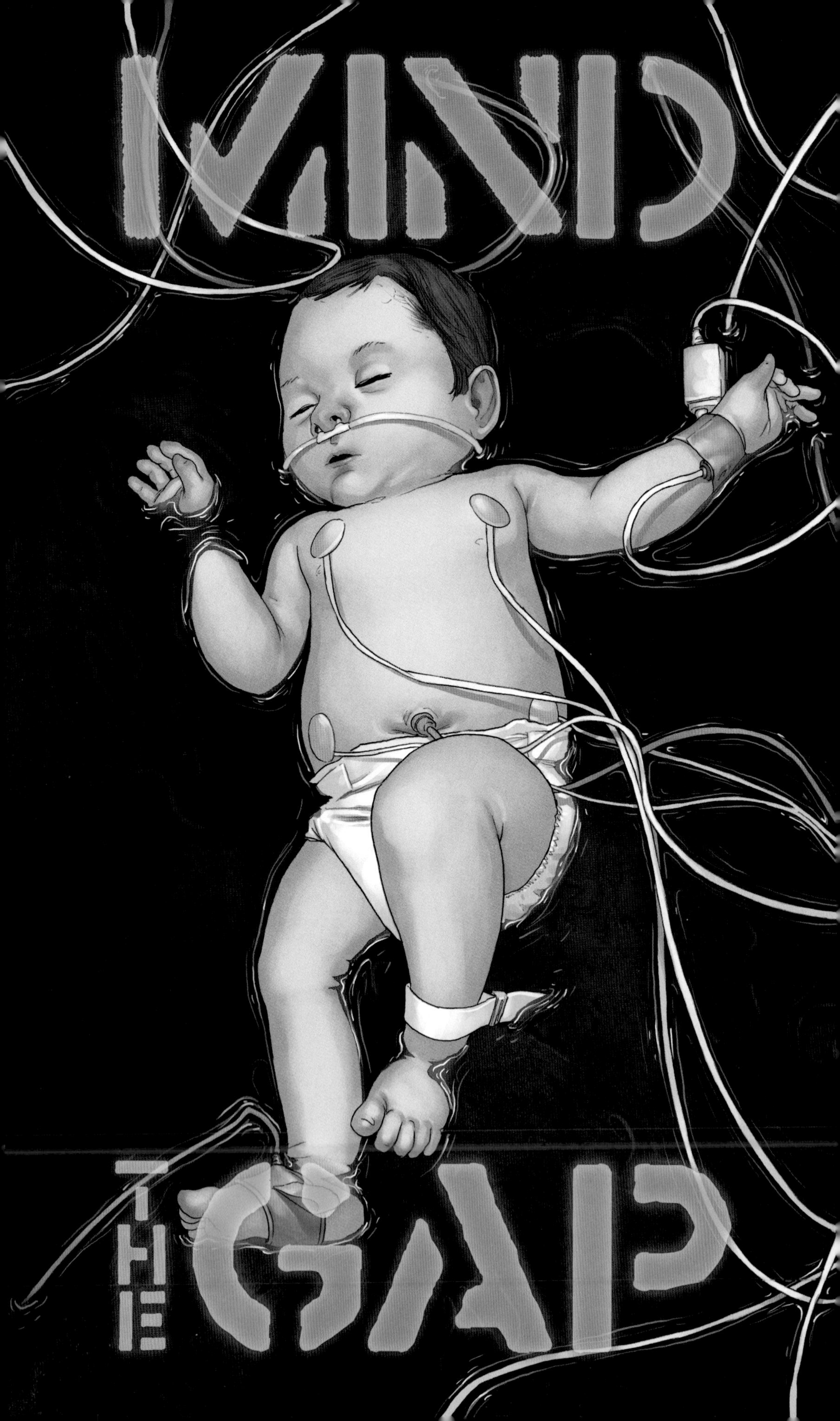
MIND
THE GAP

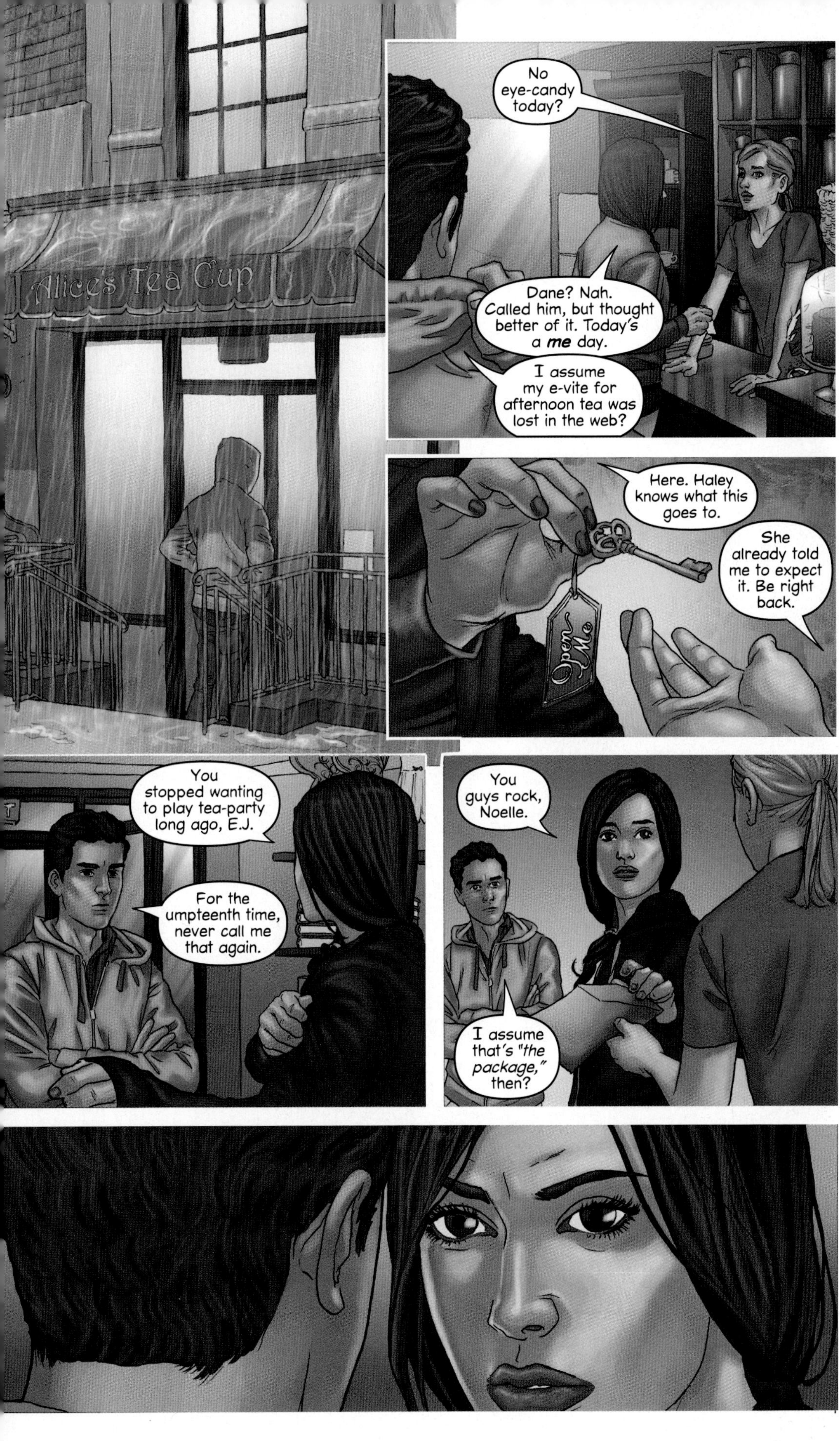
Alice's Tea Cup
No eye-candy today?
Dane? Nah. Called him, but thought better of it. Today's a *me* day.
I assume my e-vite for afternoon tea was lost in the web?
Here. Haley knows what this goes to.
Open Me
She already told me to expect it. Be right back.
You stopped wanting to play tea-party long ago, E.J.
For the umpteenth time, never call me that again.
You guys rock, Noelle.
I assume that's *"the package,"* then?

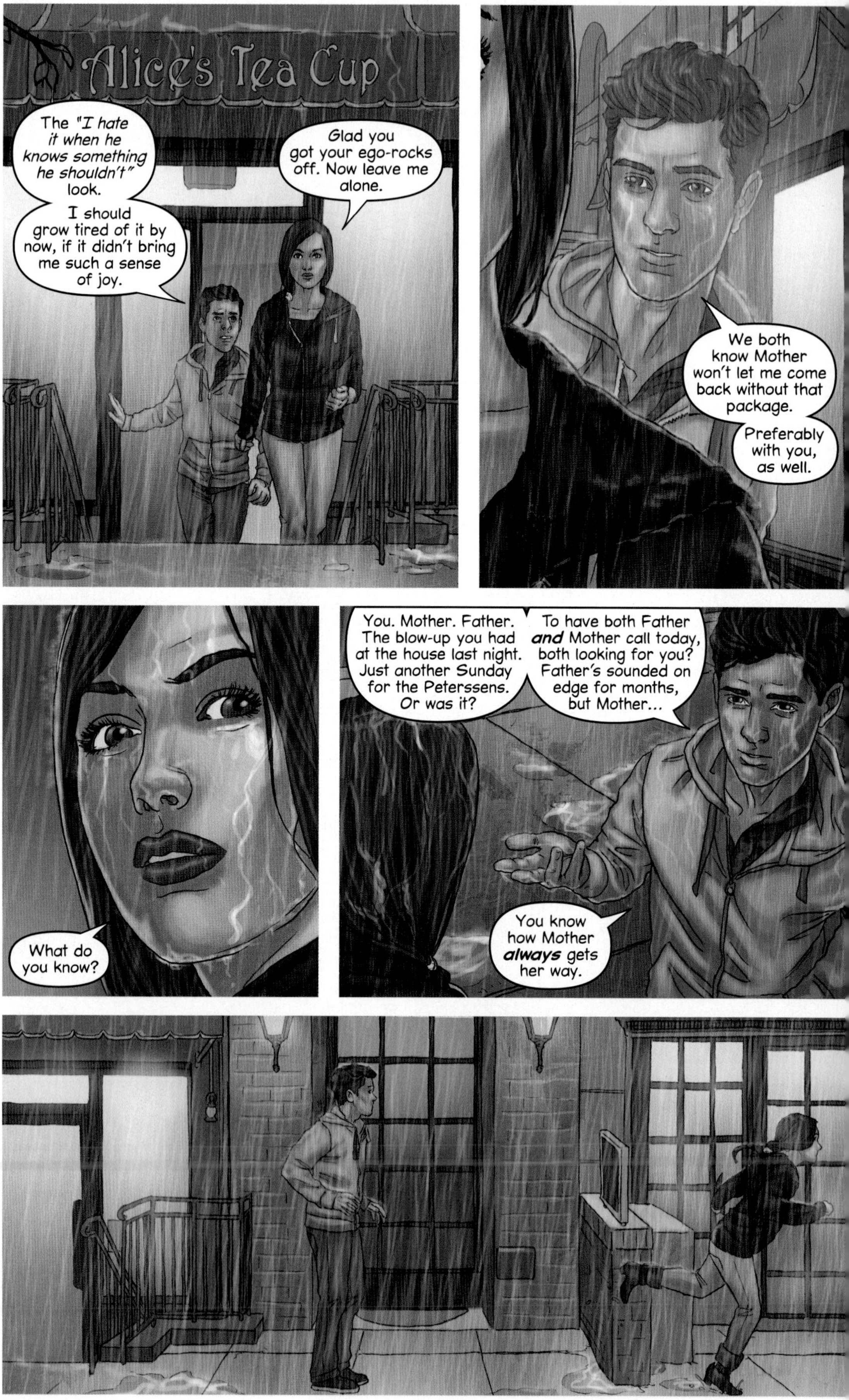
Alice's Tea Cup
The "I hate it when he knows something he shouldn't" look.
I should grow tired of it by now, if it didn't bring me such a sense of joy.
Glad you got your ego-rocks off. Now leave me alone.
We both know Mother won't let me come back without that package.
Preferably with you, as well.
What do you know?
You. Mother. Father. The blow-up you had at the house last night. Just another Sunday for the Peterssens. Or was it?
To have both Father **and** Mother call today, both looking for you? Father's sounded on edge for months, but Mother...
You know how Mother **always** gets her way.

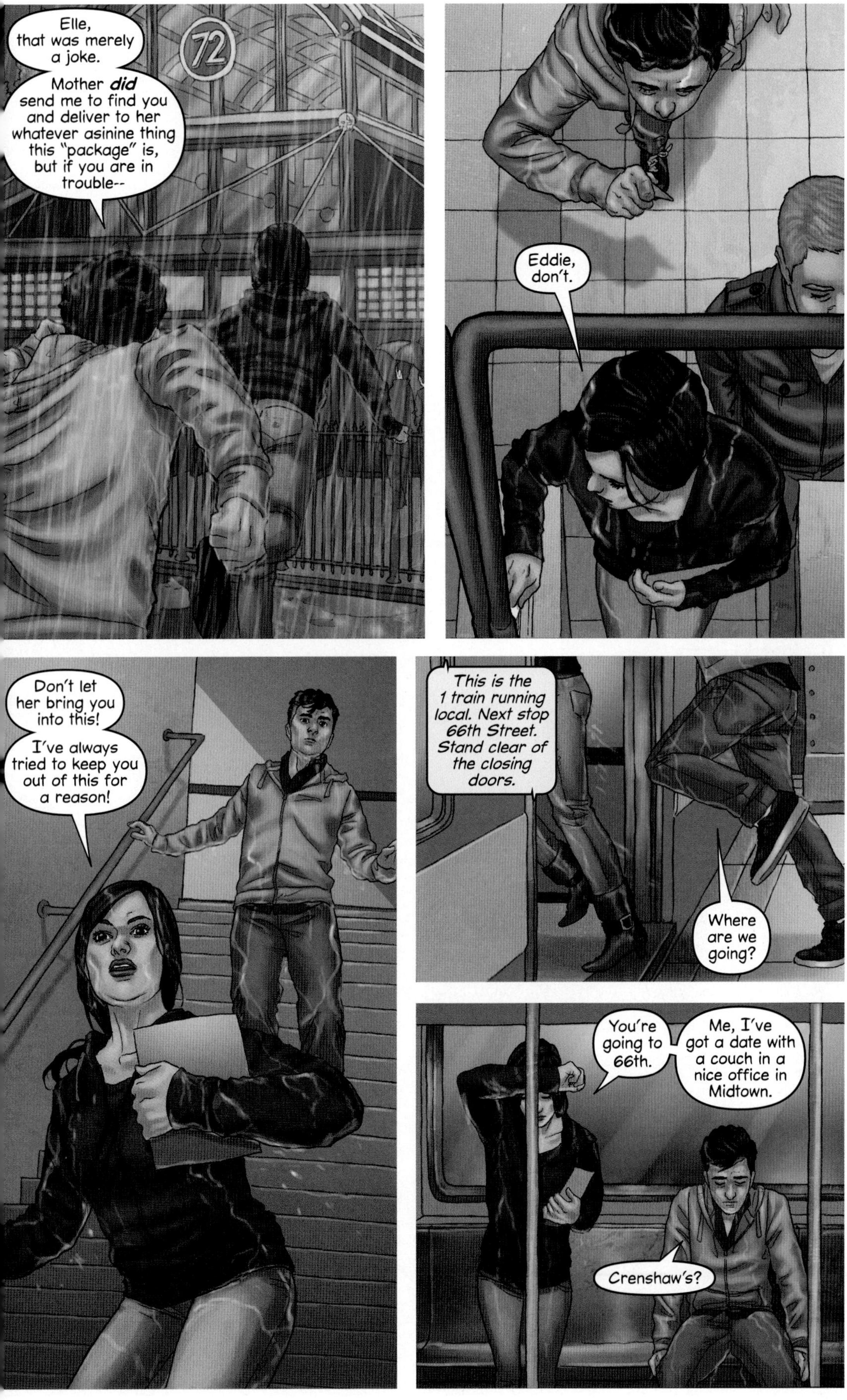
Elle, that was merely a joke.
Mother **did** send me to find you and deliver to her whatever asinine thing this "package" is, but if you are in trouble--
Eddie, don't.
Don't let her bring you into this!
I've always tried to keep you out of this for a reason!
This is the 1 train running local. Next stop 66th Street. Stand clear of the closing doors.
Where are we going?
You're going to 66th.
Me, I've got a date with a couch in a nice office in Midtown.
Crenshaw's?

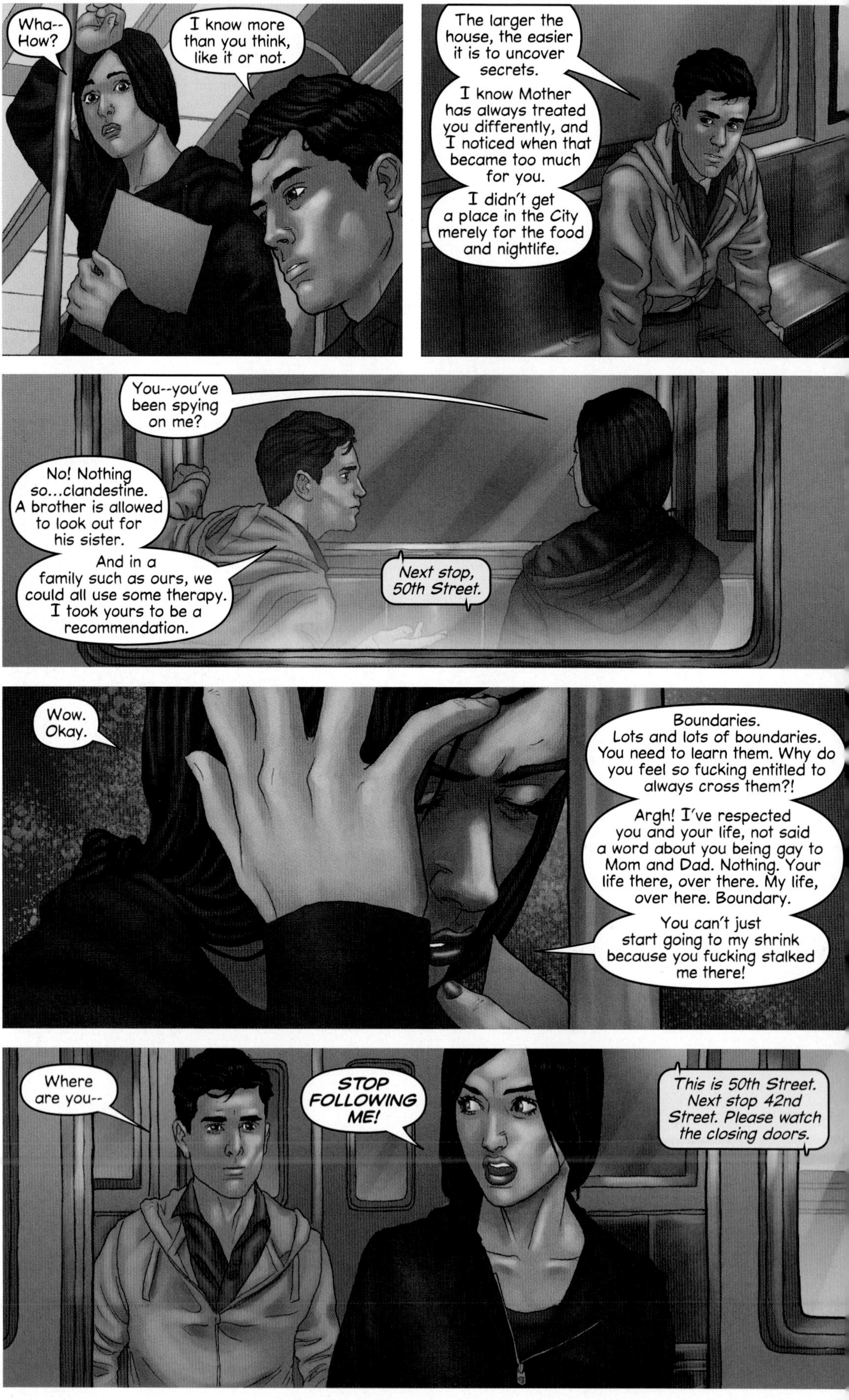
Wha-- How?
I know more than you think, like it or not.
The larger the house, the easier it is to uncover secrets.
I know Mother has always treated you differently, and I noticed when that became too much for you.
I didn't get a place in the City merely for the food and nightlife.
You--you've been spying on me?
No! Nothing so...clandestine. A brother is allowed to look out for his sister.
And in a family such as ours, we could all use some therapy. I took yours to be a recommendation.
Next stop, 50th Street.
Wow. Okay.
Boundaries. Lots and lots of boundaries. You need to learn them. Why do you feel so fucking entitled to always cross them?!
Argh! I've respected you and your life, not said a word about you being gay to Mom and Dad. Nothing. Your life there, over there. My life, over here. Boundary.
You can't just start going to my shrink because you fucking stalked me there!
Where are you--
STOP FOLLOWING ME!
This is 50th Street. Next stop 42nd Street. Please watch the closing doors.

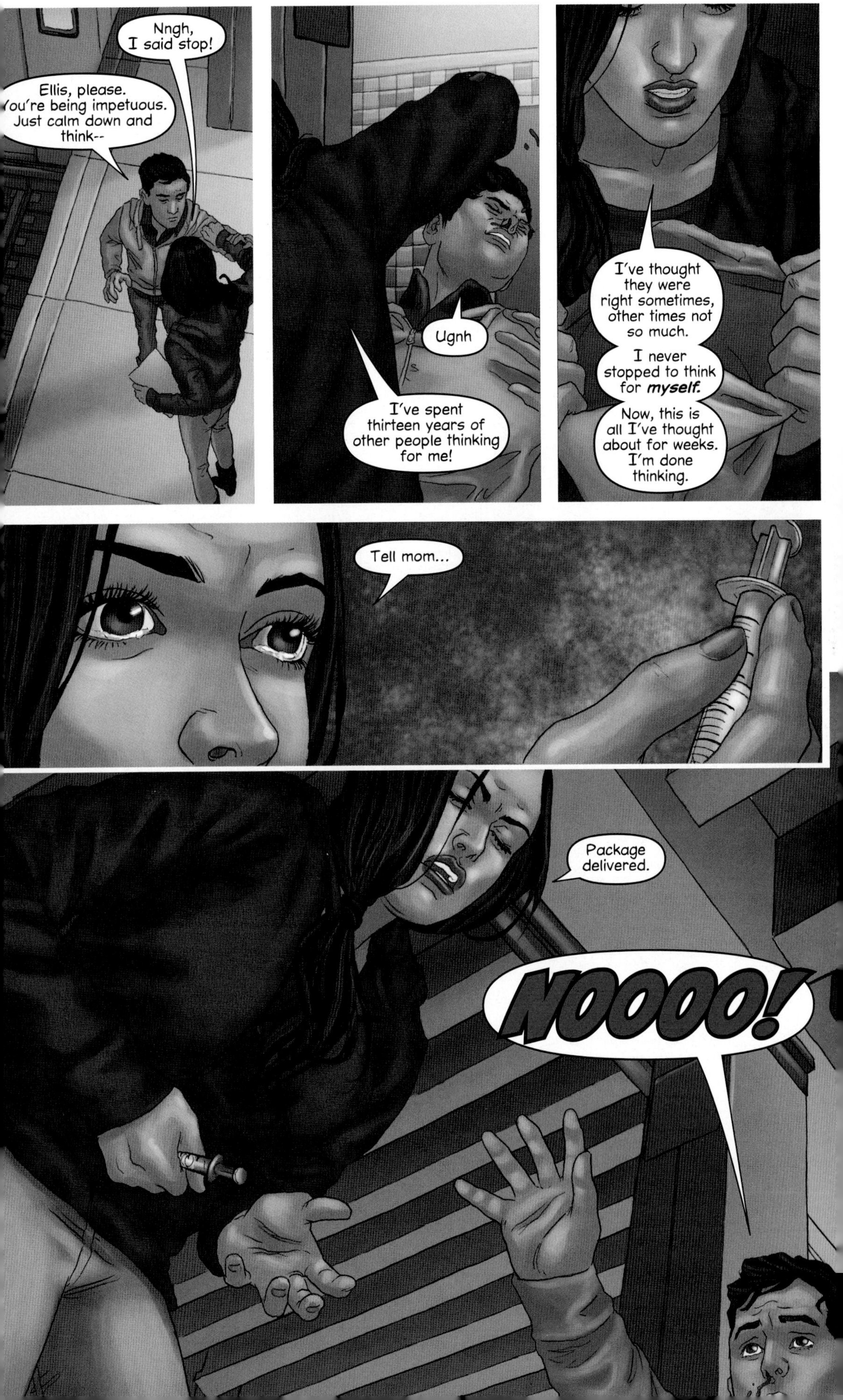
Nngh, I said stop!
Ellis, please. You're being impetuous. Just calm down and think--
Ugnh
I've spent thirteen years of other people thinking for me!
I've thought they were right sometimes, other times not so much.
I never stopped to think for *myself.*
Now, this is all I've thought about for weeks. I'm done thinking.
Tell mom...
Package delivered.
NOOOO!

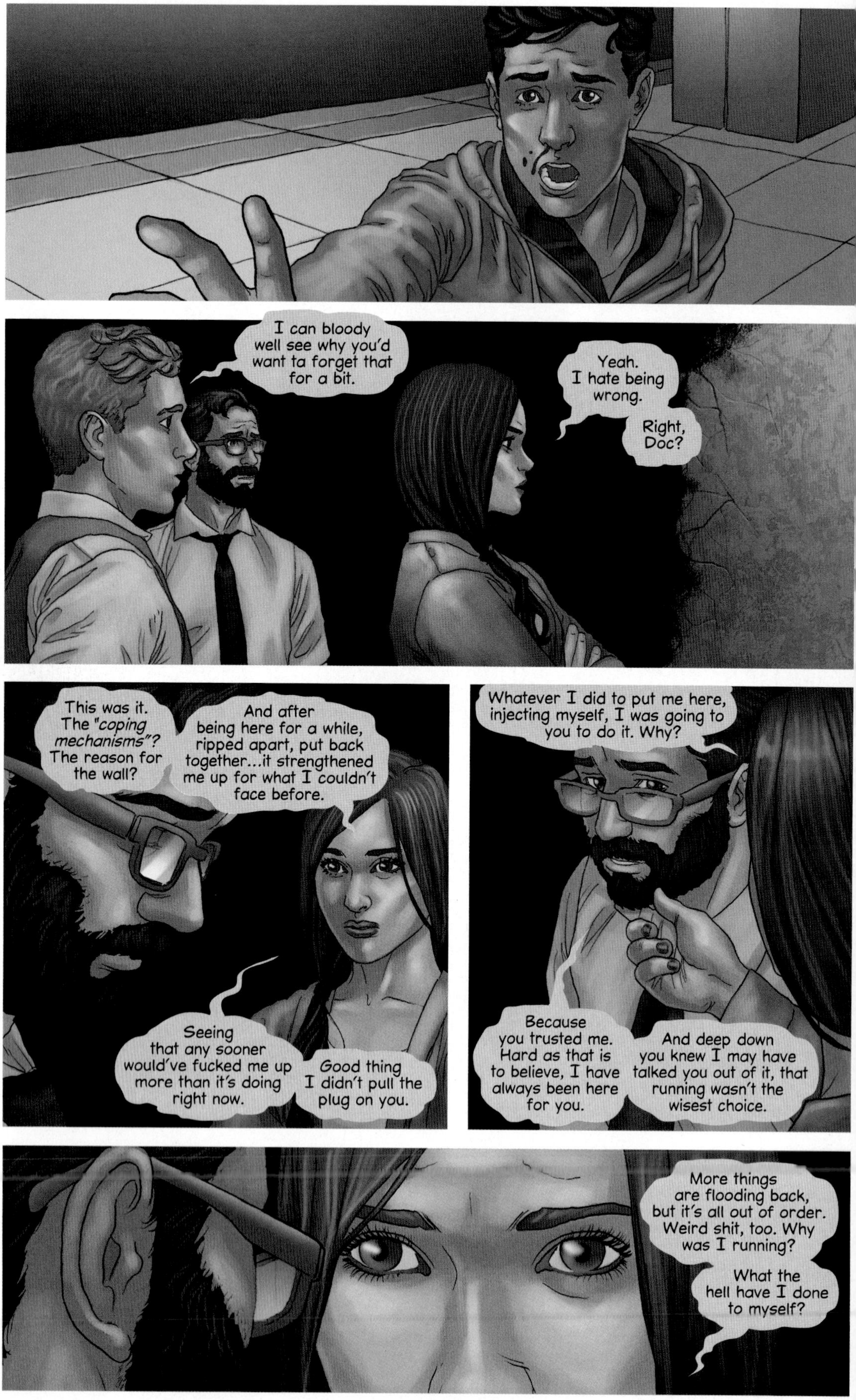
I can bloody well see why you'd want ta forget that for a bit.
Yeah. I hate being wrong.
Right, Doc?
This was it. The *"coping mechanisms"*? The reason for the wall?
And after being here for a while, ripped apart, put back together...it strengthened me up for what I couldn't face before.
Seeing that any sooner would've fucked me up more than it's doing right now.
Good thing I didn't pull the plug on you.
Whatever I did to put me here, injecting myself, I was going to you to do it. Why?
Because you trusted me. Hard as that is to believe, I have always been here for you.
And deep down you knew I may have talked you out of it, that running wasn't the wisest choice.
More things are flooding back, but it's all out of order. Weird shit, too. Why was I running?
What the hell have I done to myself?

R.I.Peterssen
PART I
"OUR FATHERS"

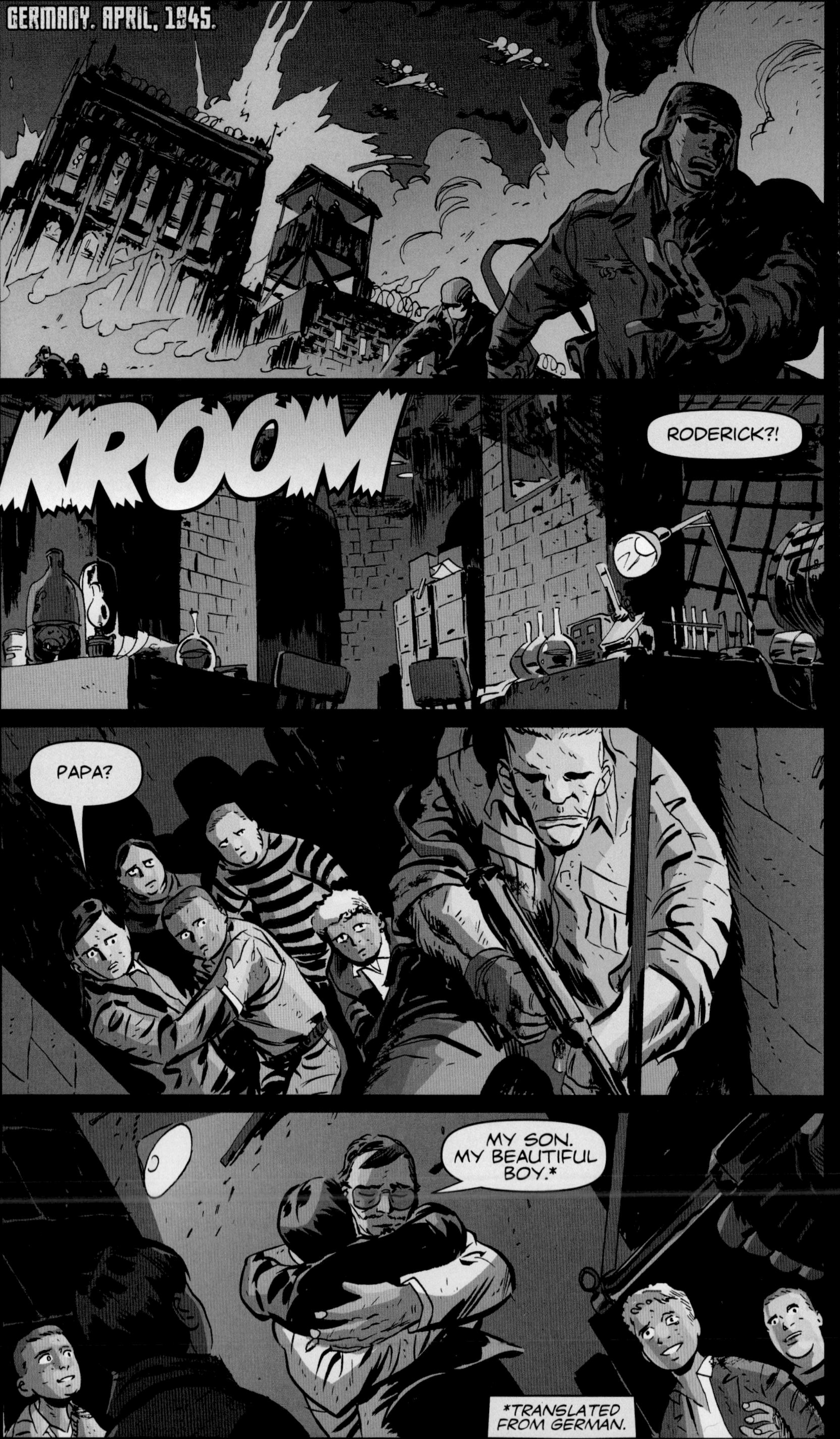
GERMANY. APRIL, 1945.
KROOM
RODERICK?!
PAPA?
MY SON. MY BEAUTIFUL BOY.*
*TRANSLATED FROM GERMAN.

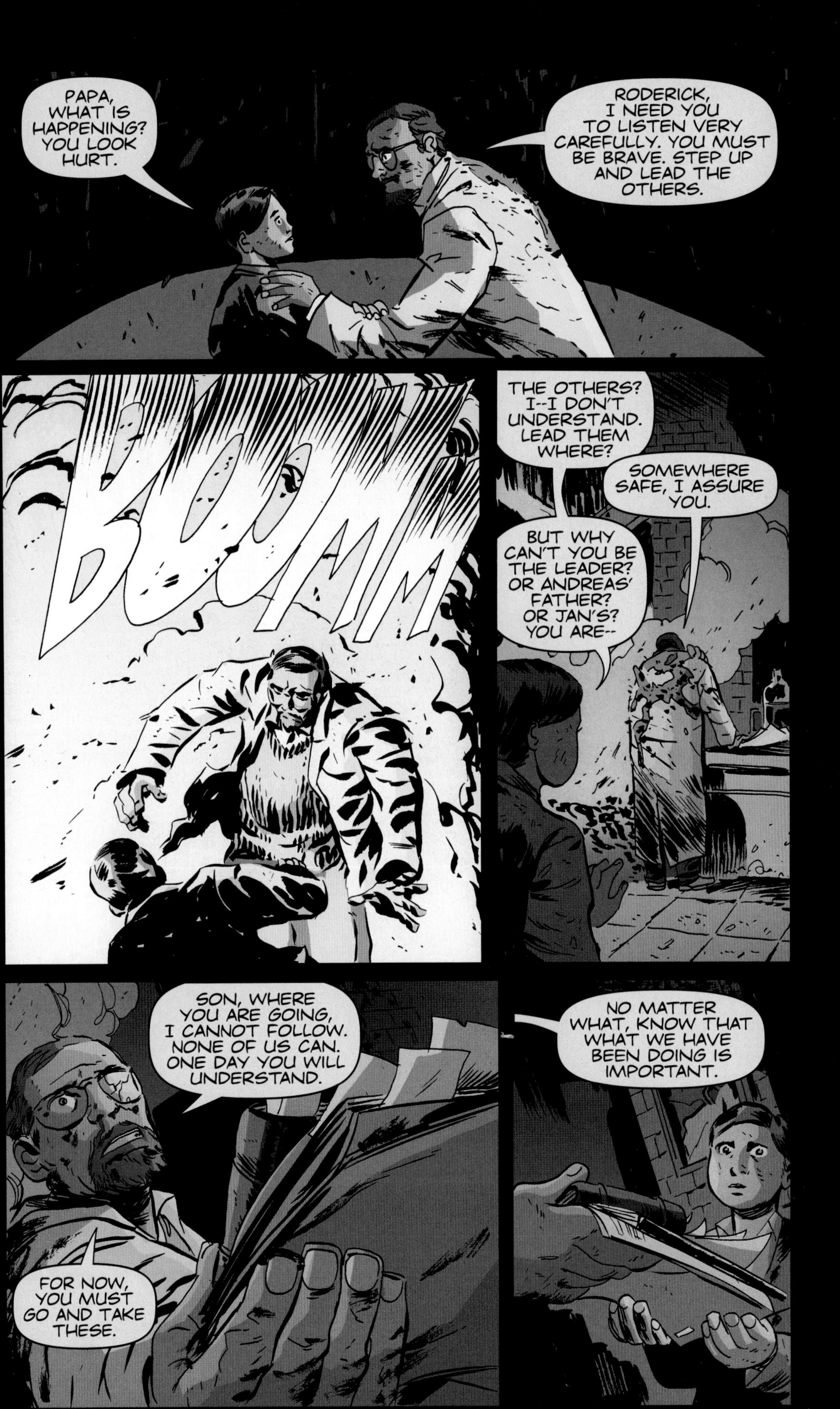
PAPA, WHAT IS HAPPENING? YOU LOOK HURT.
RODERICK, I NEED YOU TO LISTEN VERY CAREFULLY. YOU MUST BE BRAVE. STEP UP AND LEAD THE OTHERS.
BOOMM
THE OTHERS? I--I DON'T UNDERSTAND. LEAD THEM WHERE?
SOMEWHERE SAFE, I ASSURE YOU.
BUT WHY CAN'T YOU BE THE LEADER? OR ANDREAS' FATHER? OR JAN'S? YOU ARE--
SON, WHERE YOU ARE GOING, I CANNOT FOLLOW. NONE OF US CAN. ONE DAY YOU WILL UNDERSTAND.
FOR NOW, YOU MUST GO AND TAKE THESE.
NO MATTER WHAT, KNOW THAT WHAT WE HAVE BEEN DOING IS IMPORTANT.

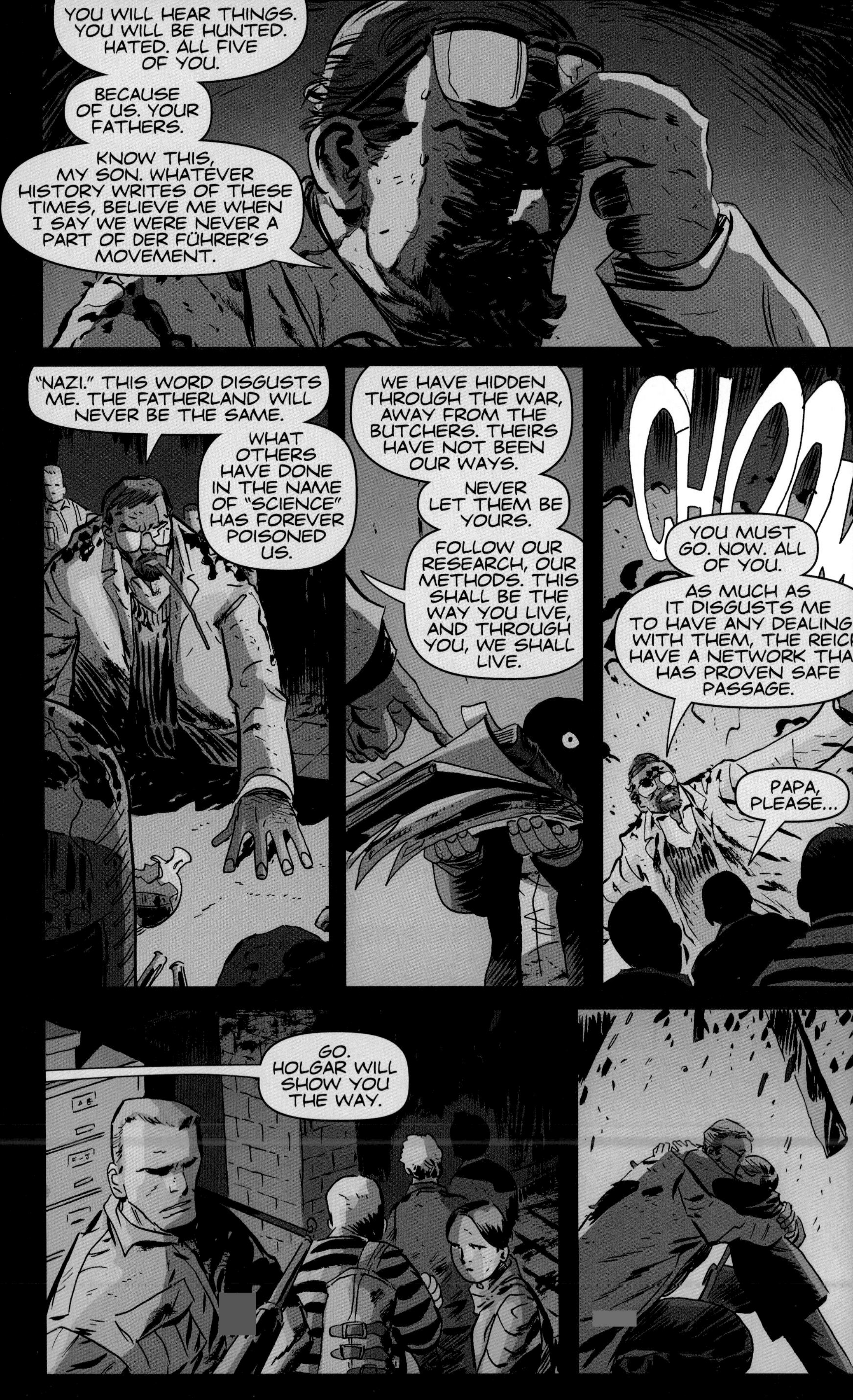
YOU WILL HEAR THINGS. YOU WILL BE HUNTED. HATED. ALL FIVE OF YOU.
BECAUSE OF US. YOUR FATHERS.
KNOW THIS, MY SON. WHATEVER HISTORY WRITES OF THESE TIMES, BELIEVE ME WHEN I SAY WE WERE NEVER A PART OF DER FÜHRER'S MOVEMENT.
"NAZI." THIS WORD DISGUSTS ME. THE FATHERLAND WILL NEVER BE THE SAME.
WHAT OTHERS HAVE DONE IN THE NAME OF "SCIENCE" HAS FOREVER POISONED US.
WE HAVE HIDDEN THROUGH THE WAR, AWAY FROM THE BUTCHERS. THEIRS HAVE NOT BEEN OUR WAYS.
NEVER LET THEM BE YOURS.
FOLLOW OUR RESEARCH, OUR METHODS. THIS SHALL BE THE WAY YOU LIVE, AND THROUGH YOU, WE SHALL LIVE.
CHOO
YOU MUST GO. NOW. ALL OF YOU.
AS MUCH AS IT DISGUSTS ME TO HAVE ANY DEALING WITH THEM, THE REIC HAVE A NETWORK THA HAS PROVEN SAFE PASSAGE.
PAPA, PLEASE...
GO. HOLGAR WILL SHOW YOU THE WAY.

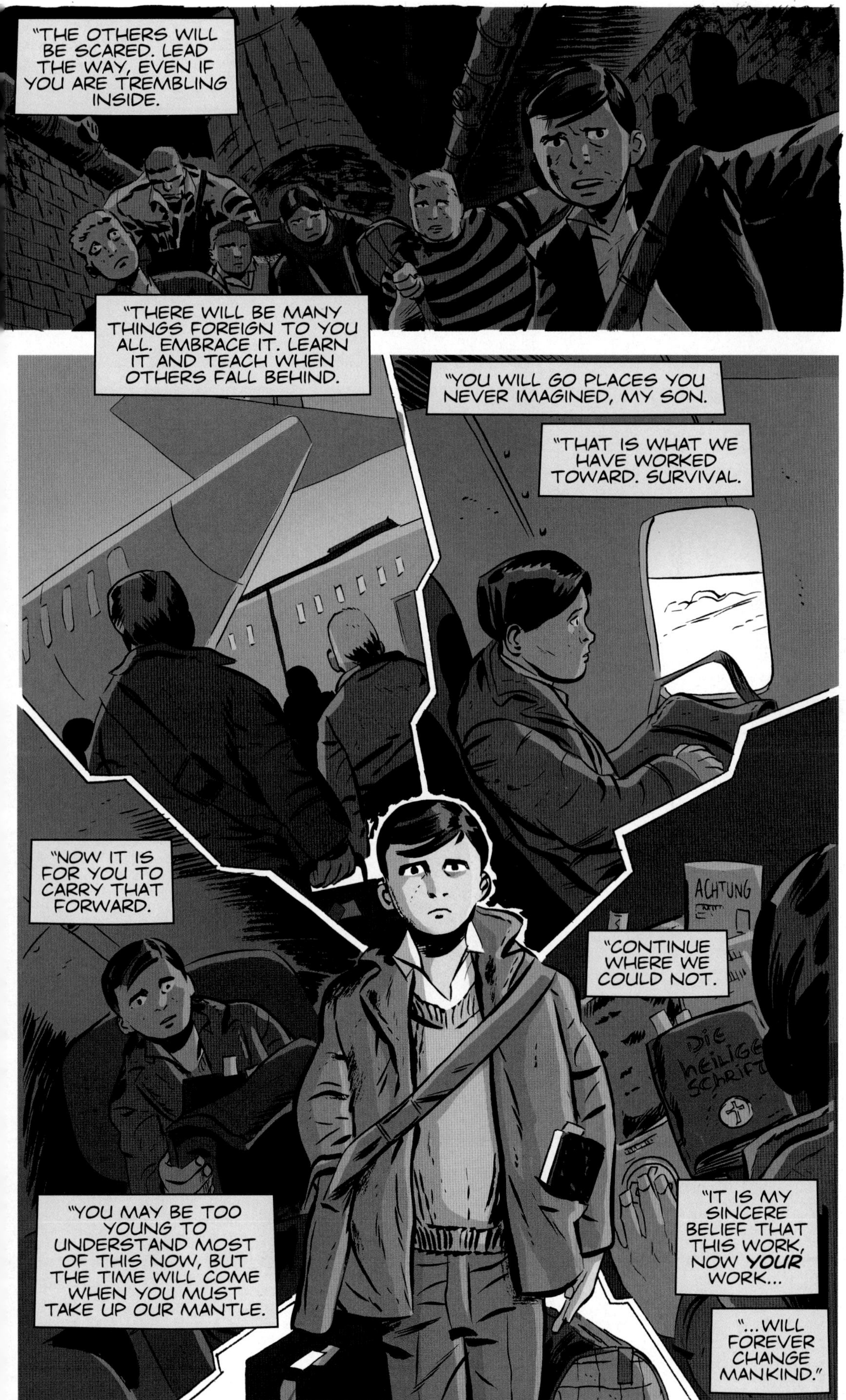
"THE OTHERS WILL BE SCARED. LEAD THE WAY, EVEN IF YOU ARE TREMBLING INSIDE.
"THERE WILL BE MANY THINGS FOREIGN TO YOU ALL. EMBRACE IT. LEARN IT AND TEACH WHEN OTHERS FALL BEHIND.
"YOU WILL GO PLACES YOU NEVER IMAGINED, MY SON.
"THAT IS WHAT WE HAVE WORKED TOWARD. SURVIVAL.
"NOW IT IS FOR YOU TO CARRY THAT FORWARD.
ACHTUNG
"CONTINUE WHERE WE COULD NOT.
Die heilige Schrift
"YOU MAY BE TOO YOUNG TO UNDERSTAND MOST OF THIS NOW, BUT THE TIME WILL COME WHEN YOU MUST TAKE UP OUR MANTLE.
"IT IS MY SINCERE BELIEF THAT THIS WORK, NOW ***YOUR*** WORK...
"...WILL FOREVER CHANGE MANKIND."

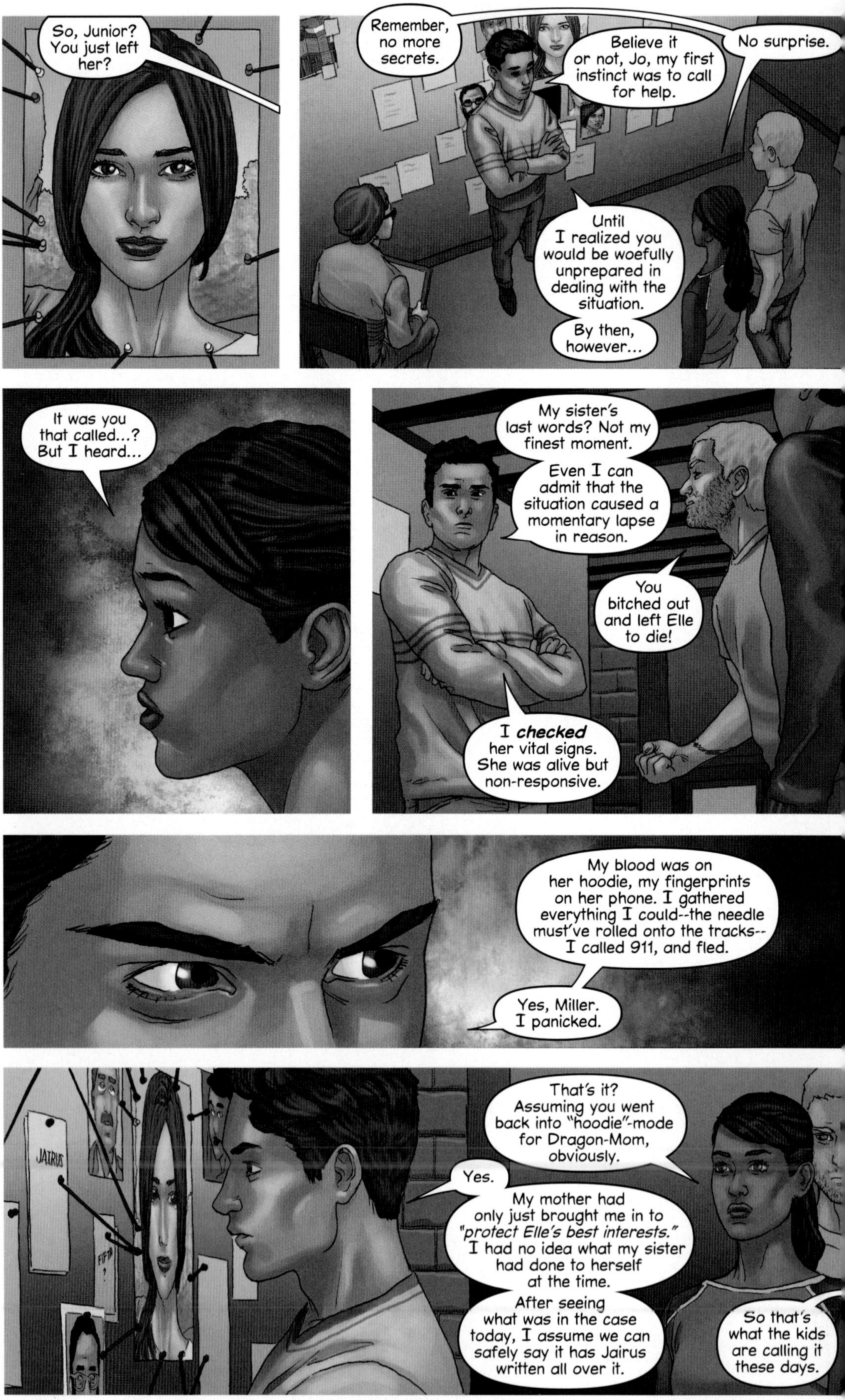

So, Junior? You just left her?
Remember, no more secrets.
Believe it or not, Jo, my first instinct was to call for help.
No surprise.
Until I realized you would be woefully unprepared in dealing with the situation.
By then, however...
It was you that called...? But I heard...
My sister's last words? Not my finest moment.
Even I can admit that the situation caused a momentary lapse in reason.
You bitched out and left Elle to die!
I *checked* her vital signs. She was alive but non-responsive.
My blood was on her hoodie, my fingerprints on her phone. I gathered everything I could--the needle must've rolled onto the tracks-- I called 911, and fled.
Yes, Miller. I panicked.
JAIRUS
That's it? Assuming you went back into "hoodie"-mode for Dragon-Mom, obviously.
Yes.
My mother had only just brought me in to *"protect Elle's best interests."* I had no idea what my sister had done to herself at the time.
After seeing what was in the case today, I assume we can safely say it has Jairus written all over it.
So that's what the kids are calling it these days.

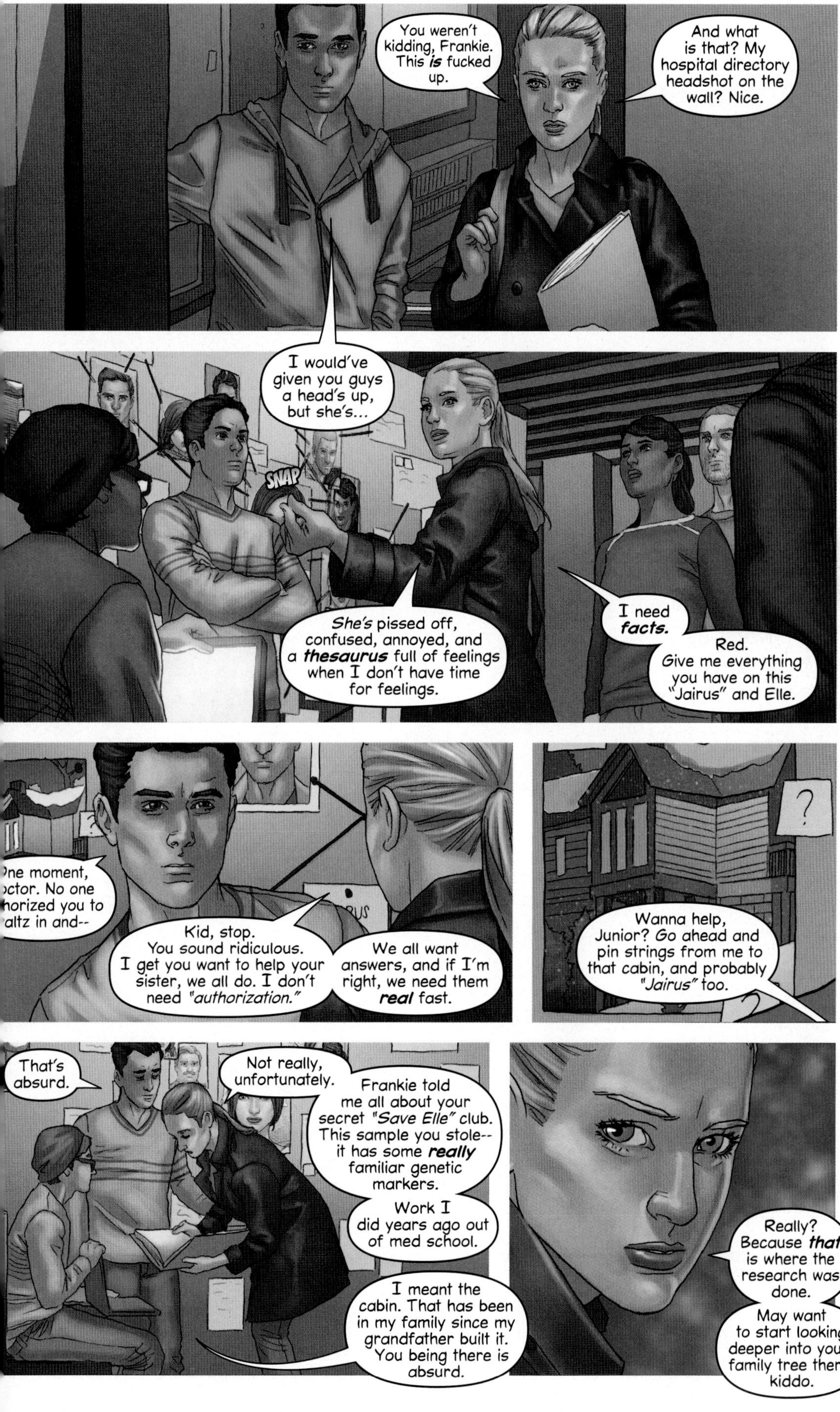

You weren't kidding, Frankie. This *is* fucked up.
And what is that? My hospital directory headshot on the wall? Nice.
I would've given you guys a head's up, but she's...
SNAP
She's pissed off, confused, annoyed, and a ***thesaurus*** full of feelings when I don't have time for feelings.
I need ***facts.***
Red. Give me everything you have on this "Jairus" and Elle.
ne moment, ctor. No one horized you to altz in and--
Kid, stop. You sound ridiculous. I get you want to help your sister, we all do. I don't need *"authorization."*
We all want answers, and if I'm right, we need them ***real*** fast.
Wanna help, Junior? *Go* ahead and pin strings from me to that cabin, and probably *"Jairus"* too.
That's absurd.
Not really, unfortunately.
Frankie told me all about your secret *"Save Elle"* club. This sample you stole-- it has some ***really*** familiar genetic markers.
Work I did years ago out of med school.
I meant the cabin. That has been in my family since my grandfather built it. You being there is absurd.
Really? Because ***that*** is where the research was done.
May want to start looking deeper into your family tree there, kiddo.

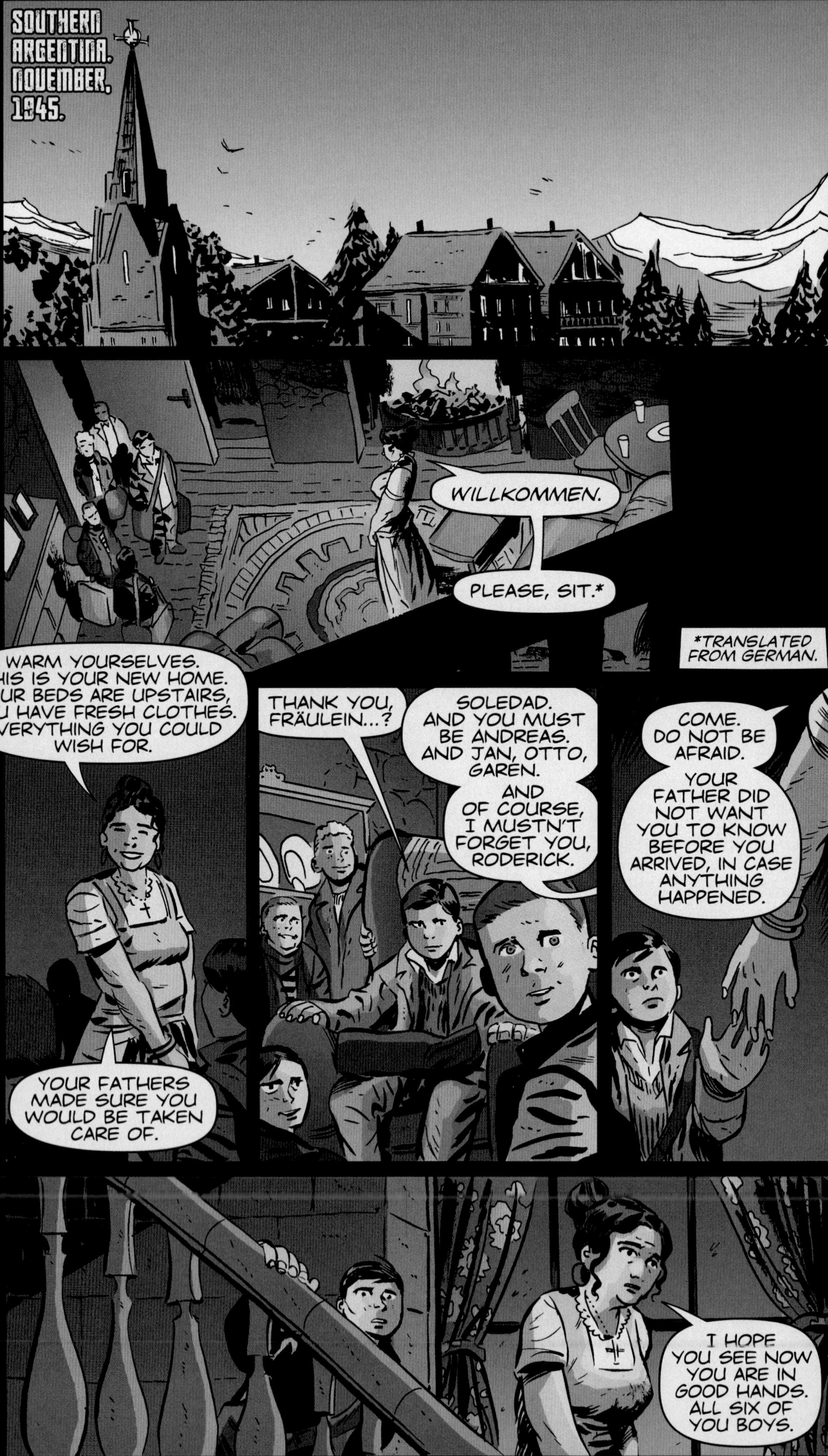
SOUTHERN ARGENTINA. NOVEMBER, 1945.
WILLKOMMEN.
PLEASE, SIT.*
*TRANSLATED FROM GERMAN.
WARM YOURSELVES. THIS IS YOUR NEW HOME. YOUR BEDS ARE UPSTAIRS, YOU HAVE FRESH CLOTHES. EVERYTHING YOU COULD WISH FOR.
YOUR FATHERS MADE SURE YOU WOULD BE TAKEN CARE OF.
THANK YOU, FRÄULEIN...?
SOLEDAD. AND YOU MUST BE ANDREAS. AND JAN, OTTO, GAREN.
AND OF COURSE, I MUSTN'T FORGET YOU, RODERICK.
COME. DO NOT BE AFRAID.
YOUR FATHER DID NOT WANT YOU TO KNOW BEFORE YOU ARRIVED, IN CASE ANYTHING HAPPENED.
I HOPE YOU SEE NOW YOU ARE IN GOOD HANDS. ALL SIX OF YOU BOYS.

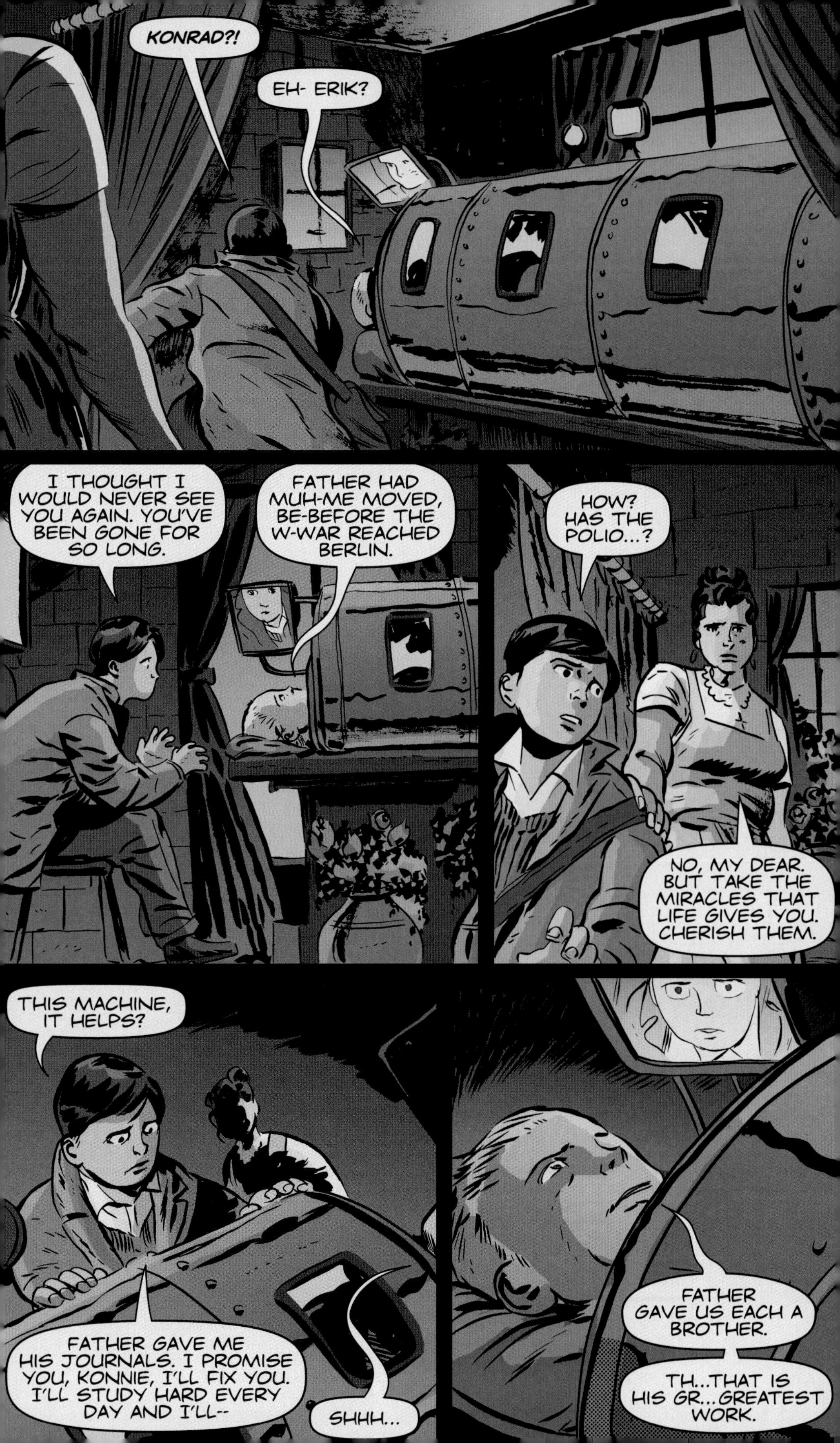
KONRAD?!
EH- ERIK?
I THOUGHT I WOULD NEVER SEE YOU AGAIN. YOU'VE BEEN GONE FOR SO LONG.
FATHER HAD MUH-ME MOVED, BE-BEFORE THE W-WAR REACHED BERLIN.
HOW? HAS THE POLIO...?
NO, MY DEAR. BUT TAKE THE MIRACLES THAT LIFE GIVES YOU. CHERISH THEM.
THIS MACHINE, IT HELPS?
FATHER GAVE ME HIS JOURNALS. I PROMISE YOU, KONNIE, I'LL FIX YOU. I'LL STUDY HARD EVERY DAY AND I'LL--
SHHH...
FATHER GAVE US EACH A BROTHER.
TH...THAT IS HIS GR...GREATEST WORK.

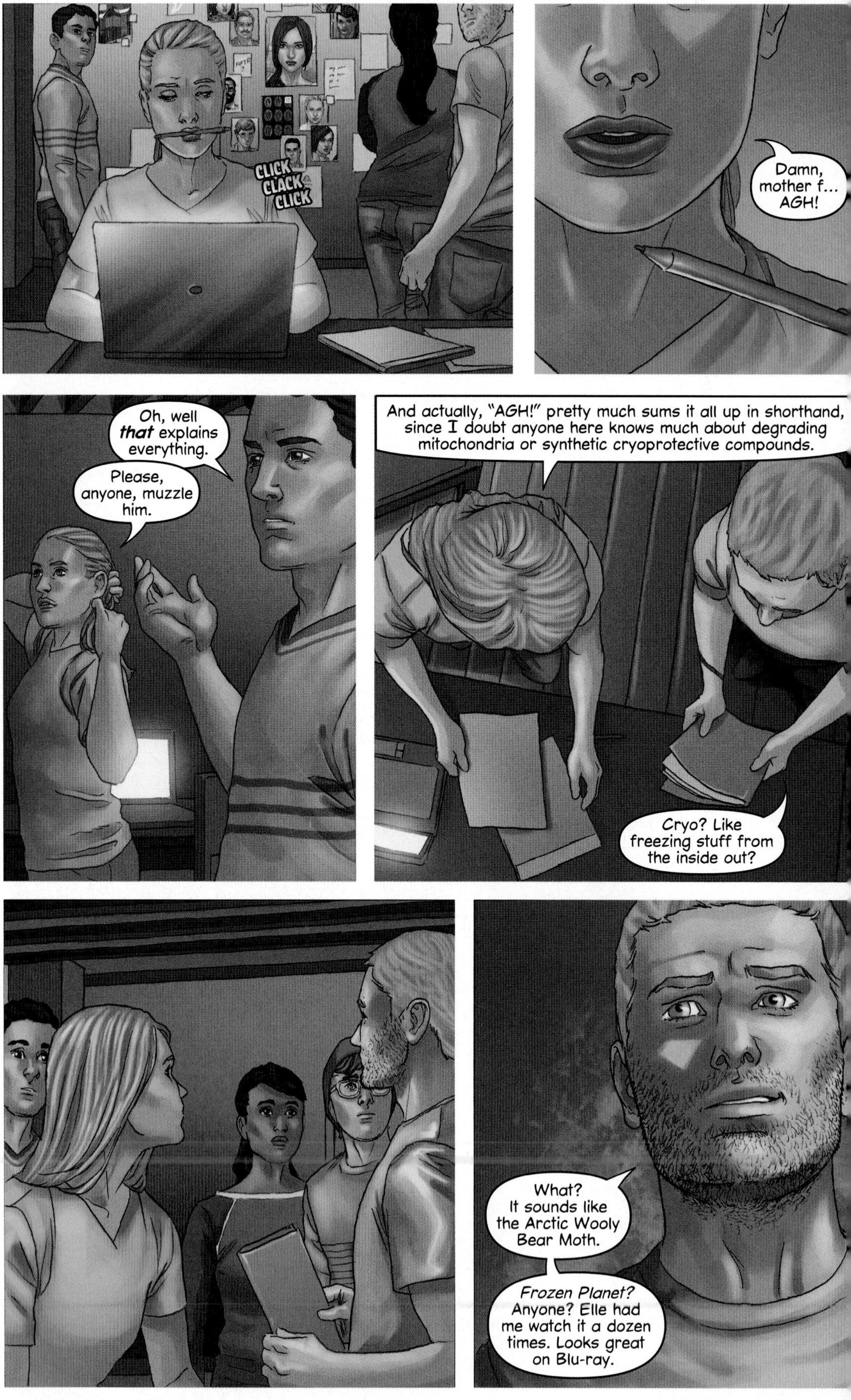
CLICK CLACK CLICK
Damn, mother f... AGH!
Oh, well *that* explains everything.
Please, anyone, muzzle him.
And actually, "AGH!" pretty much sums it all up in shorthand, since I doubt anyone here knows much about degrading mitochondria or synthetic cryoprotective compounds.
Cryo? Like freezing stuff from the inside out?
What? It sounds like the Arctic Wooly Bear Moth.
Frozen Planet? Anyone? Elle had me watch it a dozen times. Looks great on Blu-ray.

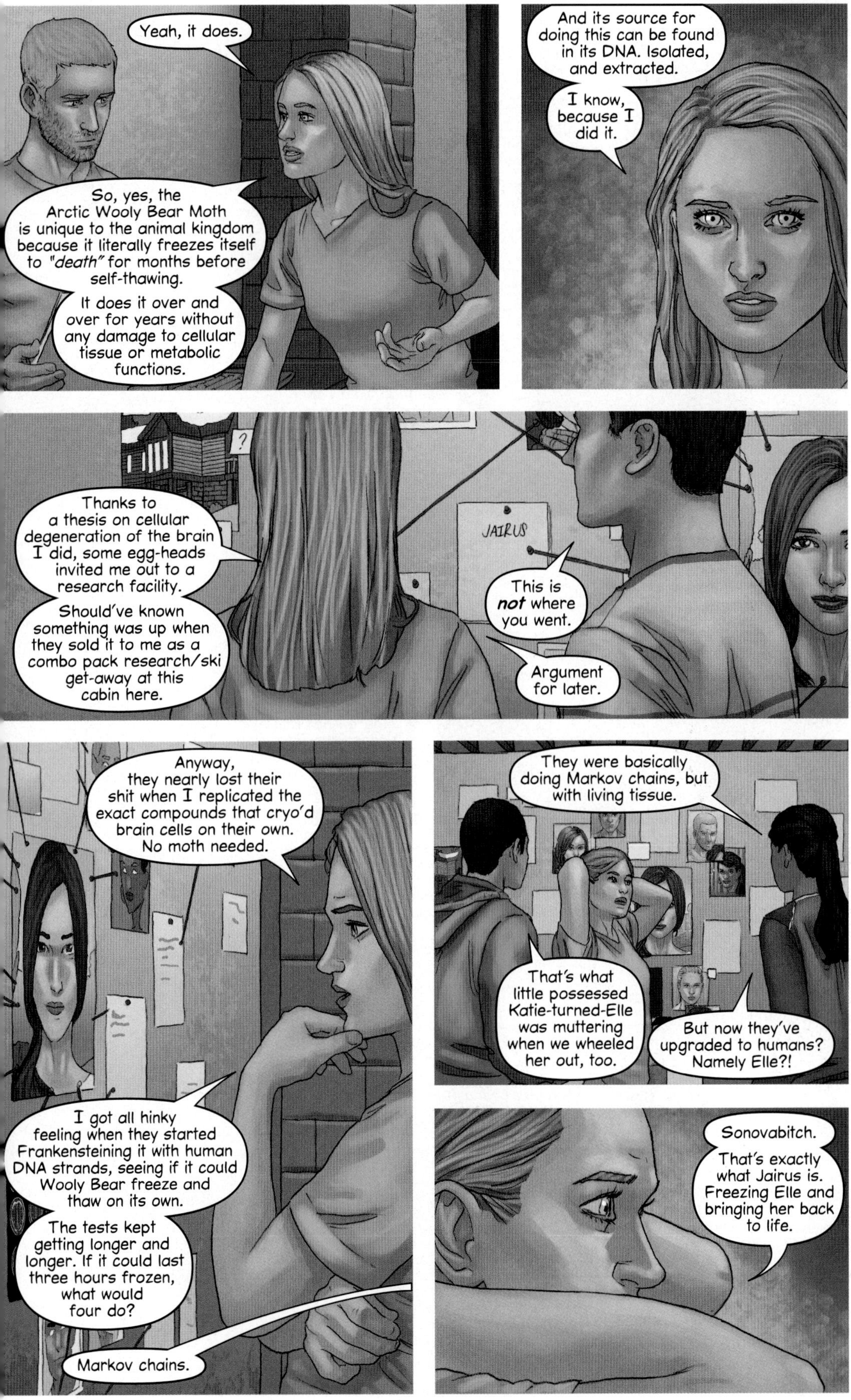
Yeah, it does.
So, yes, the Arctic Wooly Bear Moth is unique to the animal kingdom because it literally freezes itself to *"death"* for months before self-thawing.
It does it over and over for years without any damage to cellular tissue or metabolic functions.
And its source for doing this can be found in its DNA. Isolated, and extracted.
I know, because I did it.
?
Thanks to a thesis on cellular degeneration of the brain I did, some egg-heads invited me out to a research facility.
Should've known something was up when they sold it to me as a combo pack research/ski get-away at this cabin here.
JAIRUS
This is ***not*** where you went.
Argument for later.
Anyway, they nearly lost their shit when I replicated the exact compounds that cryo'd brain cells on their own. No moth needed.
I got all hinky feeling when they started Frankensteining it with human DNA strands, seeing if it could Wooly Bear freeze and thaw on its own.
The tests kept getting longer and longer. If it could last three hours frozen, what would four do?
Markov chains.
They were basically doing Markov chains, but with living tissue.
That's what little possessed Katie-turned-Elle was muttering when we wheeled her out, too.
But now they've upgraded to humans? Namely Elle?!
Sonovabitch.
That's exactly what Jairus is. Freezing Elle and bringing her back to life.

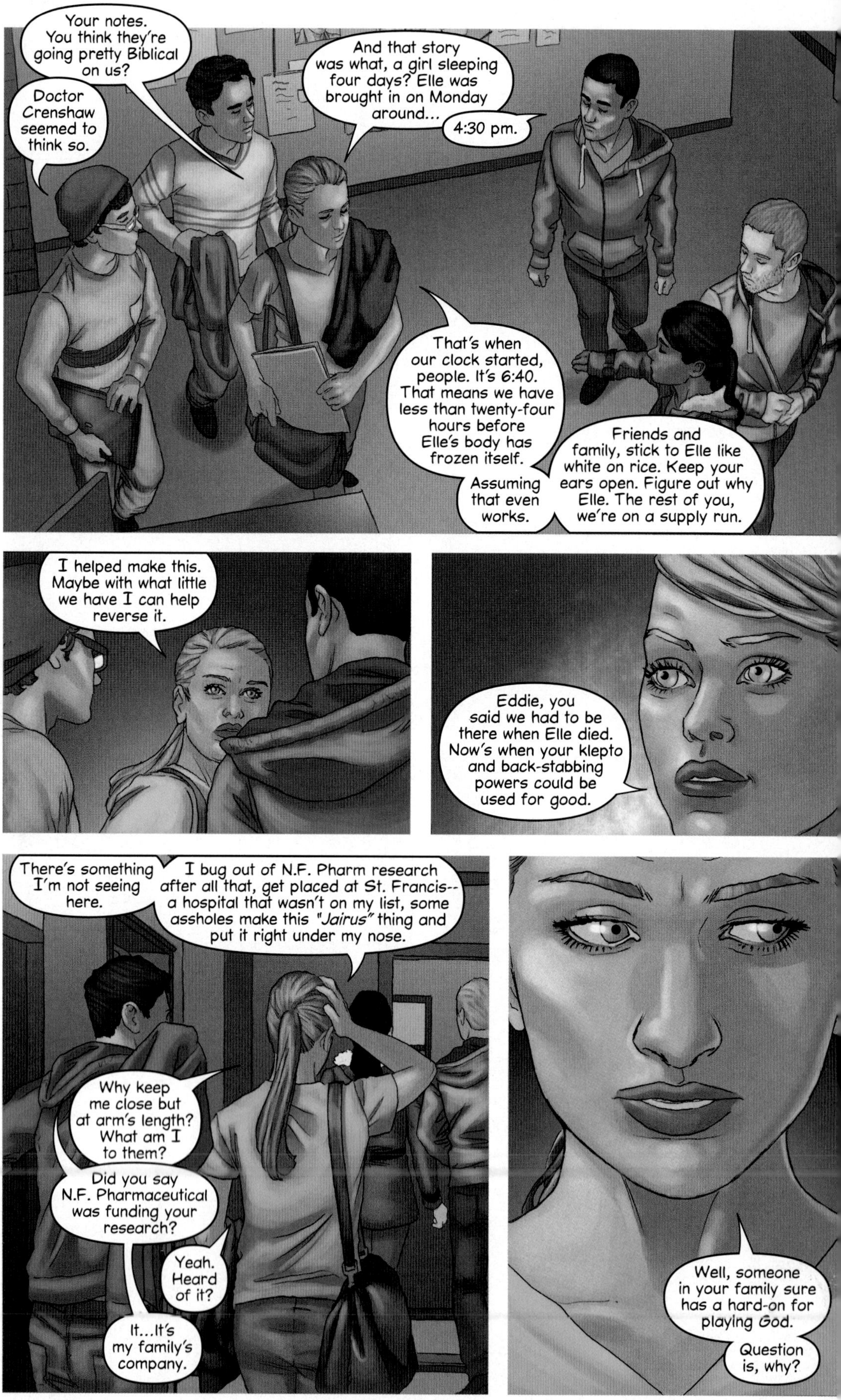
Your notes. You think they're going pretty Biblical on us?
Doctor Crenshaw seemed to think so.
And that story was what, a girl sleeping four days? Elle was brought in on Monday around...
4:30 pm.
That's when our clock started, people. It's 6:40. That means we have less than twenty-four hours before Elle's body has frozen itself.
Assuming that even works.
Friends and family, stick to Elle like white on rice. Keep your ears open. Figure out why Elle. The rest of you, we're on a supply run.
I helped make this. Maybe with what little we have I can help reverse it.
Eddie, you said we had to be there when Elle died. Now's when your klepto and back-stabbing powers could be used for good.
There's something I'm not seeing here.
I bug out of N.F. Pharm research after all that, get placed at St. Francis-- a hospital that wasn't on my list, some assholes make this "Jairus" thing and put it right under my nose.
Why keep me close but at arm's length? What am I to them?
Did you say N.F. Pharmaceutical was funding your research?
Yeah. Heard of it?
It...It's my family's company.
Well, someone in your family sure has a hard-on for playing God.
Question is, why?

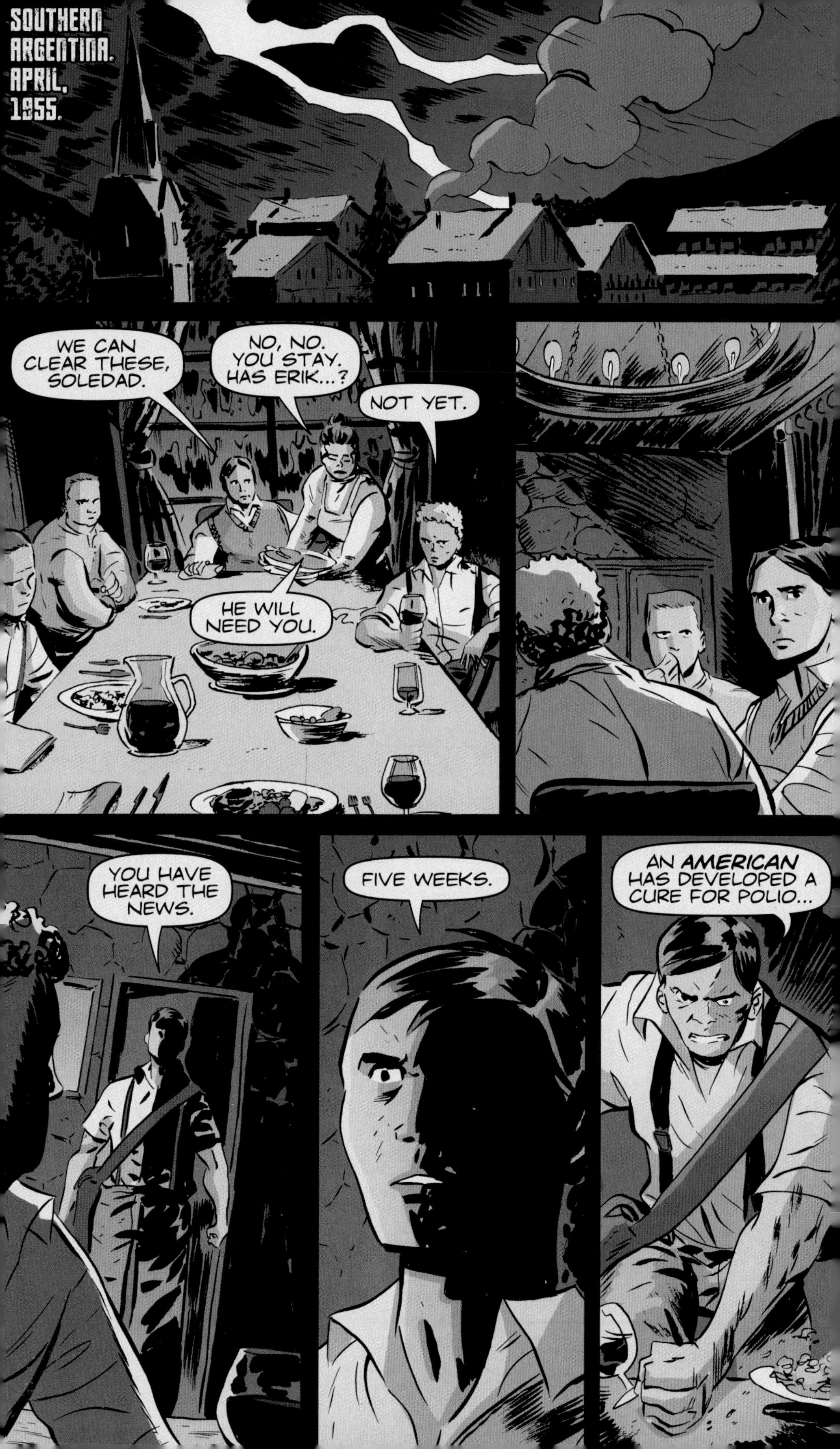
SOUTHERN ARGENTINA. APRIL, 1955.
WE CAN CLEAR THESE, SOLEDAD.
NO, NO. YOU STAY. HAS ERIK...?
NOT YET.
HE WILL NEED YOU.
YOU HAVE HEARD THE NEWS.
FIVE WEEKS.
AN AMERICAN HAS DEVELOPED A CURE FOR POLIO...

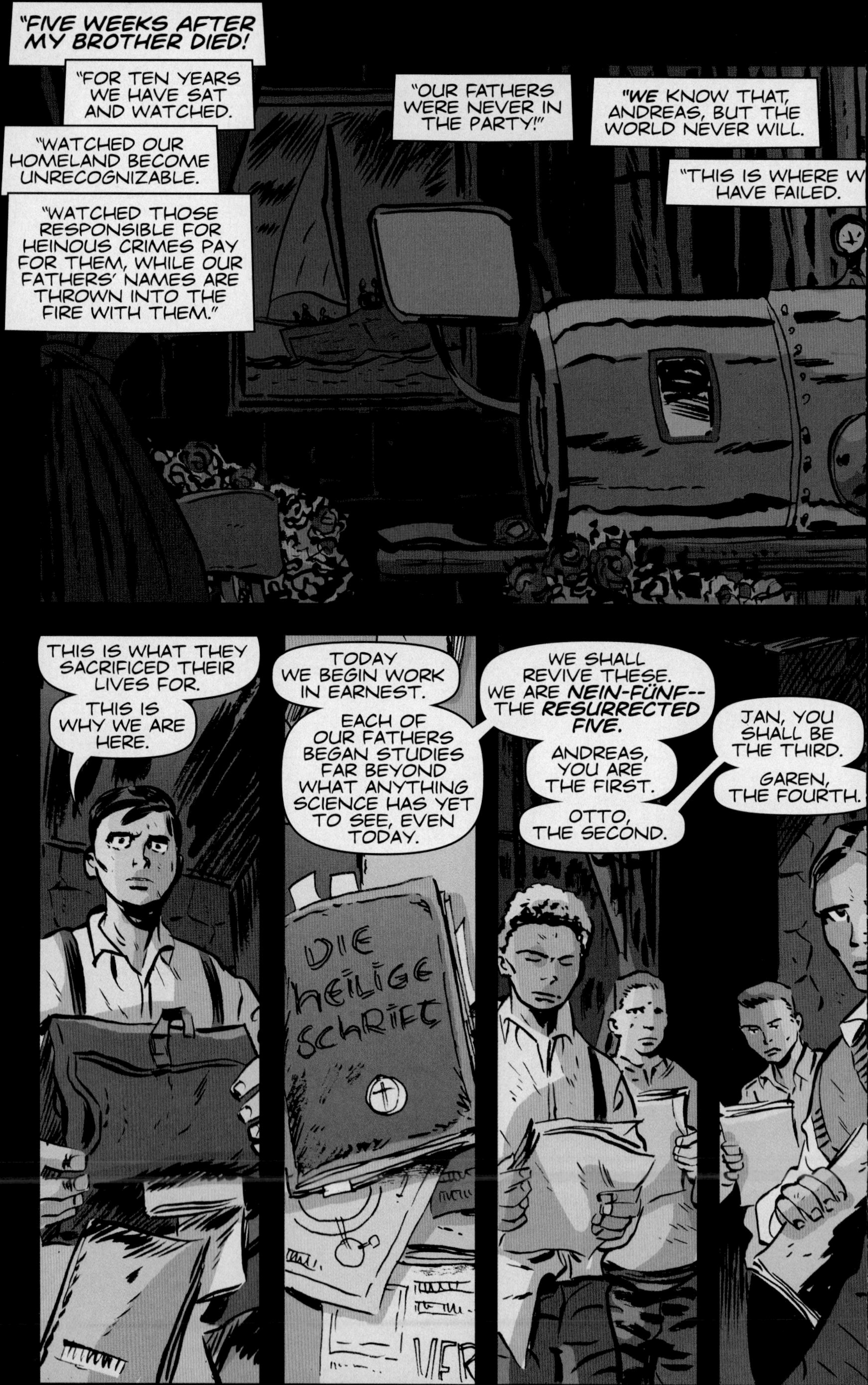
"FIVE WEEKS AFTER MY BROTHER DIED!
"FOR TEN YEARS WE HAVE SAT AND WATCHED.
"WATCHED OUR HOMELAND BECOME UNRECOGNIZABLE.
"WATCHED THOSE RESPONSIBLE FOR HEINOUS CRIMES PAY FOR THEM, WHILE OUR FATHERS' NAMES ARE THROWN INTO THE FIRE WITH THEM."
"OUR FATHERS WERE NEVER IN THE PARTY!"
"WE KNOW THAT, ANDREAS, BUT THE WORLD NEVER WILL.
"THIS IS WHERE W
HAVE FAILED.
THIS IS WHAT THEY SACRIFICED THEIR LIVES FOR.
THIS IS WHY WE ARE HERE.
TODAY WE BEGIN WORK IN EARNEST.
EACH OF OUR FATHERS BEGAN STUDIES FAR BEYOND WHAT ANYTHING SCIENCE HAS YET TO SEE, EVEN TODAY.
DIE HEILIGE SCHRIFT
WE SHALL REVIVE THESE. WE ARE NEIN-FÜNF-- THE RESURRECTED FIVE.
ANDREAS, YOU ARE THE FIRST.
OTTO, THE SECOND.
JAN, YOU SHALL BE THE THIRD.
GAREN, THE FOURTH.

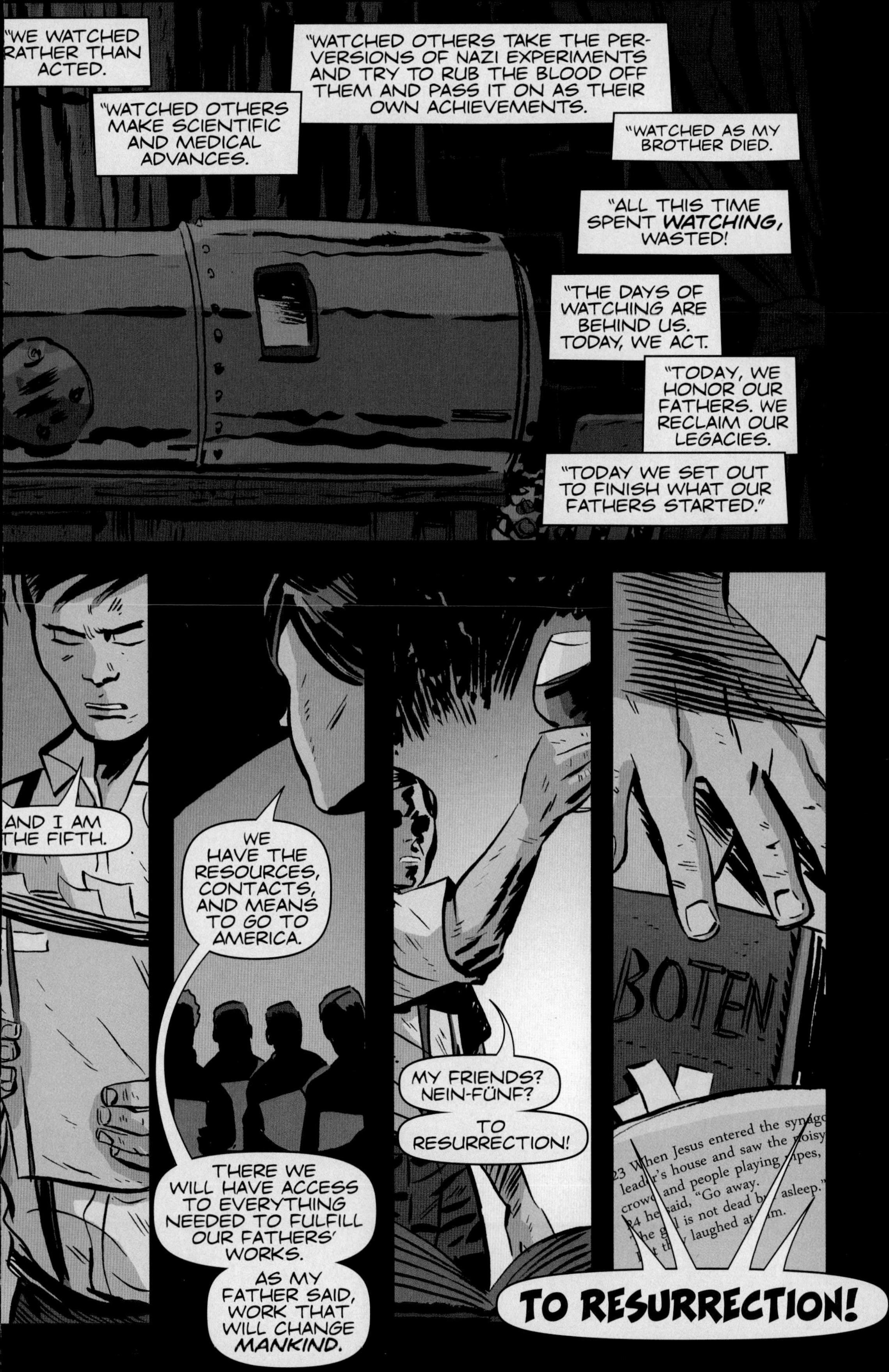
"WE WATCHED RATHER THAN ACTED.
"WATCHED OTHERS MAKE SCIENTIFIC AND MEDICAL ADVANCES.
"WATCHED OTHERS TAKE THE PERVERSIONS OF NAZI EXPERIMENTS AND TRY TO RUB THE BLOOD OFF THEM AND PASS IT ON AS THEIR OWN ACHIEVEMENTS.
"WATCHED AS MY BROTHER DIED.
"ALL THIS TIME SPENT *WATCHING*, WASTED!
"THE DAYS OF WATCHING ARE BEHIND US. TODAY, WE ACT.
"TODAY, WE HONOR OUR FATHERS. WE RECLAIM OUR LEGACIES.
"TODAY WE SET OUT TO FINISH WHAT OUR FATHERS STARTED."
AND I AM THE FIFTH.
WE HAVE THE RESOURCES, CONTACTS, AND MEANS TO GO TO AMERICA.
THERE WE WILL HAVE ACCESS TO EVERYTHING NEEDED TO FULFILL OUR FATHERS' WORKS.
AS MY FATHER SAID, WORK THAT WILL CHANGE *MANKIND*.
MY FRIENDS? NEIN-FÜNF?
TO RESURRECTION!
BOTEN
TO RESURRECTION!

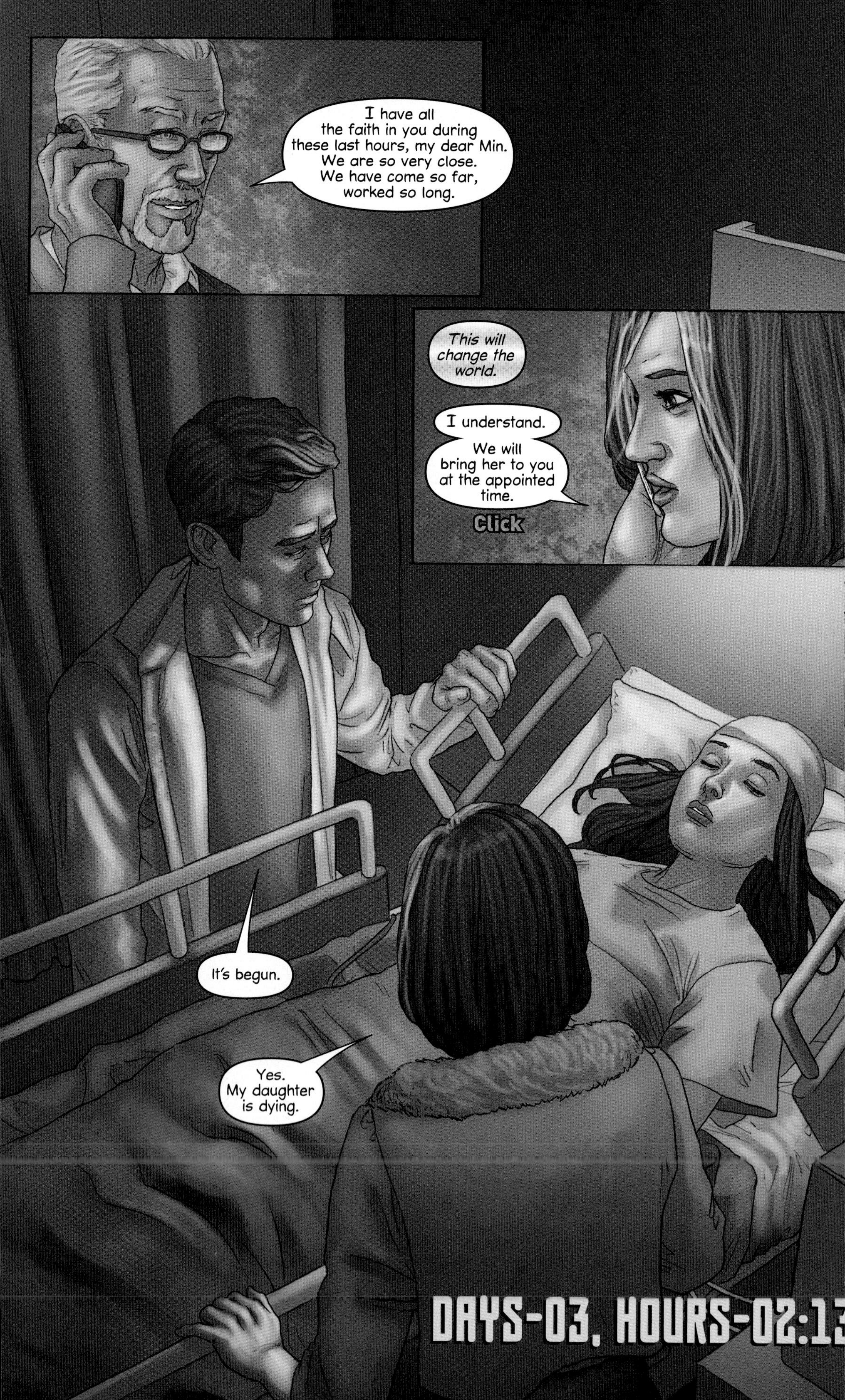
I have all the faith in you during these last hours, my dear Min. We are so very close. We have come so far, worked so long.
This will change the world.
I understand.
We will bring her to you at the appointed time.
Click
It's begun.
Yes. My daughter is dying.
DAYS-03, HOURS-02:13

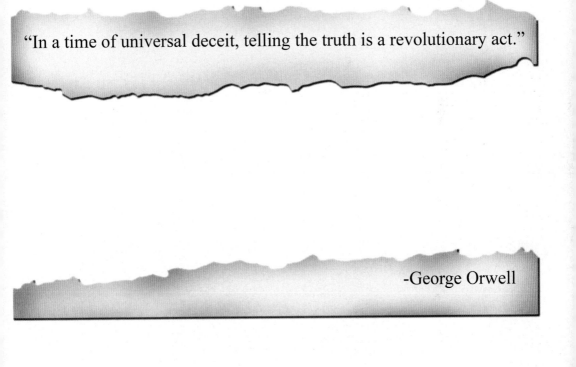

"In a time of universal deceit, telling the truth is a revolutionary act."

-George Orwell

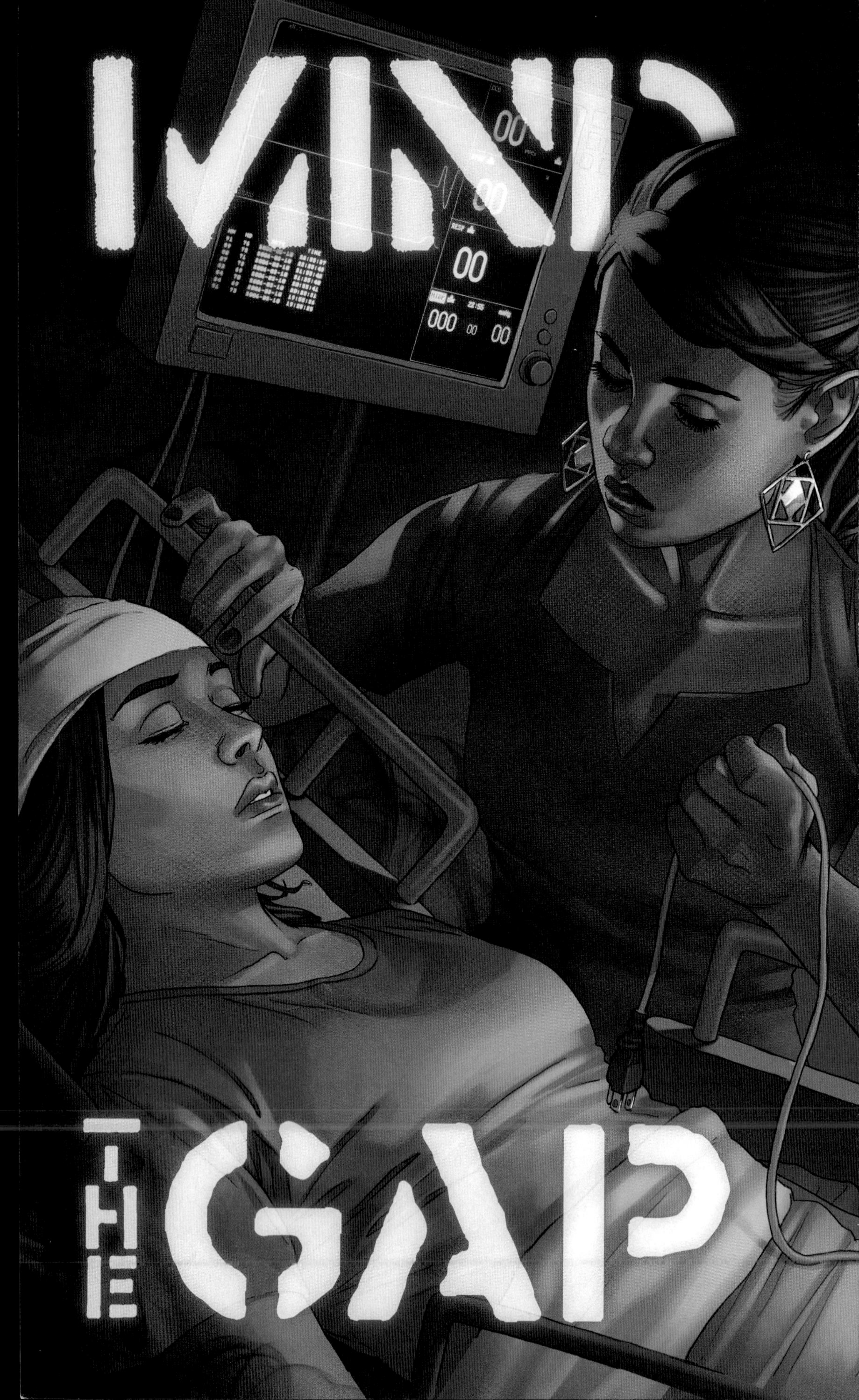
MIND
THE
GAP

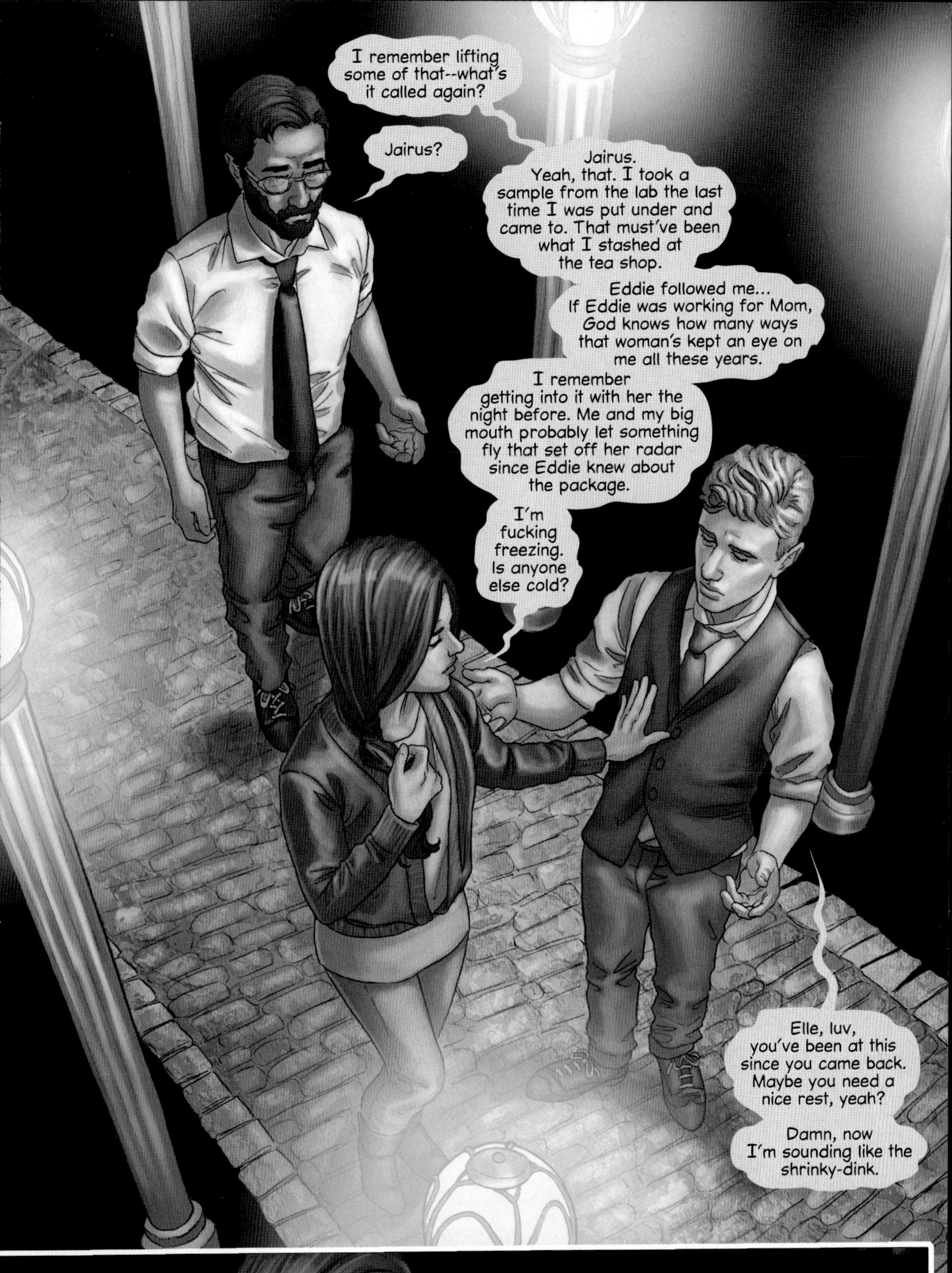
I remember lifting some of that--what's it called again?
Jairus?
Jairus. Yeah, that. I took a sample from the lab the last time I was put under and came to. That must've been what I stashed at the tea shop.
Eddie followed me... If Eddie was working for Mom, God knows how many ways that woman's kept an eye on me all these years.
I remember getting into it with her the night before. Me and my big mouth probably let something fly that set off her radar since Eddie knew about the package.
I'm fucking freezing. Is anyone else cold?
Elle, luv, you've been at this since you came back. Maybe you need a nice rest, yeah?
Damn, now I'm sounding like the shrinky-dink.

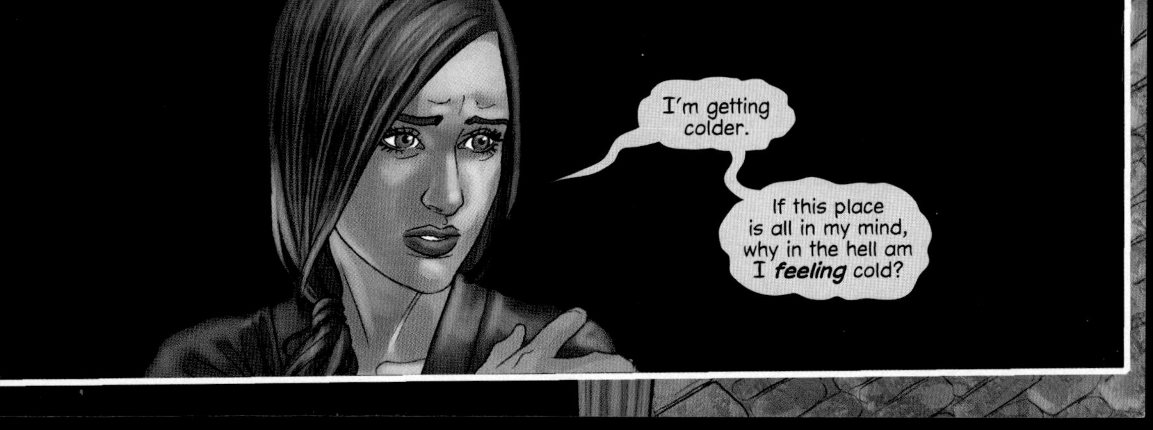
I'm getting colder.
If this place is all in my mind, why in the hell am I *feeling* cold?

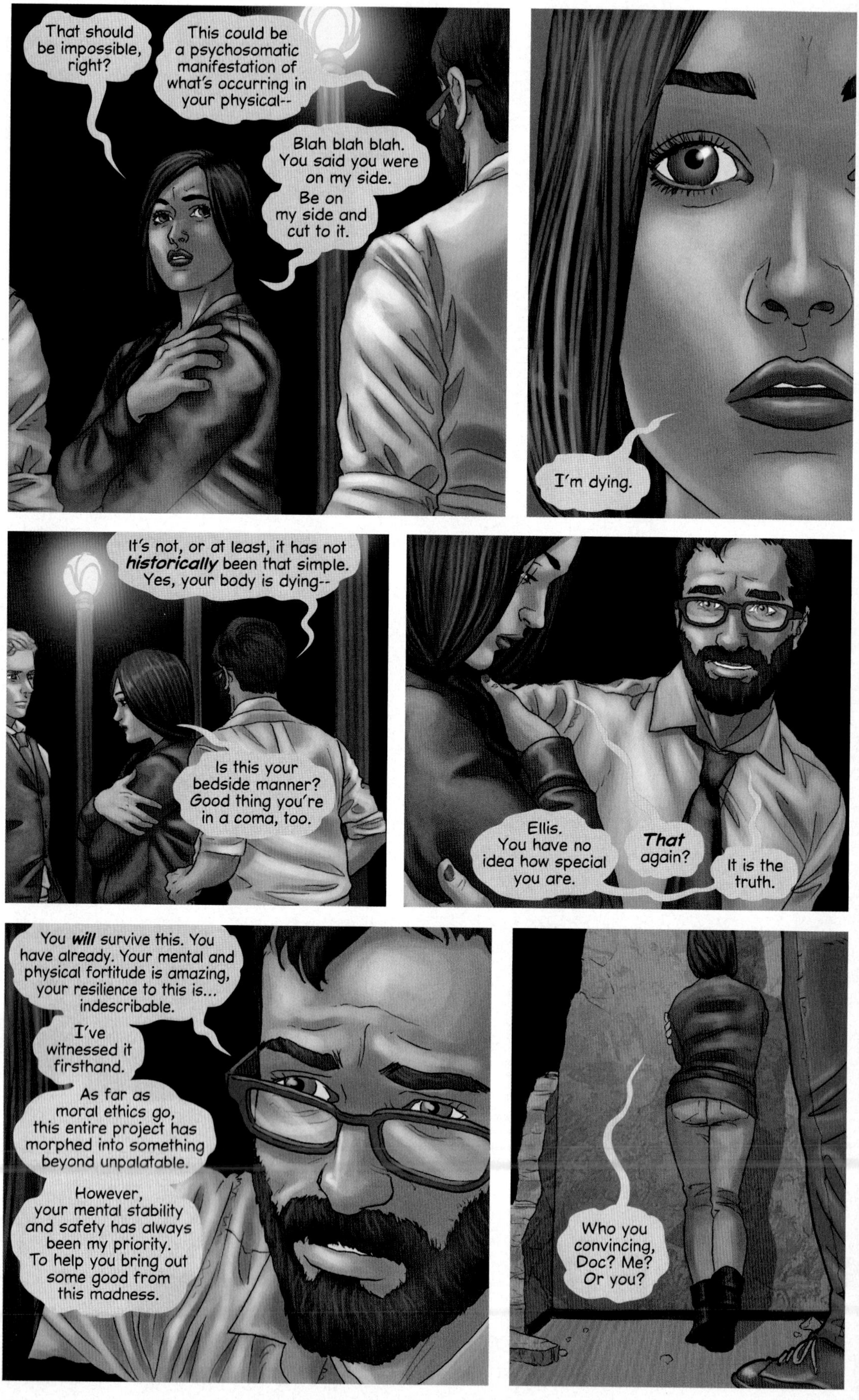
That should be impossible, right?
This could be a psychosomatic manifestation of what's occurring in your physical--
Blah blah blah. You said you were on my side.
Be on my side and cut to it.
I'm dying.
It's not, or at least, it has not *historically* been that simple. Yes, your body is dying--
Is this your bedside manner? Good thing you're in a coma, too.
Ellis. You have no idea how special you are.
That again?
It is the truth.
You *will* survive this. You have already. Your mental and physical fortitude is amazing, your resilience to this is... indescribable.
I've witnessed it firsthand.
As far as moral ethics go, this entire project has morphed into something beyond unpalatable.
However, your mental stability and safety has always been my priority. To help you bring out some good from this madness.
Who you convincing, Doc? Me? Or you?

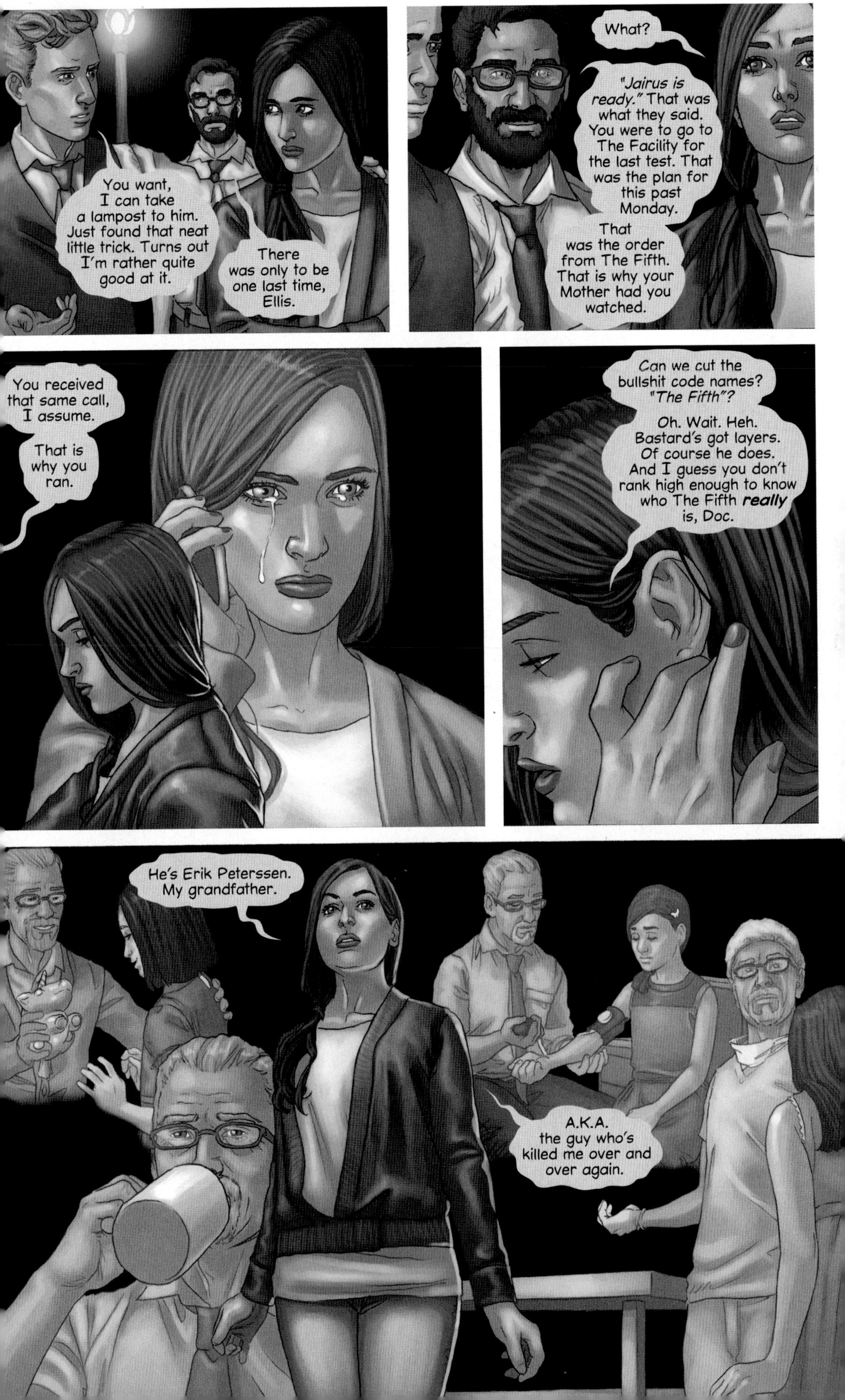
You want, I can take a lampost to him. Just found that neat little trick. Turns out I'm rather quite good at it.
There was only to be one last time, Ellis.
What?
"Jairus is ready." That was what they said. You were to go to The Facility for the last test. That was the plan for this past Monday.
That was the order from The Fifth. That is why your Mother had you watched.
You received that same call, I assume.
That is why you ran.
Can we cut the bullshit code names? "The Fifth"?
Oh. Wait. Heh. Bastard's got layers. Of course he does. And I guess you don't rank high enough to know who The Fifth **really** is, Doc.
He's Erik Peterssen. My grandfather.
A.K.A. the guy who's killed me over and over again.

R.I.Peterssen
PART 2
"THE WINDOW"

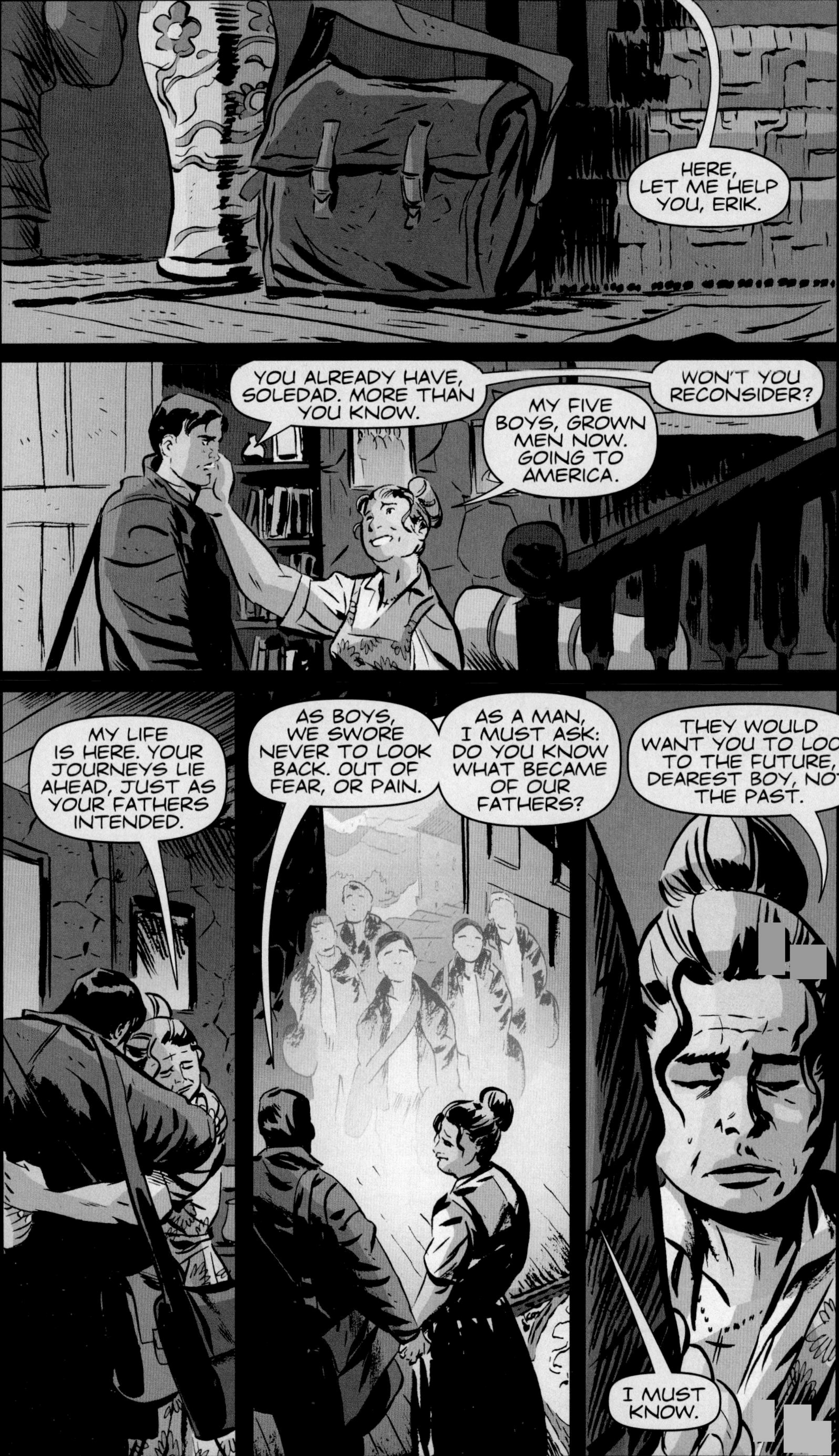
HERE, LET ME HELP YOU, ERIK.
YOU ALREADY HAVE, SOLEDAD. MORE THAN YOU KNOW.
MY FIVE BOYS, GROWN MEN NOW. GOING TO AMERICA.
WON'T YOU RECONSIDER?
MY LIFE IS HERE. YOUR JOURNEYS LIE AHEAD, JUST AS YOUR FATHERS INTENDED.
AS BOYS, WE SWORE NEVER TO LOOK BACK. OUT OF FEAR, OR PAIN.
AS A MAN, I MUST ASK: DO YOU KNOW WHAT BECAME OF OUR FATHERS?
THEY WOULD WANT YOU TO LOOK TO THE FUTURE, DEAREST BOY, NOT THE PAST.
I MUST KNOW.

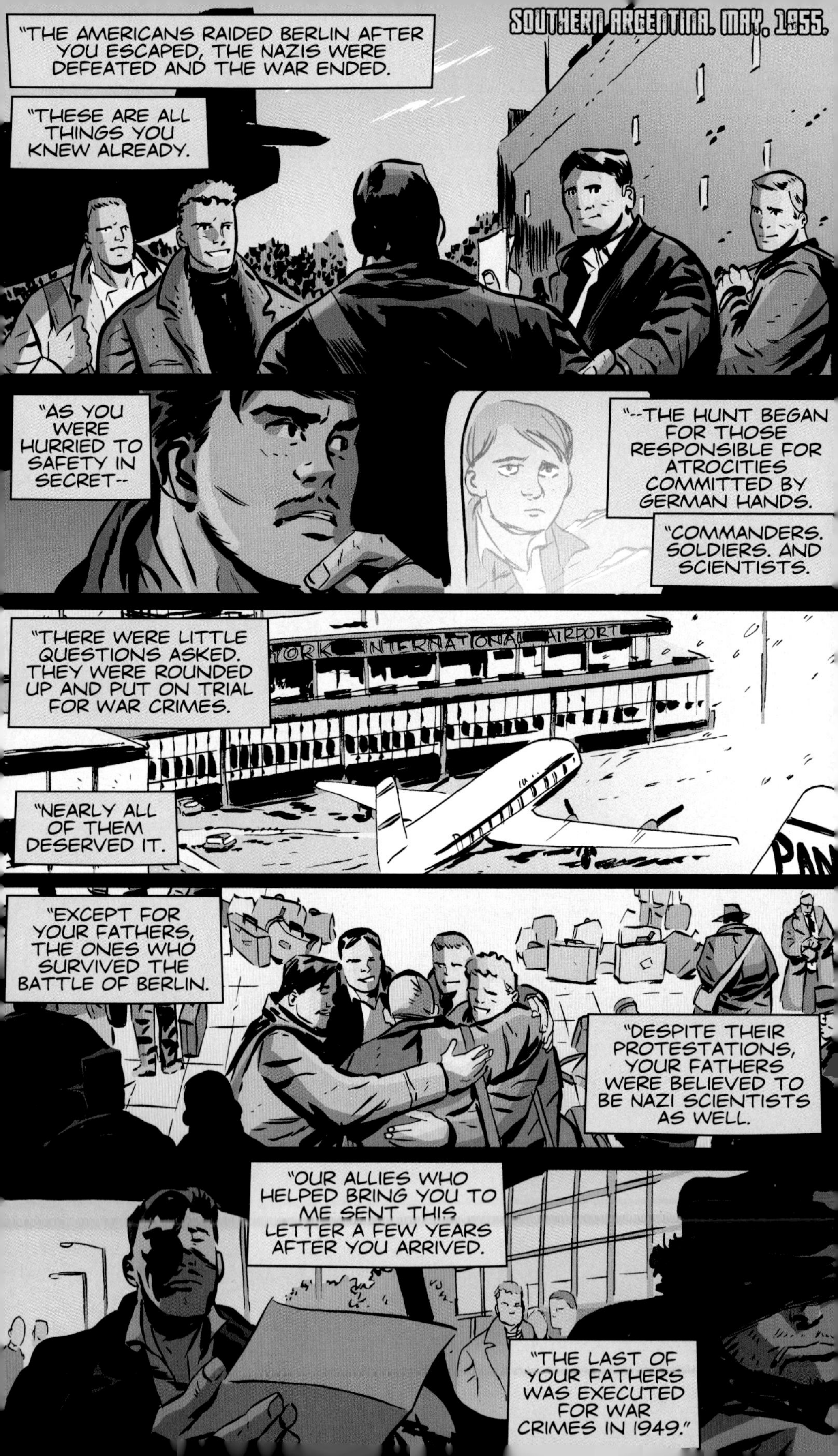
SOUTHERN ARGENTINA. MAY, 1955.
"THE AMERICANS RAIDED BERLIN AFTER YOU ESCAPED, THE NAZIS WERE DEFEATED AND THE WAR ENDED.
"THESE ARE ALL THINGS YOU KNEW ALREADY.
"AS YOU WERE HURRIED TO SAFETY IN SECRET--
"--THE HUNT BEGAN FOR THOSE RESPONSIBLE FOR ATROCITIES COMMITTED BY GERMAN HANDS.
"COMMANDERS. SOLDIERS. AND SCIENTISTS.
"THERE WERE LITTLE QUESTIONS ASKED. THEY WERE ROUNDED UP AND PUT ON TRIAL FOR WAR CRIMES.
INTERNATIONAL AIRPORT
"NEARLY ALL OF THEM DESERVED IT.
"EXCEPT FOR YOUR FATHERS, THE ONES WHO SURVIVED THE BATTLE OF BERLIN.
"DESPITE THEIR PROTESTATIONS, YOUR FATHERS WERE BELIEVED TO BE NAZI SCIENTISTS AS WELL.
"OUR ALLIES WHO HELPED BRING YOU TO ME SENT THIS LETTER A FEW YEARS AFTER YOU ARRIVED.
"THE LAST OF YOUR FATHERS WAS EXECUTED FOR WAR CRIMES IN 1949."

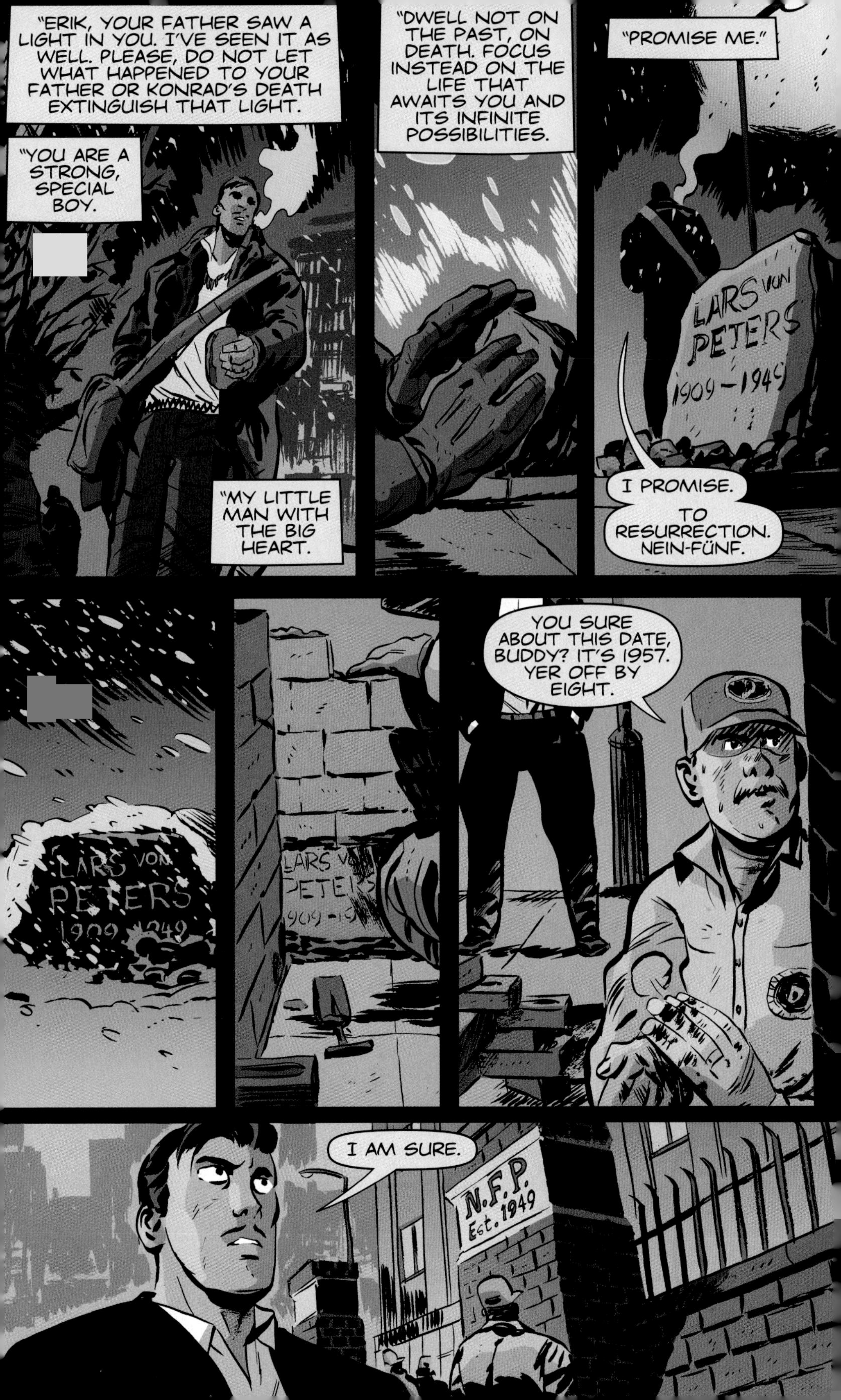
"ERIK, YOUR FATHER SAW A LIGHT IN YOU. I'VE SEEN IT AS WELL. PLEASE, DO NOT LET WHAT HAPPENED TO YOUR FATHER OR KONRAD'S DEATH EXTINGUISH THAT LIGHT.
"YOU ARE A STRONG, SPECIAL BOY.
"MY LITTLE MAN WITH THE BIG HEART.
"DWELL NOT ON THE PAST, ON DEATH. FOCUS INSTEAD ON THE LIFE THAT AWAITS YOU AND ITS INFINITE POSSIBILITIES.
"PROMISE ME."
LARS VON PETERS 1909 – 1949
I PROMISE.
TO RESURRECTION. NEIN-FÜNF.
LARS VON PETERS 1909 – 1949
YOU SURE ABOUT THIS DATE, BUDDY? IT'S 1957. YER OFF BY EIGHT.
I AM SURE.
N.F.P. Est. 1949

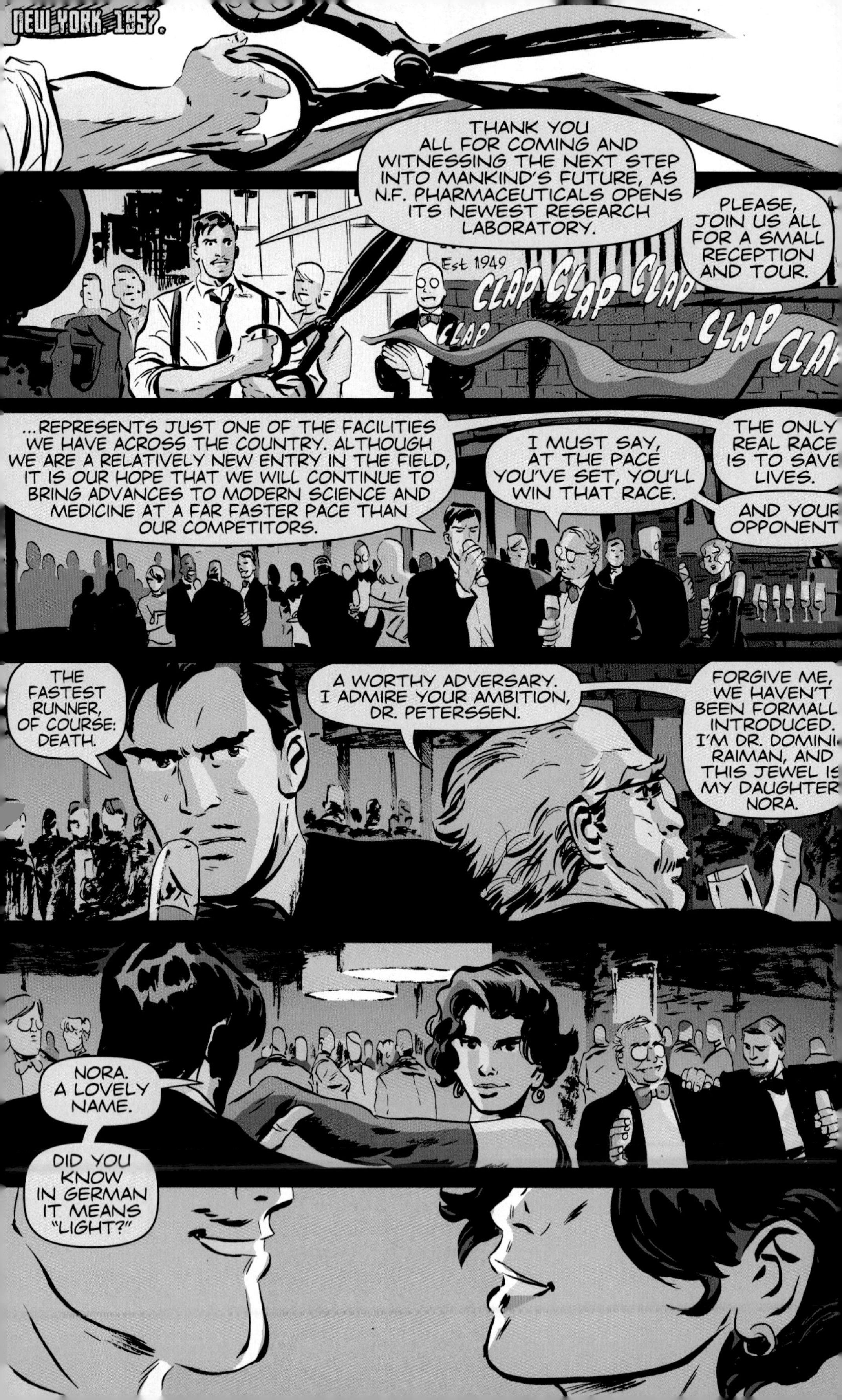
NEW YORK, 1957.
THANK YOU ALL FOR COMING AND WITNESSING THE NEXT STEP INTO MANKIND'S FUTURE, AS N.F. PHARMACEUTICALS OPENS ITS NEWEST RESEARCH LABORATORY.
PLEASE, JOIN US ALL FOR A SMALL RECEPTION AND TOUR.
Est 1949
CLAP CLAP CLAP CLAP CLAP CLAP
...REPRESENTS JUST ONE OF THE FACILITIES WE HAVE ACROSS THE COUNTRY. ALTHOUGH WE ARE A RELATIVELY NEW ENTRY IN THE FIELD, IT IS OUR HOPE THAT WE WILL CONTINUE TO BRING ADVANCES TO MODERN SCIENCE AND MEDICINE AT A FAR FASTER PACE THAN OUR COMPETITORS.
I MUST SAY, AT THE PACE YOU'VE SET, YOU'LL WIN THAT RACE.
THE ONLY REAL RACE IS TO SAVE LIVES.
AND YOUR OPPONENT
THE FASTEST RUNNER, OF COURSE: DEATH.
A WORTHY ADVERSARY. I ADMIRE YOUR AMBITION, DR. PETERSSEN.
FORGIVE ME, WE HAVEN'T BEEN FORMALL INTRODUCED. I'M DR. DOMINI RAIMAN, AND THIS JEWEL IS MY DAUGHTER NORA.
NORA. A LOVELY NAME.
DID YOU KNOW IN GERMAN IT MEANS "LIGHT?"

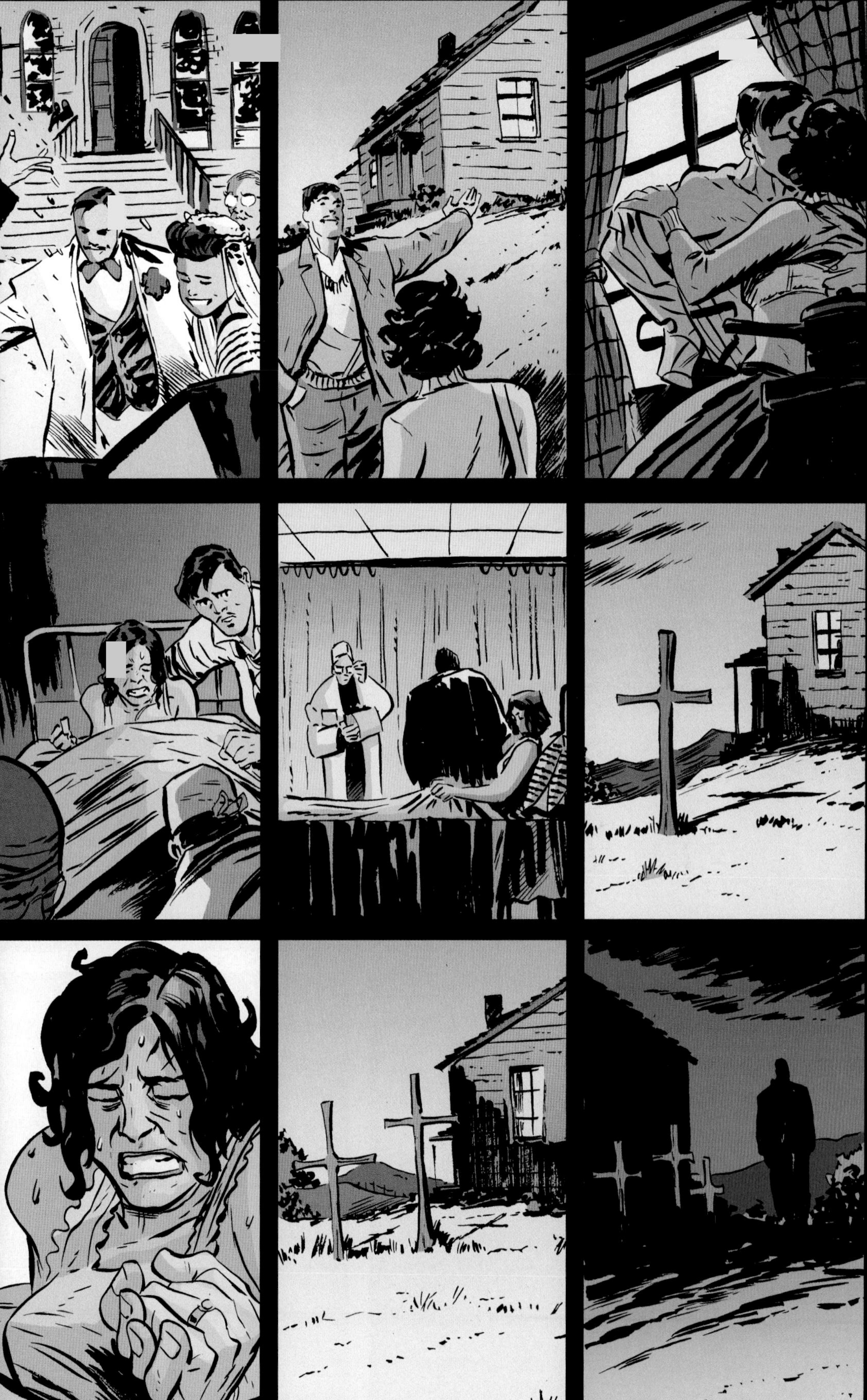

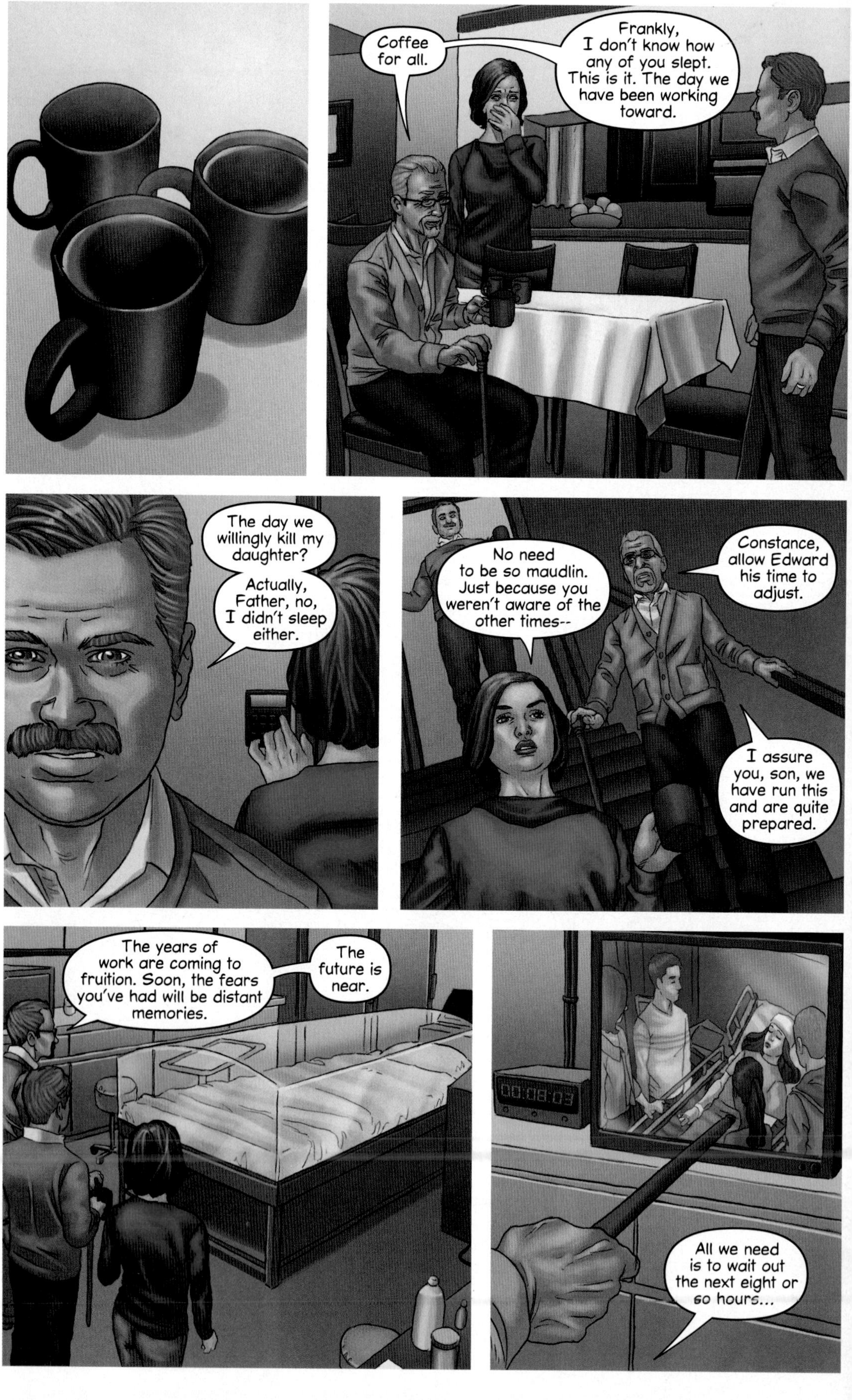
Coffee for all.
Frankly, I don't know how any of you slept. This is it. The day we have been working toward.
The day we willingly kill my daughter?
Actually, Father, no, I didn't sleep either.
No need to be so maudlin. Just because you weren't aware of the other times--
Constance, allow Edward his time to adjust.
I assure you, son, we have run this and are quite prepared.
The years of work are coming to fruition. Soon, the fears you've had will be distant memories.
The future is near.
00:08:03
All we need is to wait out the next eight or so hours...

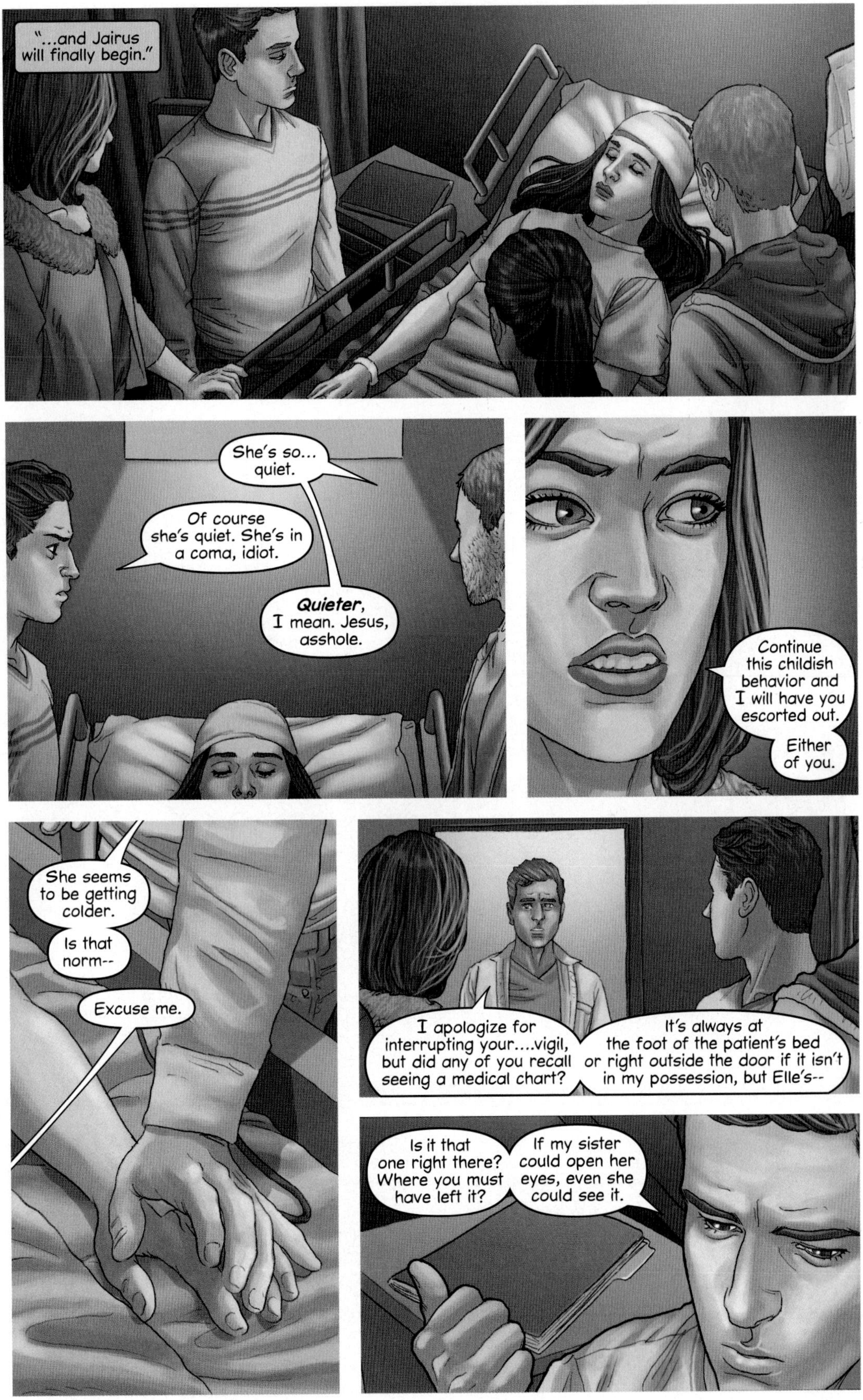
"...and Jairus will finally begin."
She's so... quiet.
Of course she's quiet. She's in a coma, idiot.
Quieter, I mean. Jesus, asshole.
Continue this childish behavior and I will have you escorted out.
Either of you.
She seems to be getting colder.
Is that norm--
Excuse me.
I apologize for interrupting your....vigil, but did any of you recall seeing a medical chart?
It's always at the foot of the patient's bed or right outside the door if it isn't in my possession, but Elle's--
Is it that one right there? Where you must have left it?
If my sister could open her eyes, even she could see it.

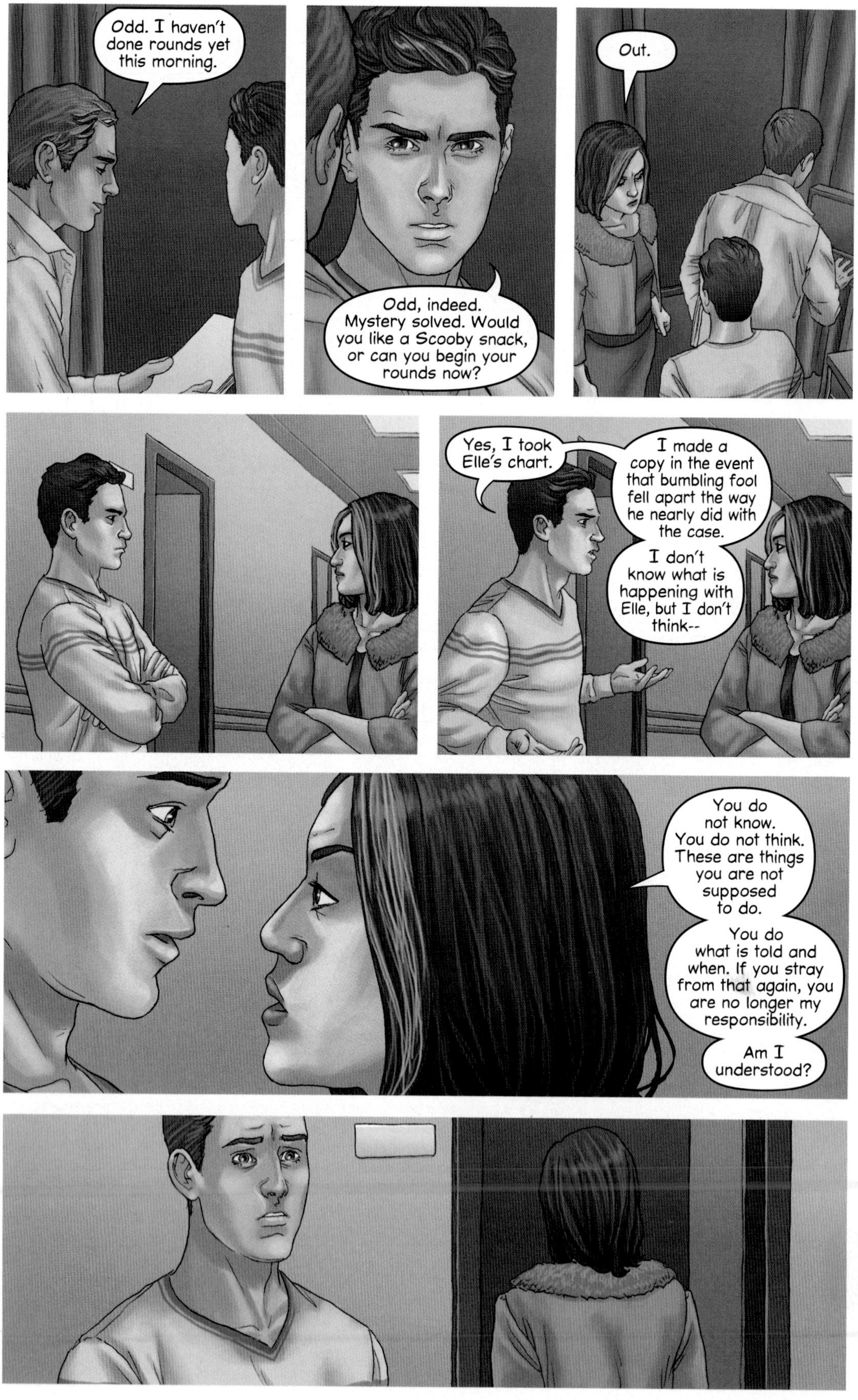

Odd. I haven't done rounds yet this morning.
Odd, indeed. Mystery solved. Would you like a Scooby snack, or can you begin your rounds now?
Out.
Yes, I took Elle's chart.
I made a copy in the event that bumbling fool fell apart the way he nearly did with the case.
I don't know what is happening with Elle, but I don't think--
You do not know. You do not think. These are things you are not supposed to do.
You do what is told and when. If you stray from that again, you are no longer my responsibility.
Am I understood?

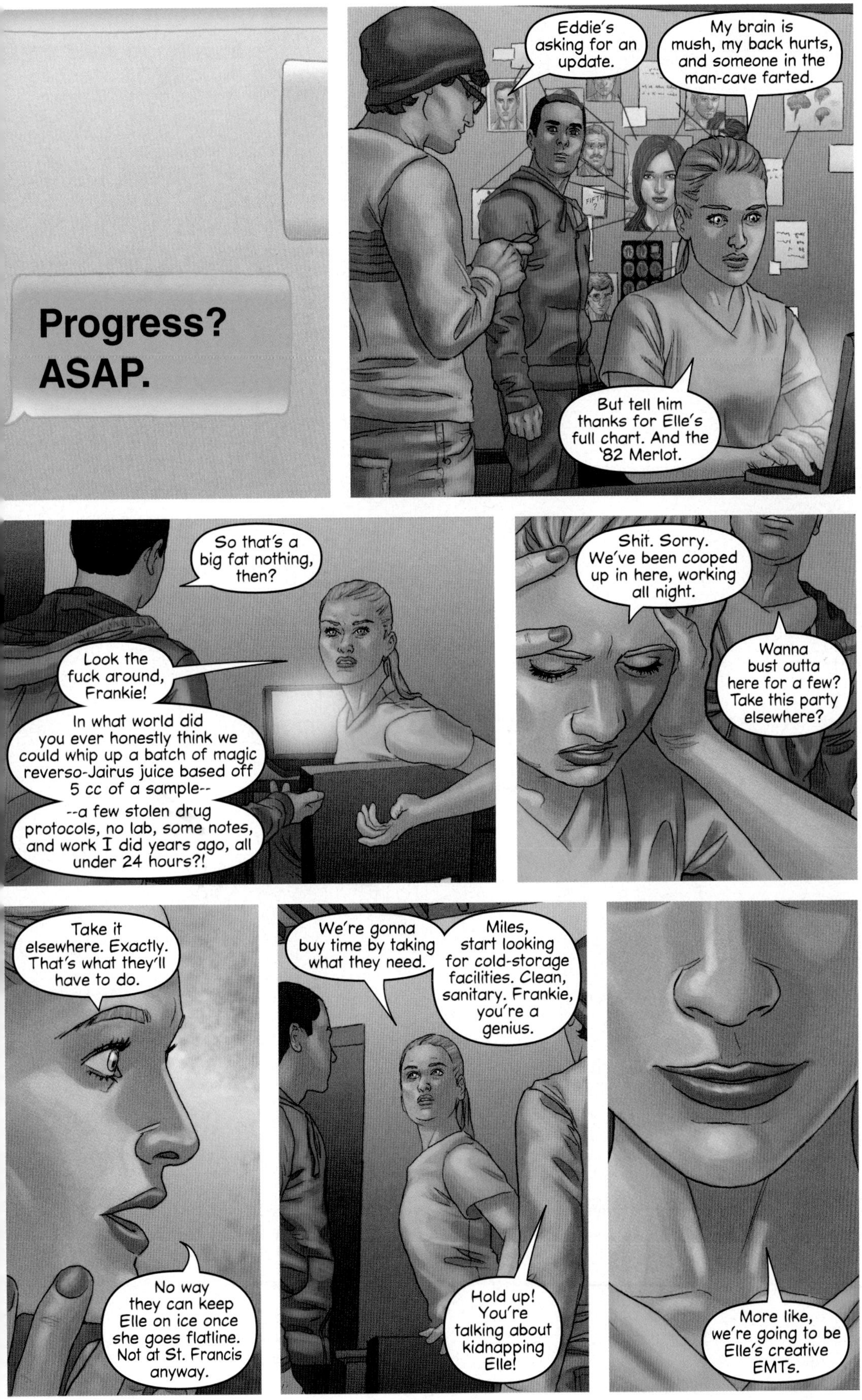
Progress?
ASAP.
Eddie's asking for an update.
My brain is mush, my back hurts, and someone in the man-cave farted.
But tell him thanks for Elle's full chart. And the '82 Merlot.
So that's a big fat nothing, then?
Look the fuck around, Frankie!
In what world did you ever honestly think we could whip up a batch of magic reverso-Jairus juice based off 5 cc of a sample--
--a few stolen drug protocols, no lab, some notes, and work I did years ago, all under 24 hours?!
Shit. Sorry. We've been cooped up in here, working all night.
Wanna bust outta here for a few? Take this party elsewhere?
Take it elsewhere. Exactly. That's what they'll have to do.
No way they can keep Elle on ice once she goes flatline. Not at St. Francis anyway.
We're gonna buy time by taking what they need.
Miles, start looking for cold-storage facilities. Clean, sanitary. Frankie, you're a genius.
Hold up! You're talking about kidnapping Elle!
More like, we're going to be Elle's creative EMTs.

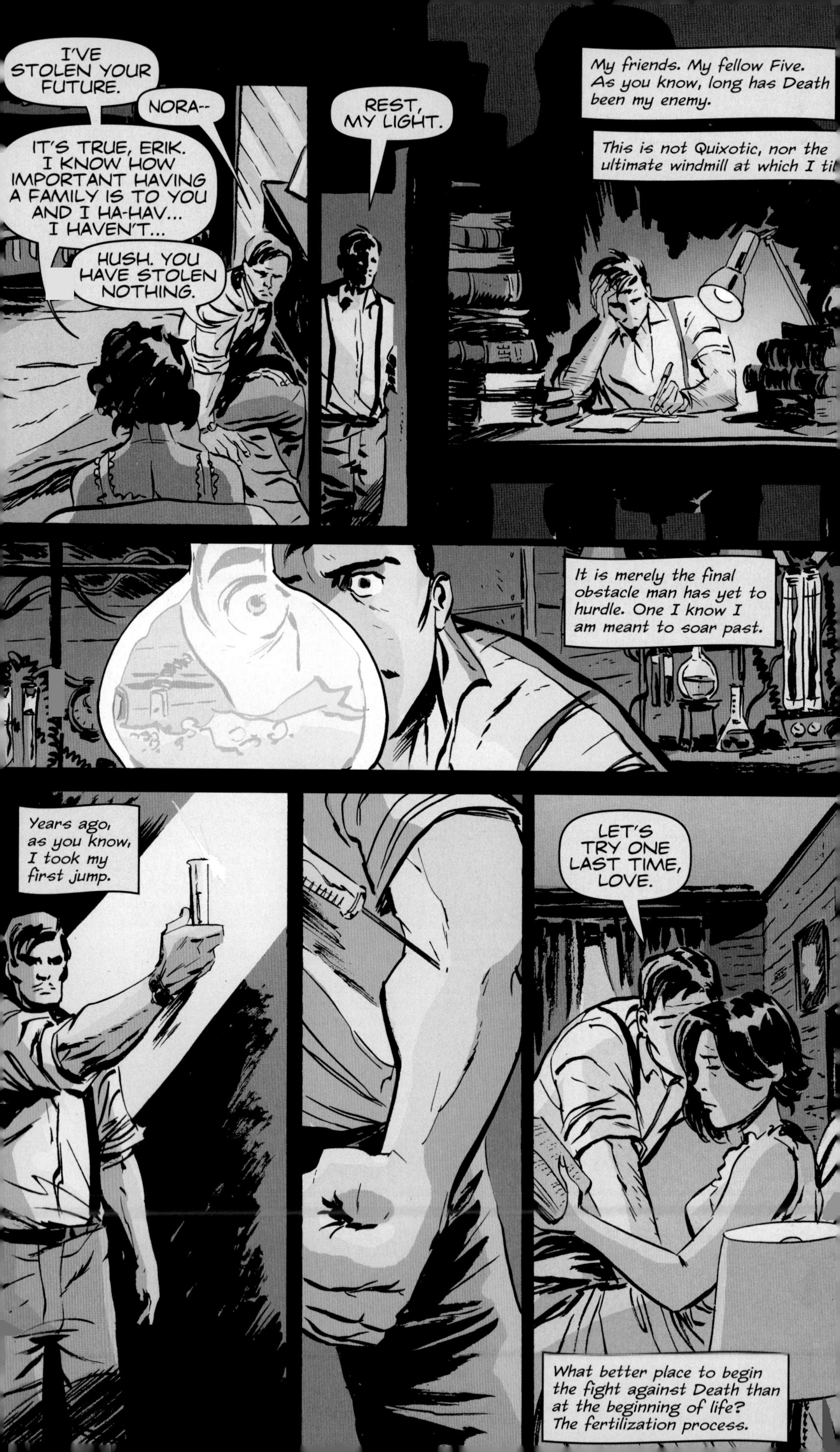

I'VE STOLEN YOUR FUTURE.
NORA--
IT'S TRUE, ERIK. I KNOW HOW IMPORTANT HAVING A FAMILY IS TO YOU AND I HA-HAV... I HAVEN'T...
HUSH. YOU HAVE STOLEN NOTHING.
REST, MY LIGHT.
My friends. My fellow Five. As you know, long has Death been my enemy.
This is not Quixotic, nor the ultimate windmill at which I ti
It is merely the final obstacle man has yet to hurdle. One I know I am meant to soar past.
Years ago, as you know, I took my first jump.
LET'S TRY ONE LAST TIME, LOVE.
What better place to begin the fight against Death than at the beginning of life? The fertilization process.

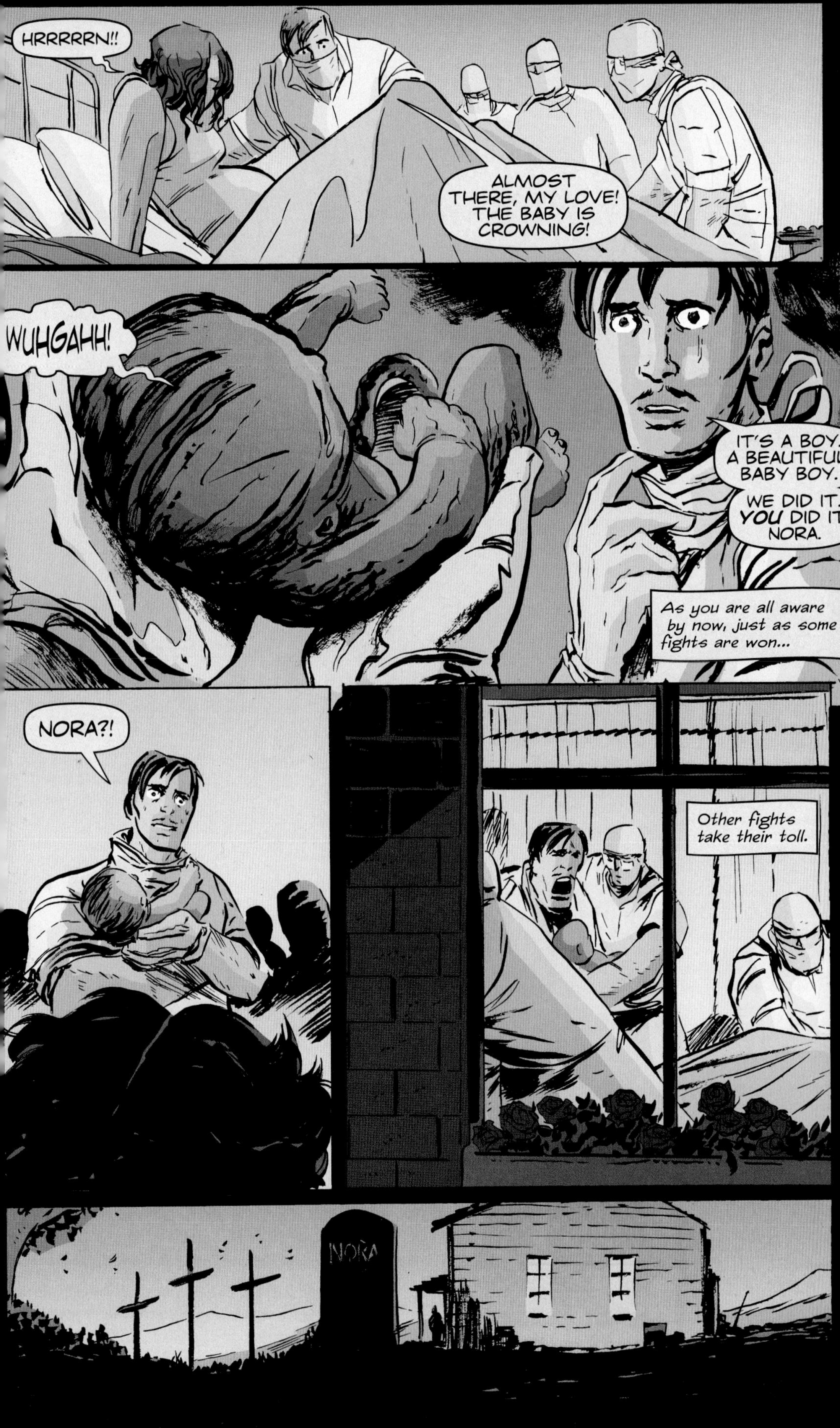
HRRRRRN!!
ALMOST THERE, MY LOVE! THE BABY IS CROWNING!
WUHGAHH!
IT'S A BOY. A BEAUTIFUL, BABY BOY.
WE DID IT. YOU DID IT, NORA.
As you are all aware by now, just as some fights are won...
NORA?!
Other fights take their toll.
NORA

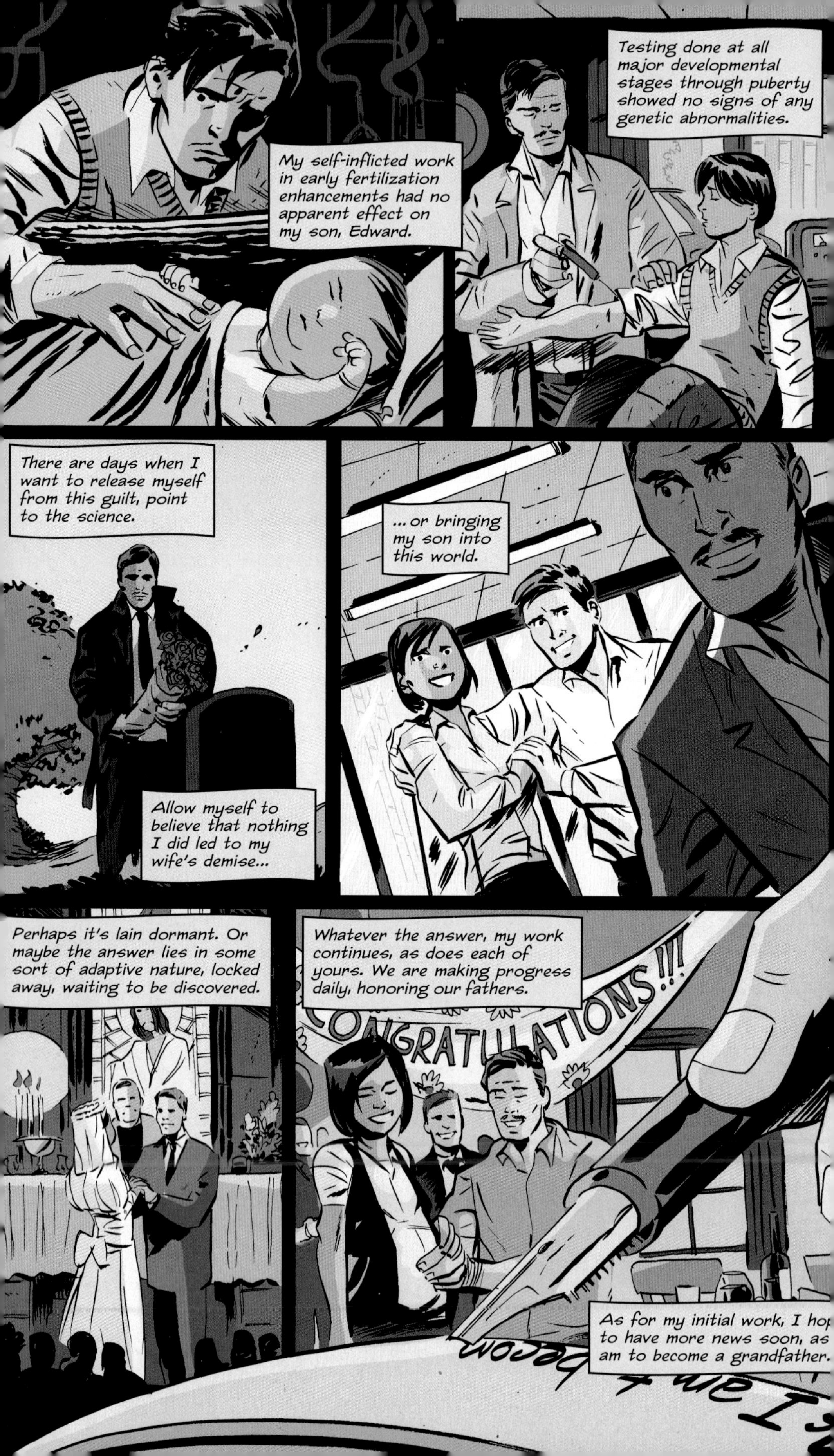
My self-inflicted work in early fertilization enhancements had no apparent effect on my son, Edward.
Testing done at all major developmental stages through puberty showed no signs of any genetic abnormalities.
There are days when I want to release myself from this guilt, point to the science.
Allow myself to believe that nothing I did led to my wife's demise...
...or bringing my son into this world.
Perhaps it's lain dormant. Or maybe the answer lies in some sort of adaptive nature, locked away, waiting to be discovered.
Whatever the answer, my work continues, as does each of yours. We are making progress daily, honoring our fathers.
CONGRATULATIONS!!!
As for my initial work, I hop
to have more news soon, as
am to become a grandfather.

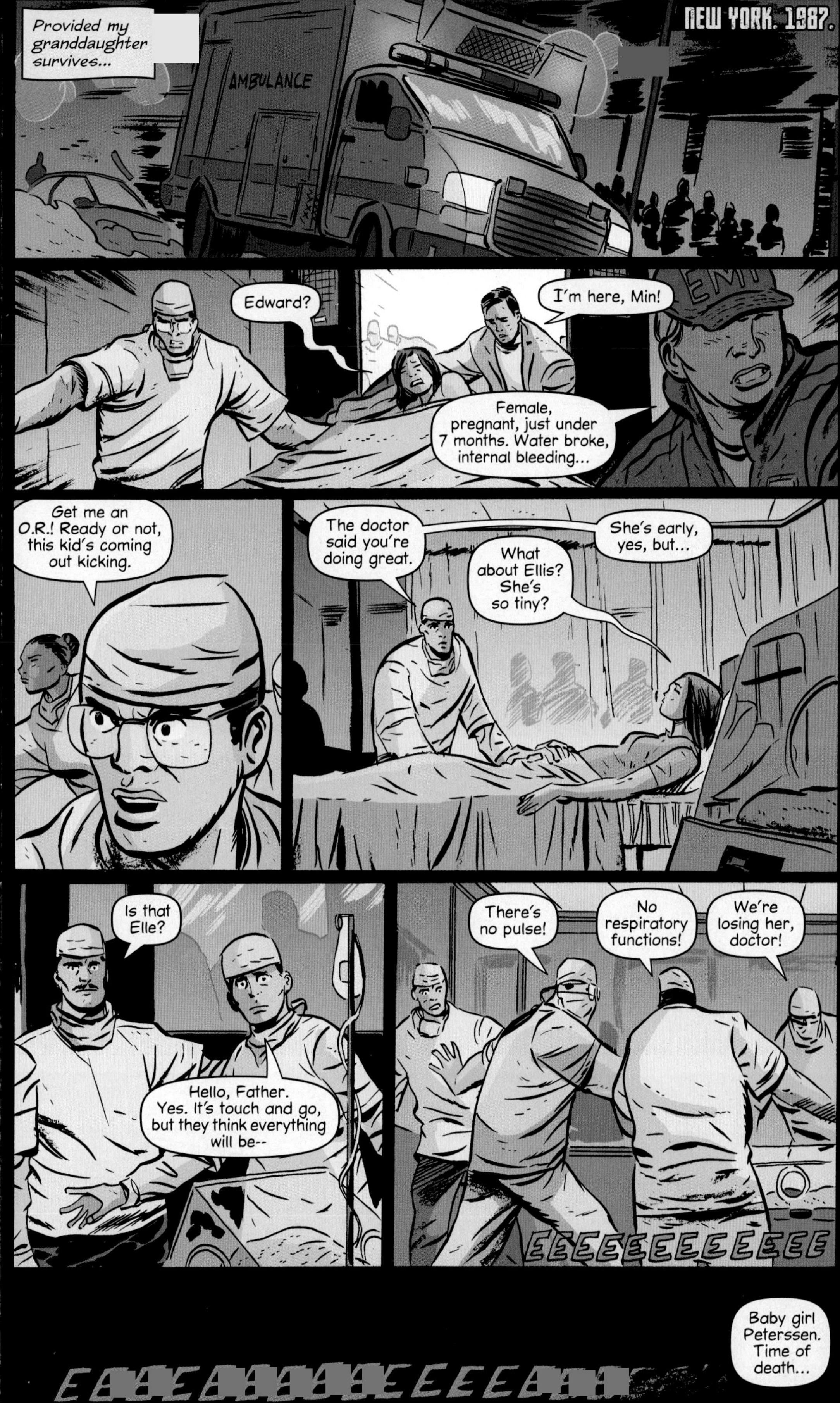

Provided my granddaughter survives...
NEW YORK. 1987.
AMBULANCE
Edward?
I'm here, Min!
EMT
Female, pregnant, just under 7 months. Water broke, internal bleeding...
Get me an O.R.! Ready or not, this kid's coming out kicking.
The doctor said you're doing great.
What about Ellis? She's so tiny?
She's early, yes, but...
Is that Elle?
Hello, Father. Yes. It's touch and go, but they think everything will be--
There's no pulse!
No respiratory functions!
We're losing her, doctor!
EEEEEEEEEEEEE
Baby girl Peterssen. Time of death...

So I can't get back into there because of what they--

Because of what **I** pumped into me?

That would be my educated guess, correct.

Seeing as we've all got degrees in ghost-minds around here.

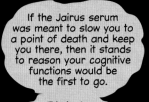

If the Jairus serum was meant to slow you to a point of death and keep you there, then it stands to reason your cognitive functions would be the first to go.

Eliminate the fight-or-flight instinct.

You docs had to know it'd take more than **that** to K.O. the fight in me.

The dose I took was a random sample, not the planned amount, right?

As far as I know.

Then the control dose is probably up with mad scientist grand-daddy, waiting for me to pull through this round before getting back on the final hamster wheel?

We can't rule that out.

Fuck that.

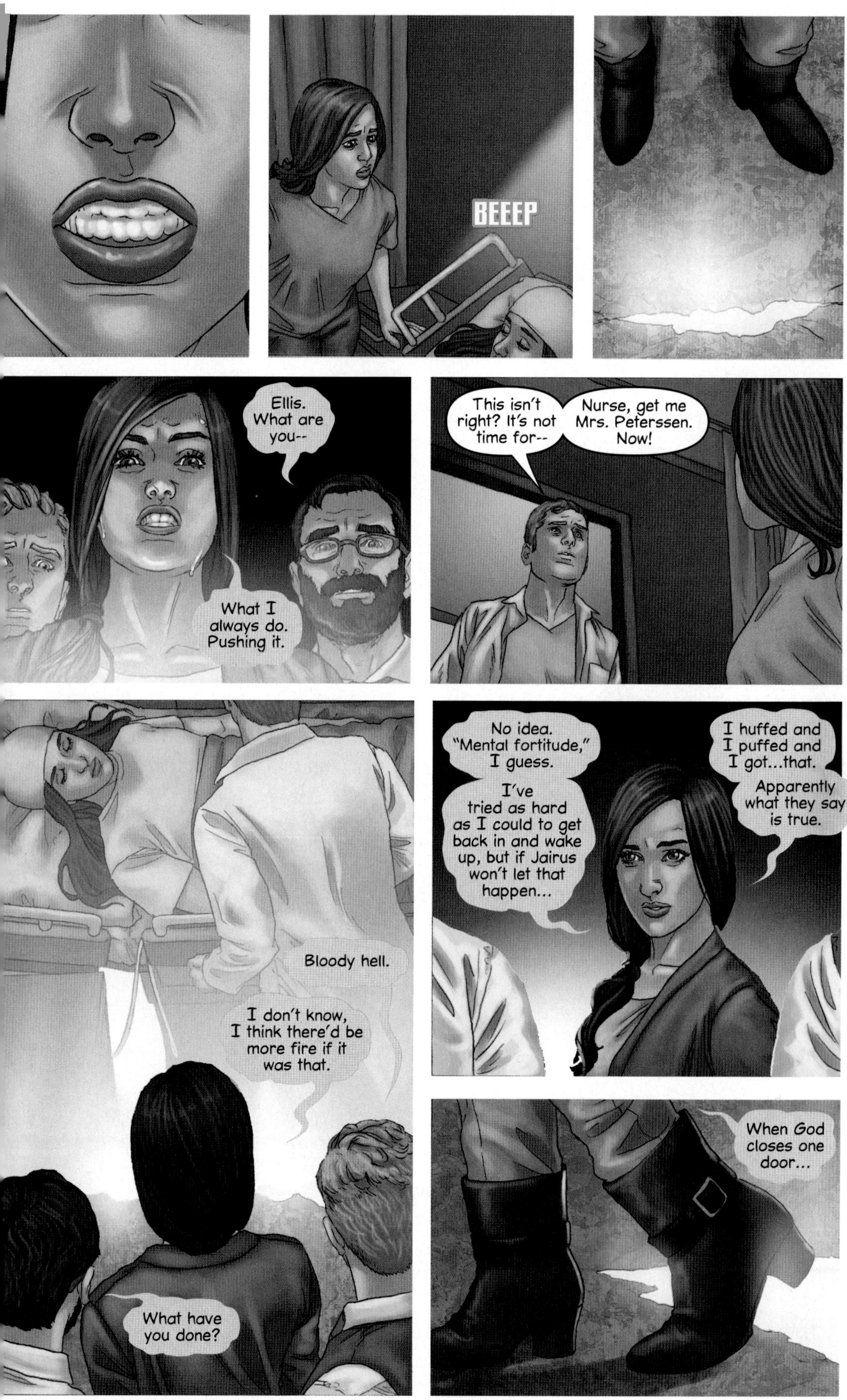
BEEEP
Ellis. What are you--
What I always do. Pushing it.
This isn't right? It's not time for--
Nurse, get me Mrs. Peterssen. Now!
Bloody hell.
I don't know, I think there'd be more fire if it was that.
What have you done?
No idea. "Mental fortitude," I guess.
I've tried as hard as I could to get back in and wake up, but if Jairus won't let that happen...
I huffed and I puffed and I got...that.
Apparently what they say is true.
When God closes one door...

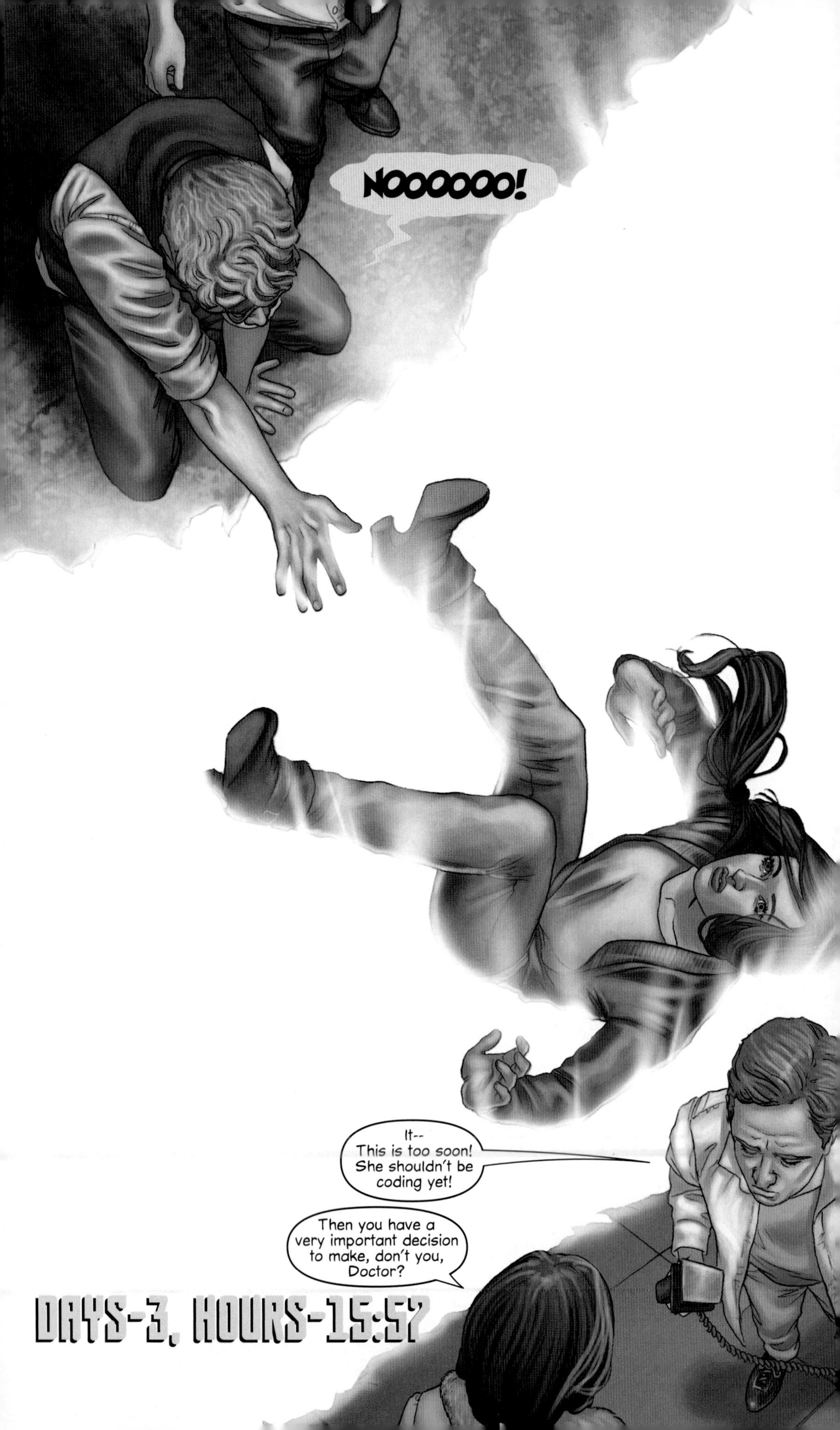
NOOOOOO!
It-- This is too soon! She shouldn't be coding yet!
Then you have a very important decision to make, don't you, Doctor?
DAYS-3, HOURS-15:57

"...for this is a righteous war and the removal of so foul a brood from off the face of the earth is a service God will bless."

- Miguel de Cervantes, *Don Quixote*

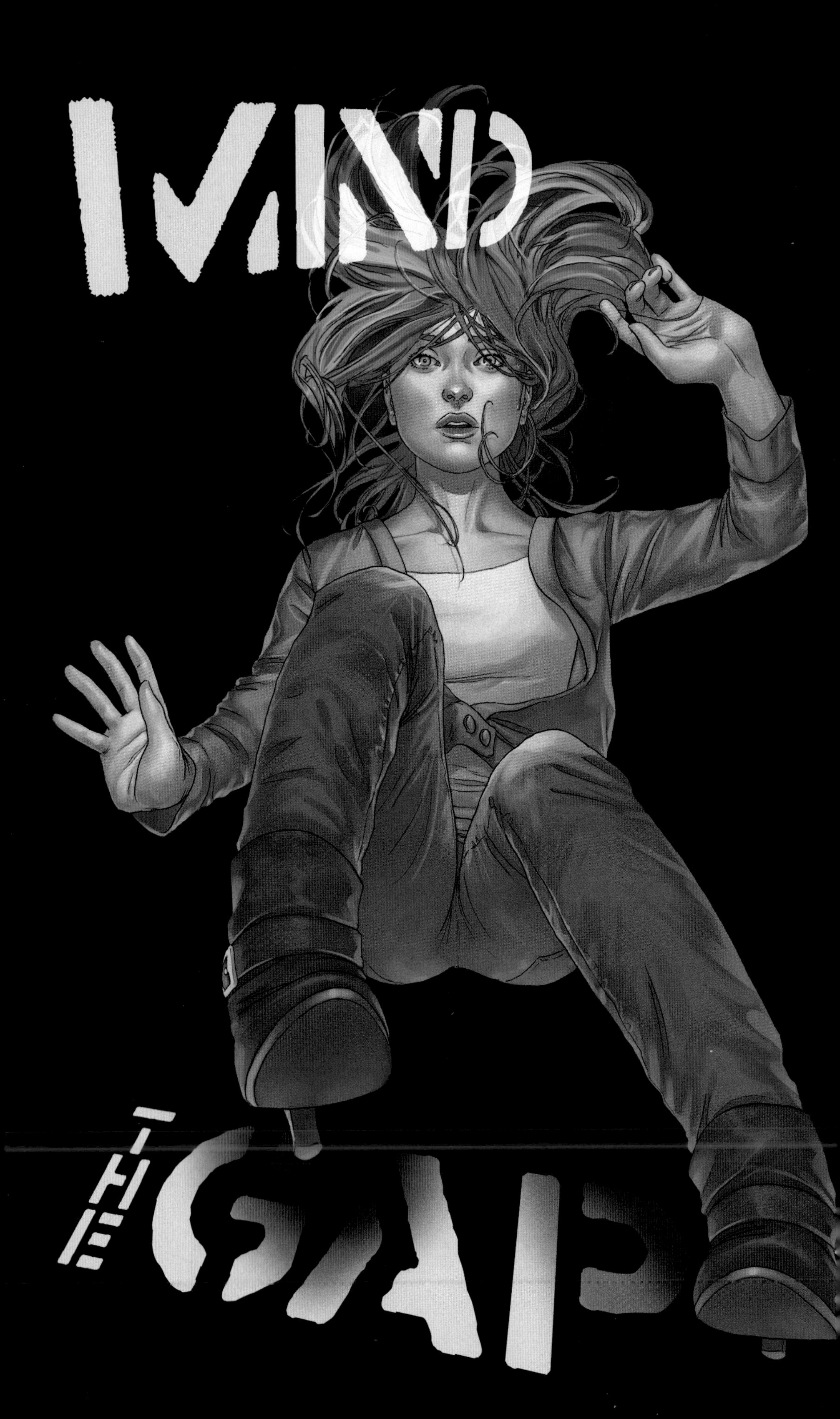
MIND
THE
GAP

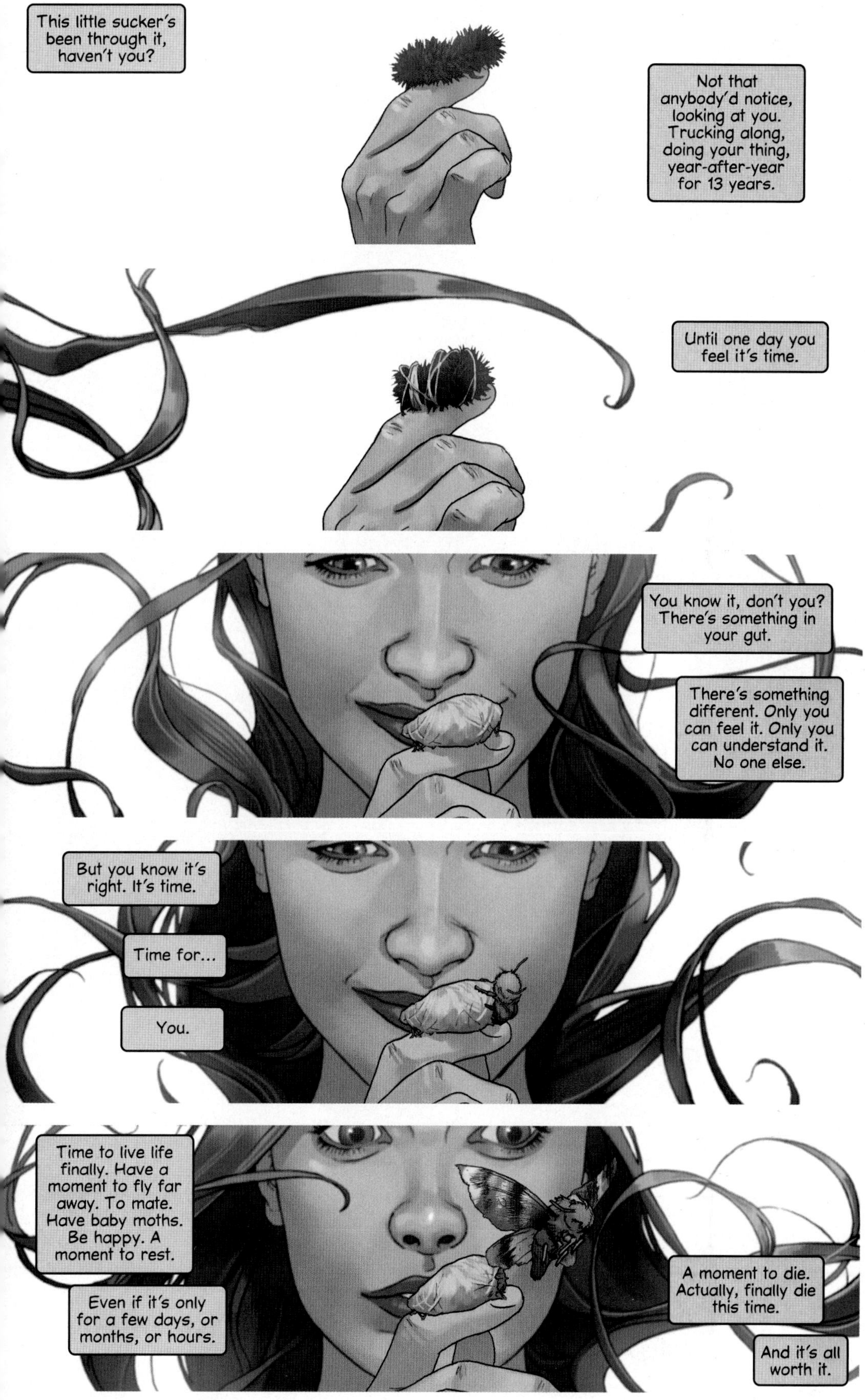
This little sucker's been through it, haven't you?
Not that anybody'd notice, looking at you. Trucking along, doing your thing, year-after-year for 13 years.
Until one day you feel it's time.
You know it, don't you? There's something in your gut.
There's something different. Only you can feel it. Only you can understand it. No one else.
But you know it's right. It's time.
Time for...
You.
Time to live life finally. Have a moment to fly far away. To mate. Have baby moths. Be happy. A moment to rest.
Even if it's only for a few days, or months, or hours.
A moment to die. Actually, finally die this time.
And it's all worth it.

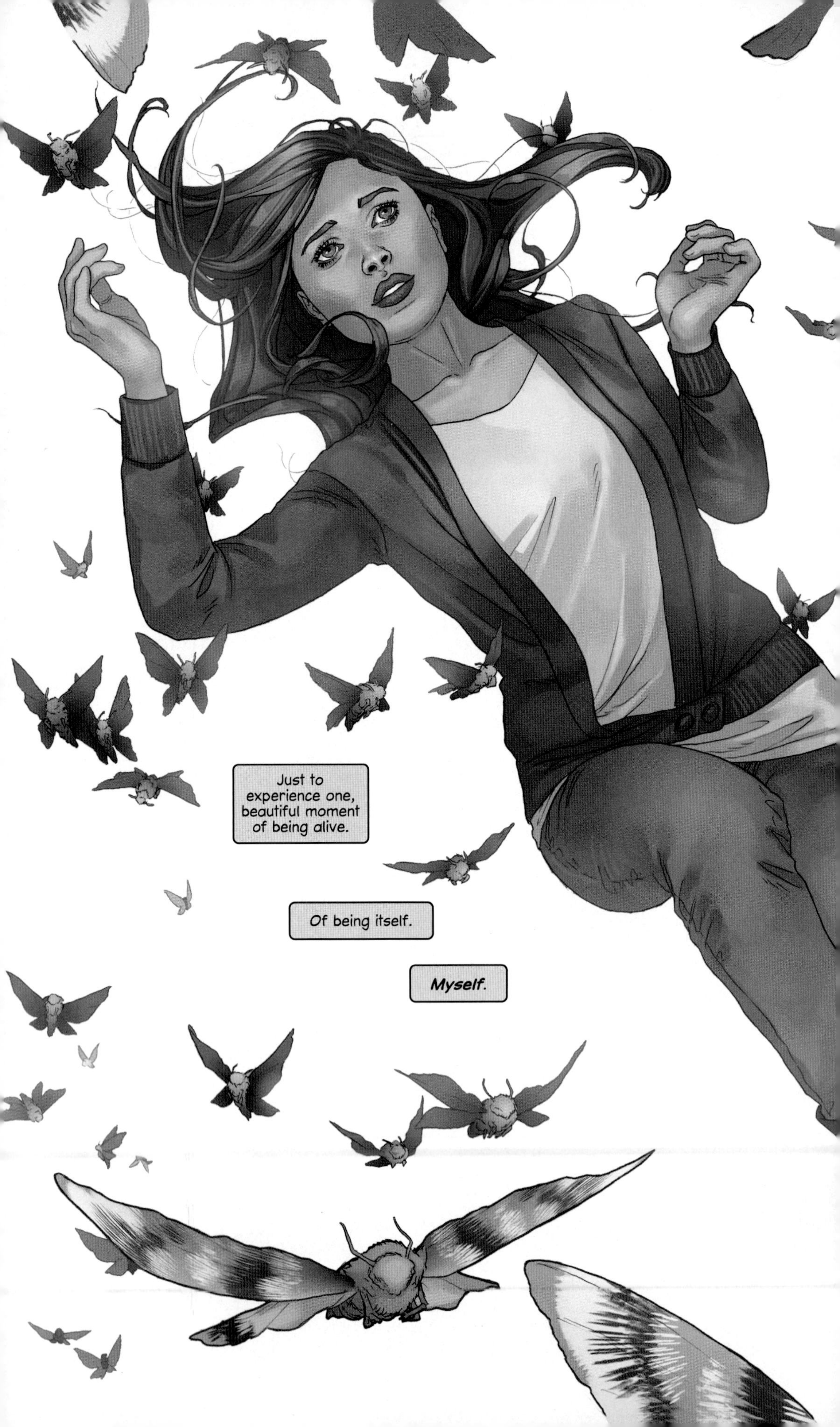
Just to experience one, beautiful moment of being alive.
Of being itself.
Myself.

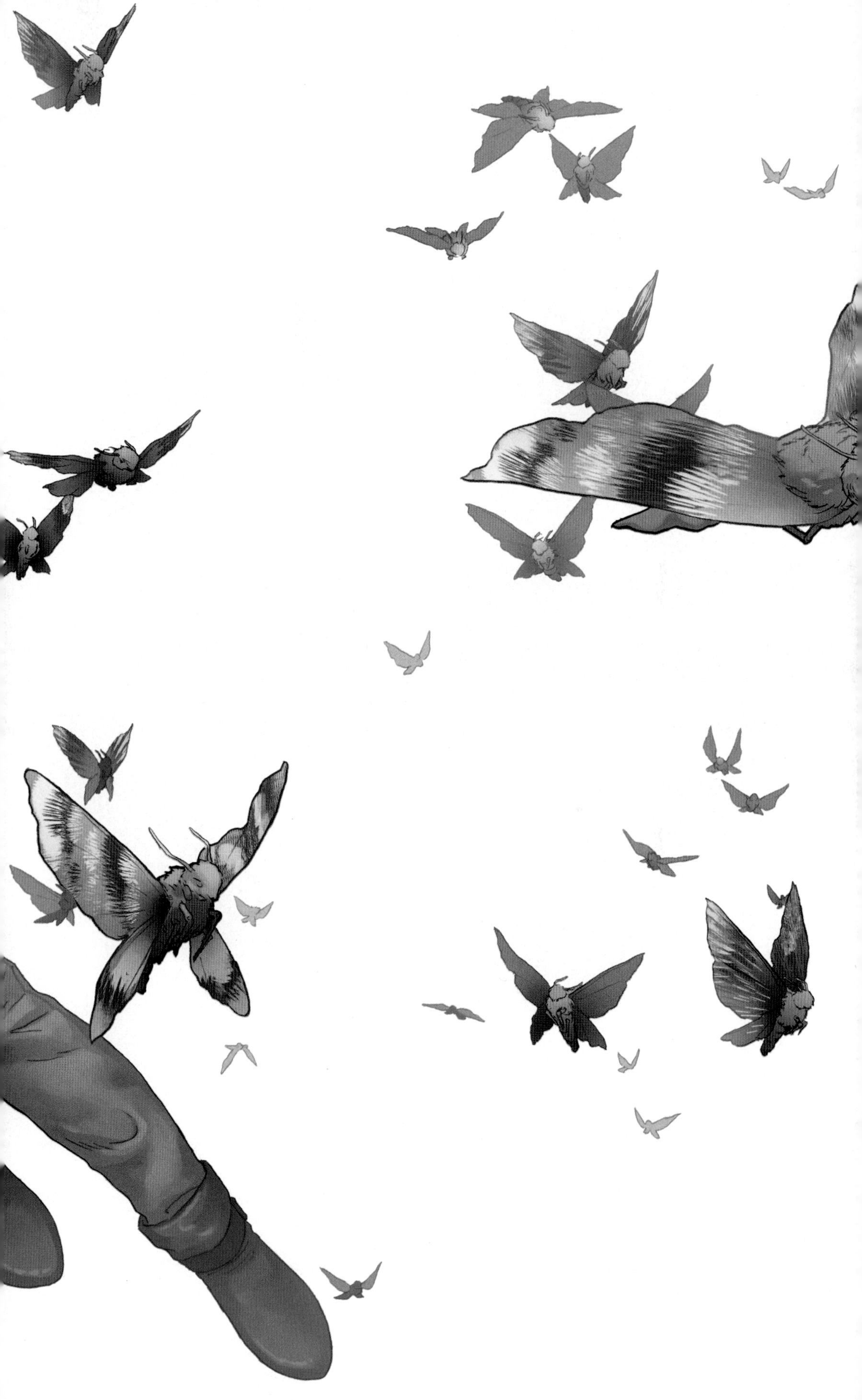

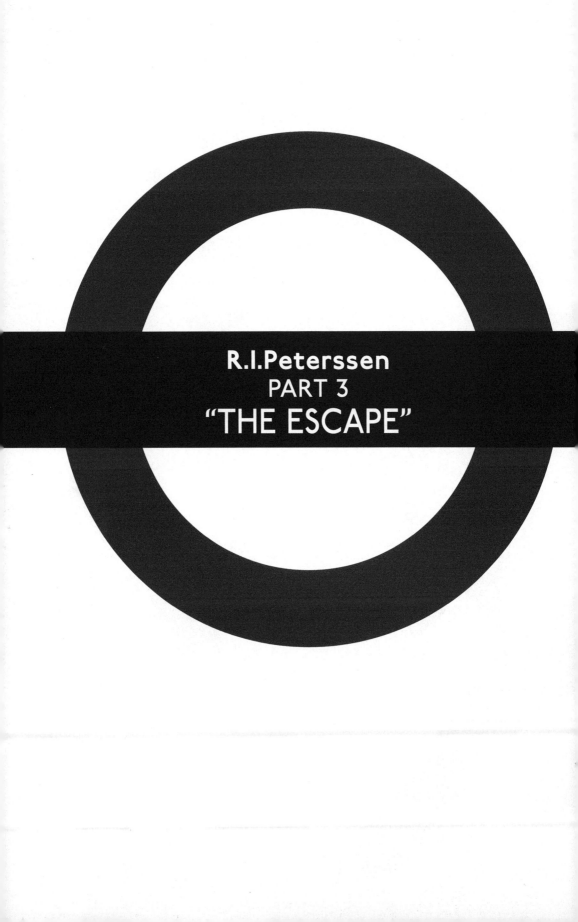

R.I.Peterssen
PART 3
"THE ESCAPE"

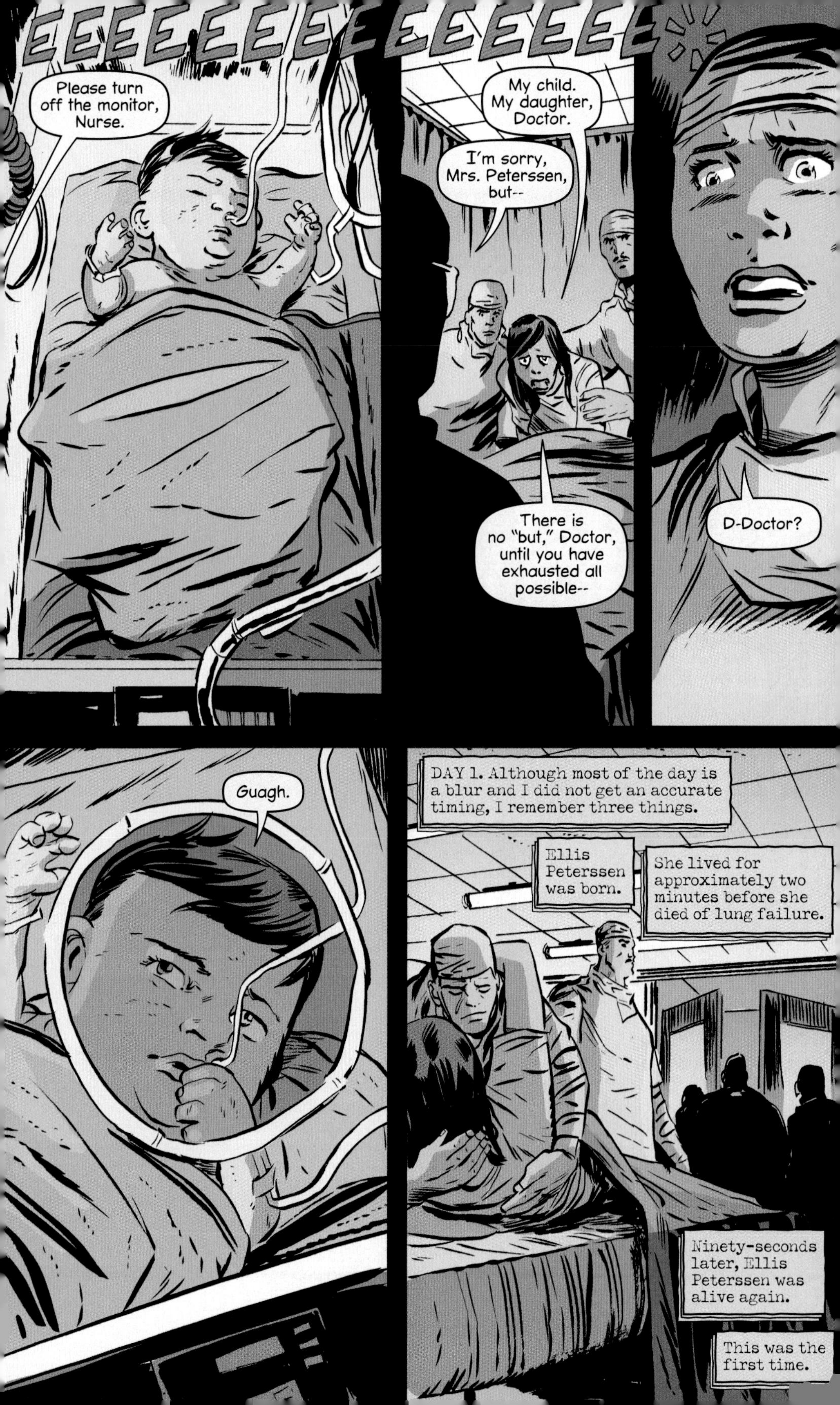
EEEEEEEEEEEEEEEE
Please turn off the monitor, Nurse.
My child. My daughter, Doctor.
I'm sorry, Mrs. Peterssen, but--
There is no "but," Doctor, until you have exhausted all possible--
D-Doctor?
Guagh.
DAY 1. Although most of the day is a blur and I did not get an accurate timing, I remember three things.
Ellis Peterssen was born.
She lived for approximately two minutes before she died of lung failure.
Ninety-seconds later, Ellis Peterssen was alive again.
This was the first time.

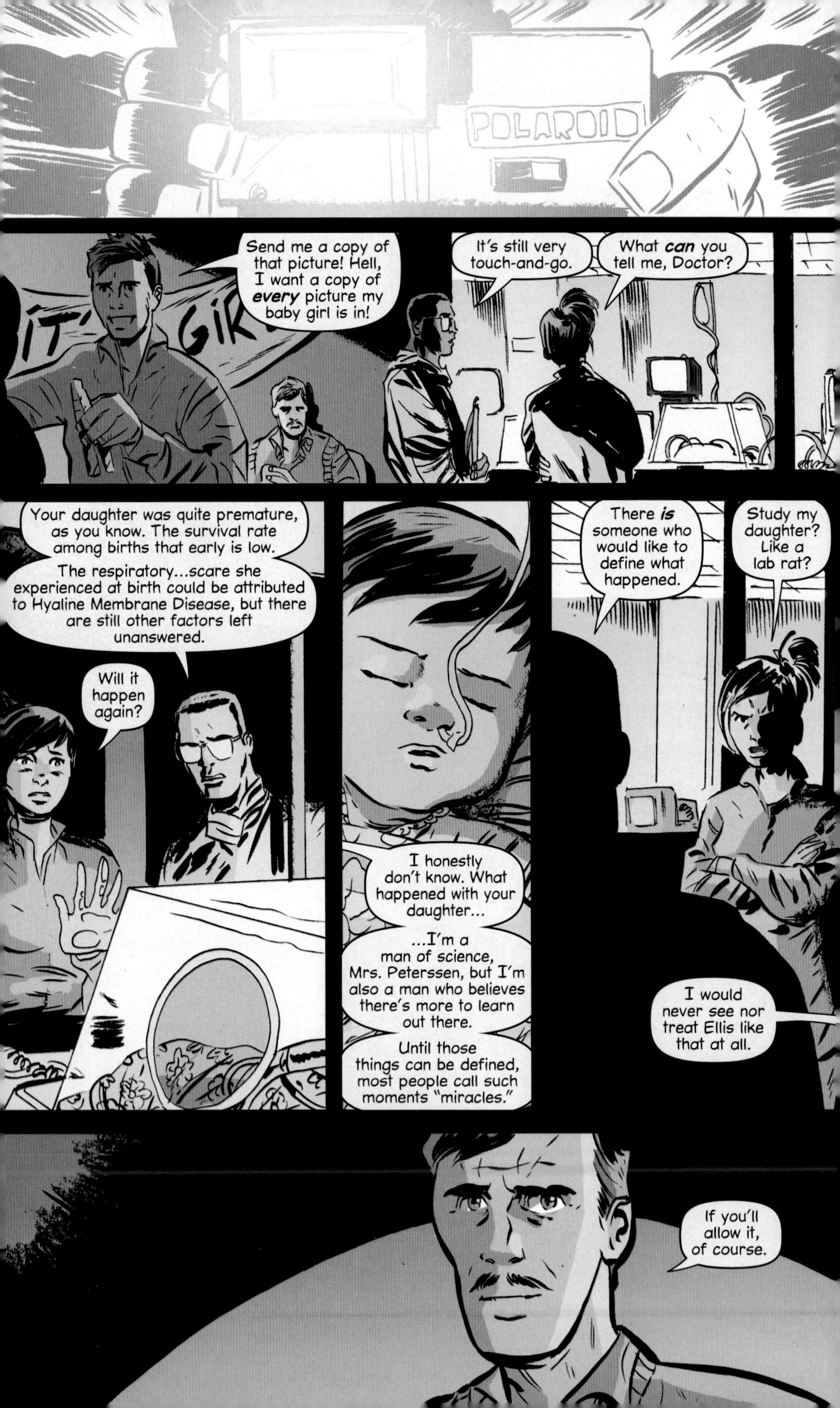

POLAROID
Send me a copy of that picture! Hell, I want a copy of ***every*** picture my baby girl is in!
It's still very touch-and-go.
What ***can*** you tell me, Doctor?
Your daughter was quite premature, as you know. The survival rate among births that early is low.
The respiratory...scare she experienced at birth could be attributed to Hyaline Membrane Disease, but there are still other factors left unanswered.
Will it happen again?
I honestly don't know. What happened with your daughter...
...I'm a man of science, Mrs. Peterssen, but I'm also a man who believes there's more to learn out there.
Until those things can be defined, most people call such moments "miracles."
There ***is*** someone who would like to define what happened.
Study my daughter? Like a lab rat?
I would never see nor treat Ellis like that at all.
If you'll allow it, of course.

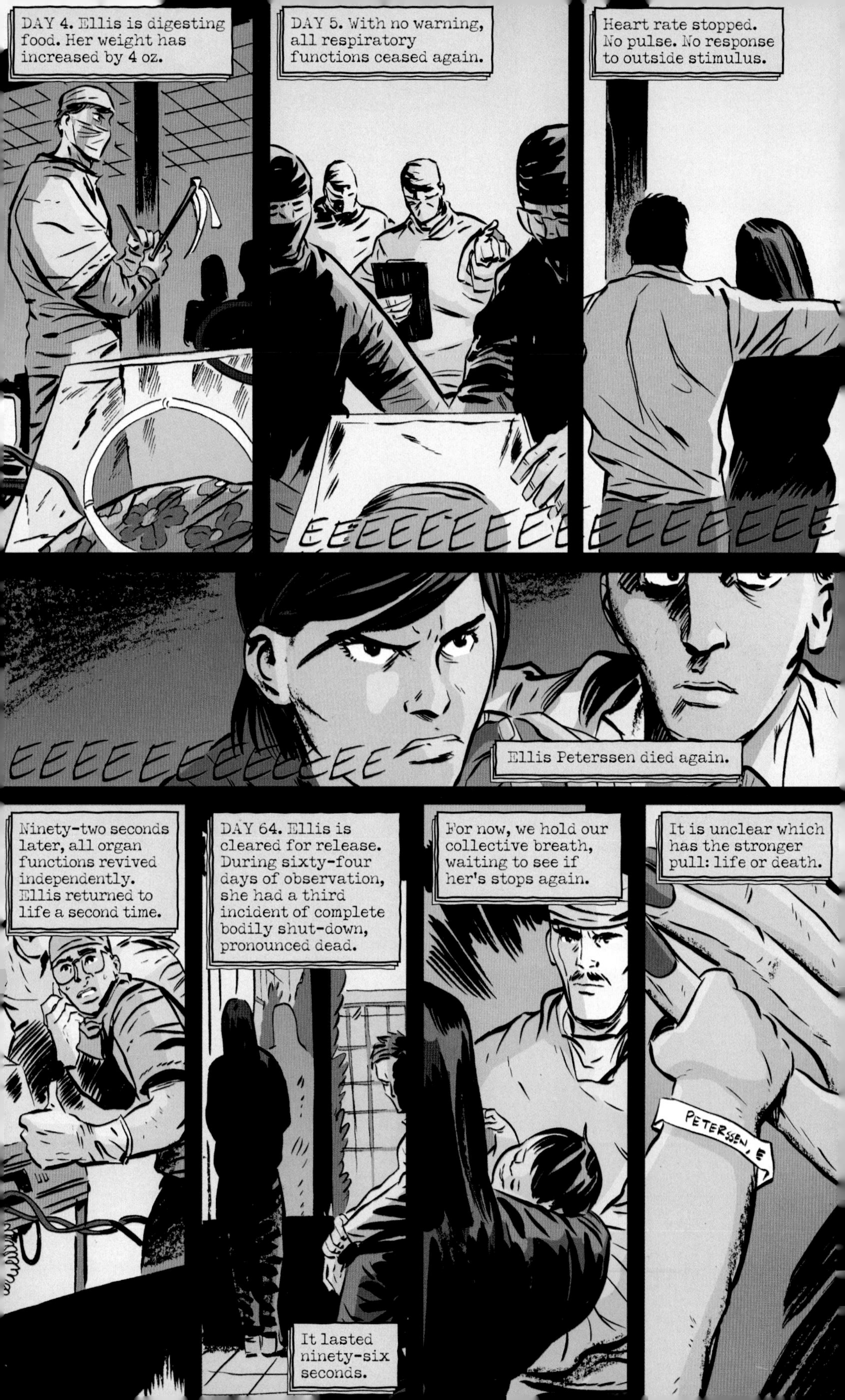
DAY 4. Ellis is digesting food. Her weight has increased by 4 oz.
DAY 5. With no warning, all respiratory functions ceased again.
EEEEEEEEEEE
Heart rate stopped. No pulse. No response to outside stimulus.
EEEEEEEEEEE
EEEEEEEEEEEEEEE
Ellis Peterssen died again.
Ninety-two seconds later, all organ functions revived independently. Ellis returned to life a second time.
DAY 64. Ellis is cleared for release. During sixty-four days of observation, she had a third incident of complete bodily shut-down, pronounced dead.
It lasted ninety-six seconds.
For now, we hold our collective breath, waiting to see if her's stops again.
It is unclear which has the stronger pull: life or death.
PETERSSEN, E

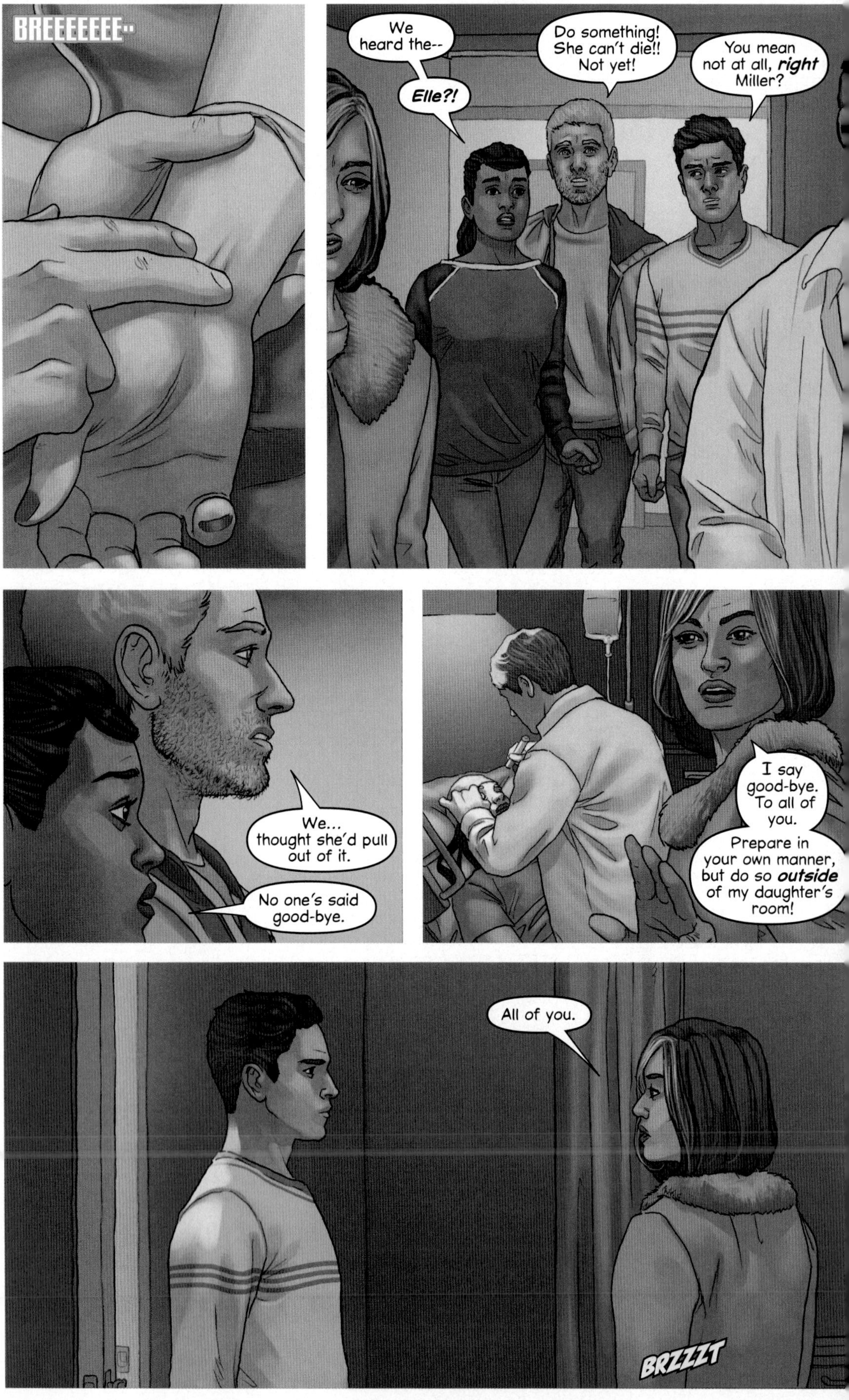
BREEEEEEE..
We heard the--
Elle?!
Do something! She can't die!! Not yet!
You mean not at all, right Miller?
We... thought she'd pull out of it.
No one's said good-bye.
I say good-bye. To all of you.
Prepare in your own manner, but do so outside of my daughter's room!
All of you.
BRZZZT

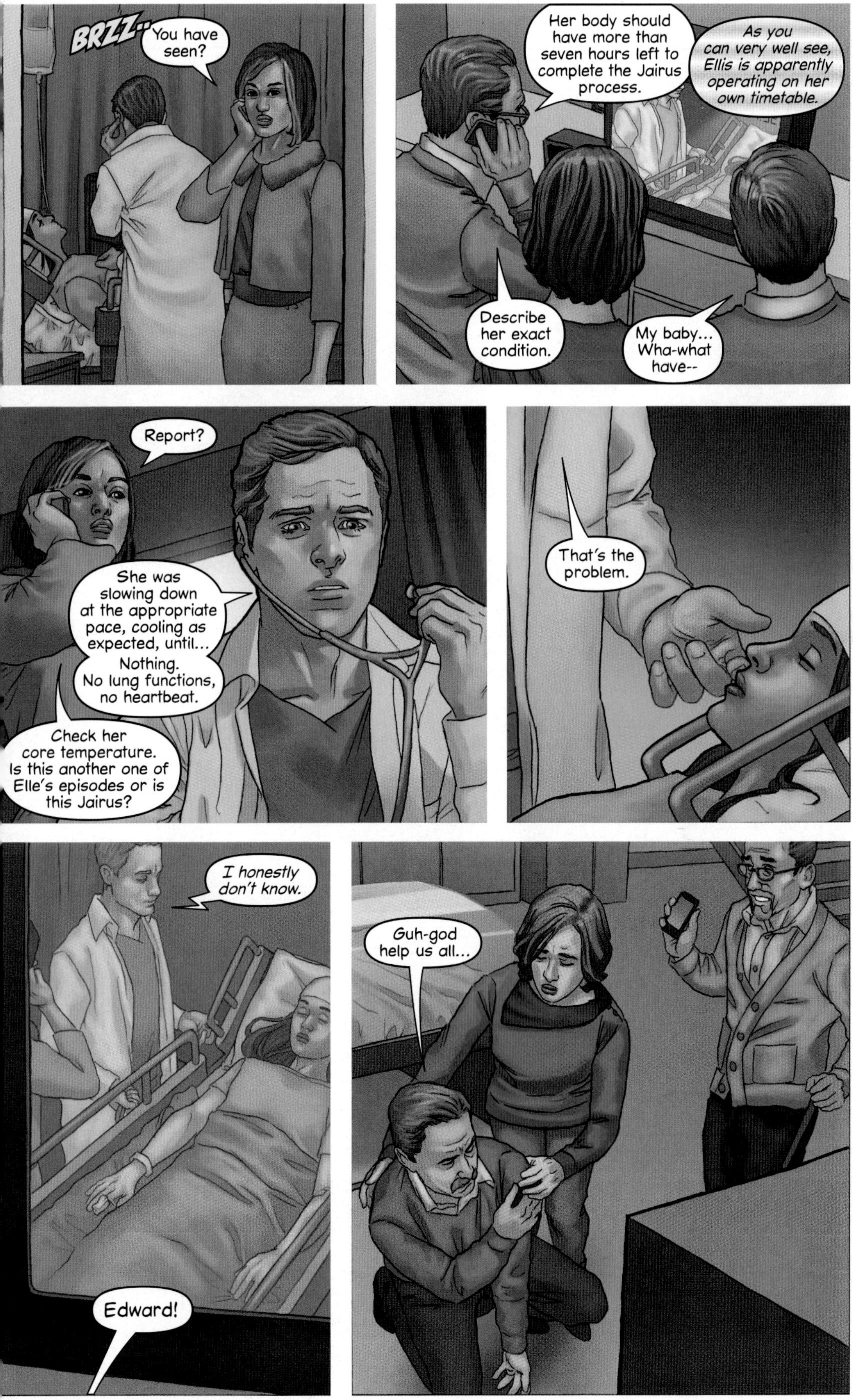
BRZZ..
You have seen?
Her body should have more than seven hours left to complete the Jairus process.
As you can very well see, Ellis is apparently operating on her own timetable.
Describe her exact condition.
My baby... Wha-what have--
Report?
She was slowing down at the appropriate pace, cooling as expected, until...
Nothing. No lung functions, no heartbeat.
Check her core temperature. Is this another one of Elle's episodes or is this Jairus?
That's the problem.
I honestly don't know.
Edward!
Guh-god help us all...

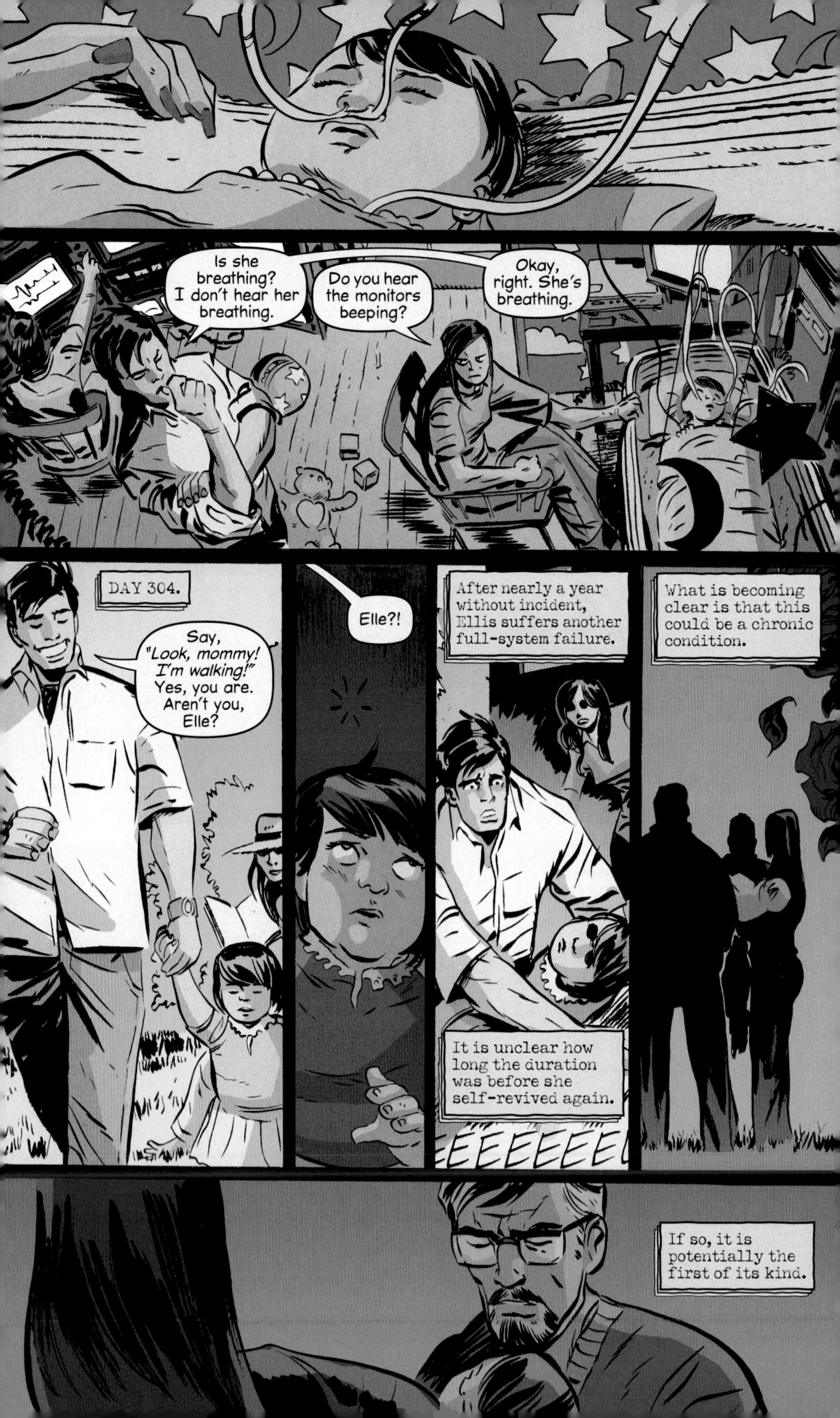

Is she breathing? I don't hear her breathing.
Do you hear the monitors beeping?
Okay, right. She's breathing.
DAY 304.
Say, "Look, mommy! I'm walking!" Yes, you are. Aren't you, Elle?
Elle?!
After nearly a year without incident, Ellis suffers another full-system failure.
It is unclear how long the duration was before she self-revived again.
EEEEEEEE
What is becoming clear is that this could be a chronic condition.
If so, it is potentially the first of its kind.

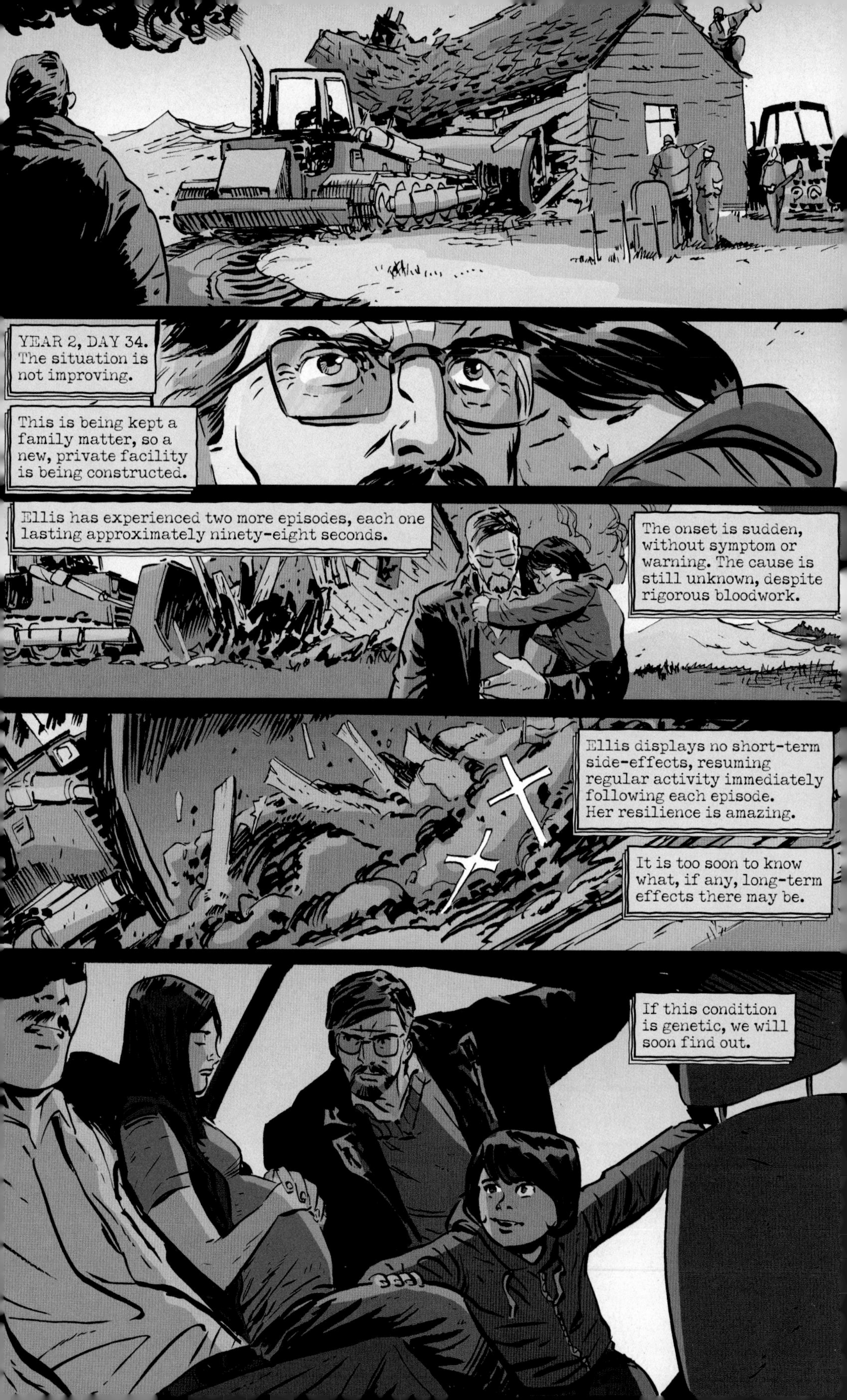

YEAR 2, DAY 34. The situation is not improving.
This is being kept a family matter, so a new, private facility is being constructed.
Ellis has experienced two more episodes, each one lasting approximately ninety-eight seconds.
The onset is sudden, without symptom or warning. The cause is still unknown, despite rigorous bloodwork.
Ellis displays no short-term side-effects, resuming regular activity immediately following each episode. Her resilience is amazing.
It is too soon to know what, if any, long-term effects there may be.
If this condition is genetic, we will soon find out.

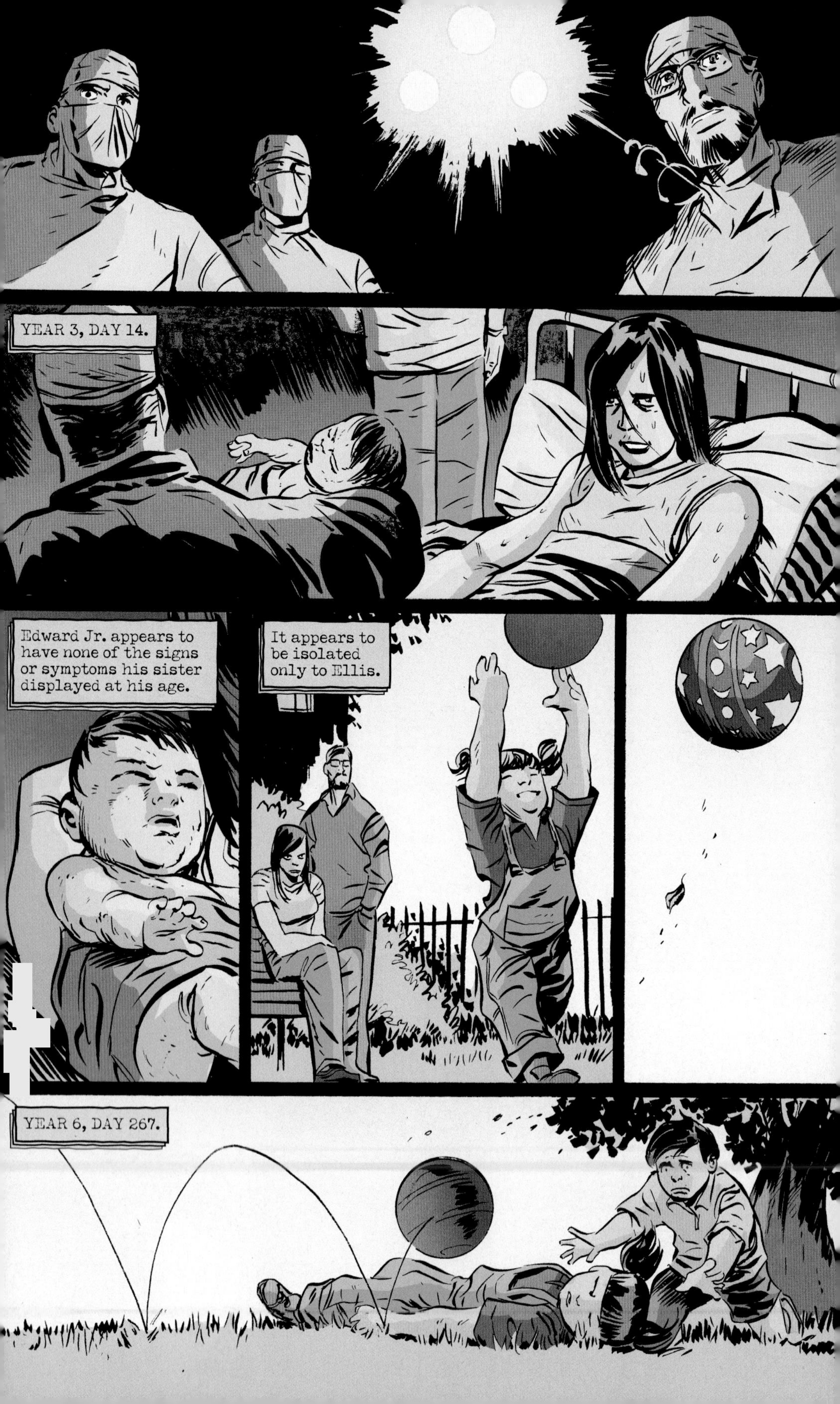
YEAR 3, DAY 14.
Edward Jr. appears to have none of the signs or symptoms his sister displayed at his age.
It appears to be isolated only to Ellis.
YEAR 6, DAY 267.

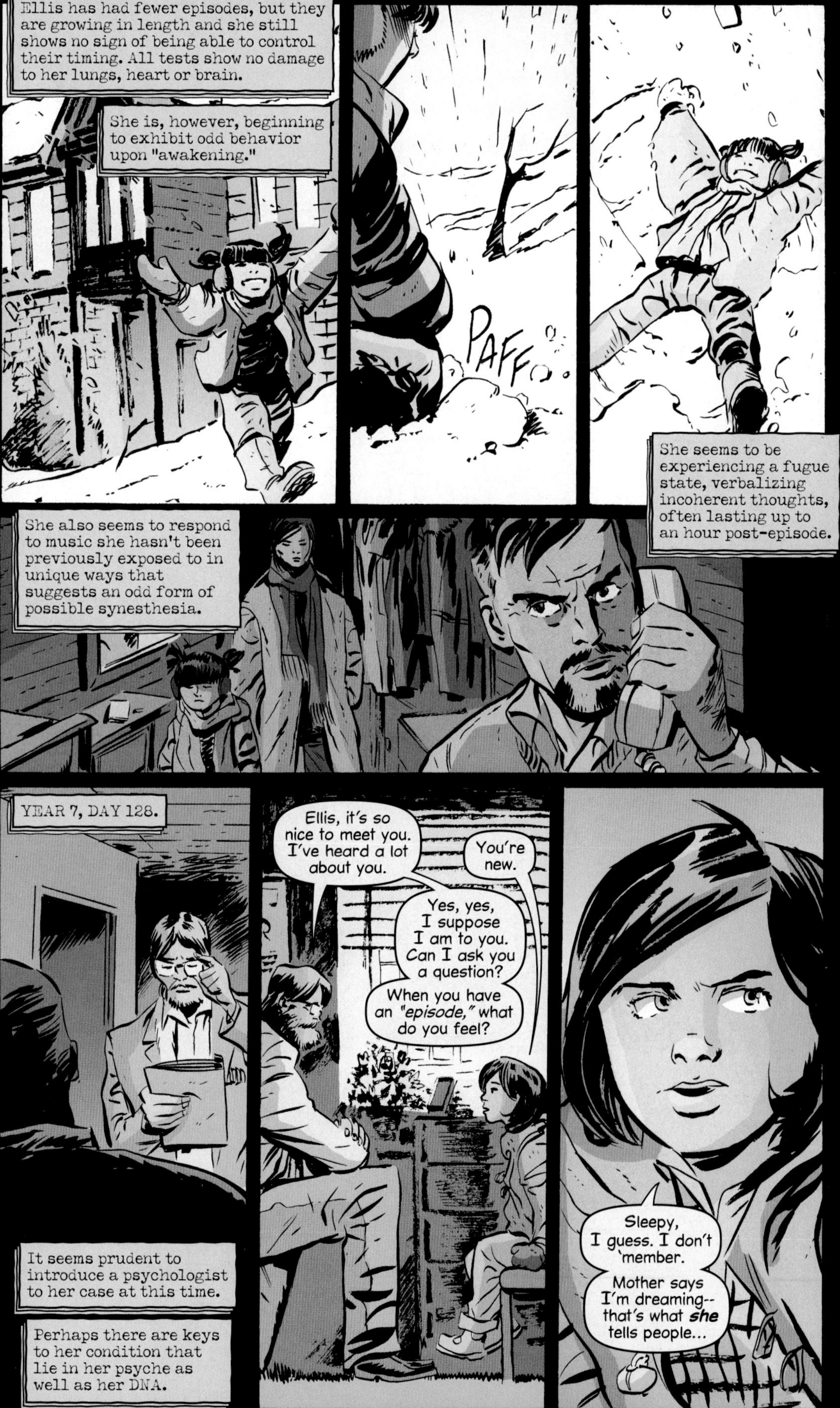

Ellis has had fewer episodes, but they are growing in length and she still shows no sign of being able to control their timing. All tests show no damage to her lungs, heart or brain.
She is, however, beginning to exhibit odd behavior upon "awakening."
PAFF
She seems to be experiencing a fugue state, verbalizing incoherent thoughts, often lasting up to an hour post-episode.
She also seems to respond to music she hasn't been previously exposed to in unique ways that suggests an odd form of possible synesthesia.
YEAR 7, DAY 128.
It seems prudent to introduce a psychologist to her case at this time.
Perhaps there are keys to her condition that lie in her psyche as well as her DNA.
Ellis, it's so nice to meet you. I've heard a lot about you.
You're new.
Yes, yes, I suppose I am to you. Can I ask you a question?
When you have an *"episode,"* what do you feel?
Sleepy, I guess. I don't 'member.
Mother says I'm dreaming-- that's what *she* tells people...

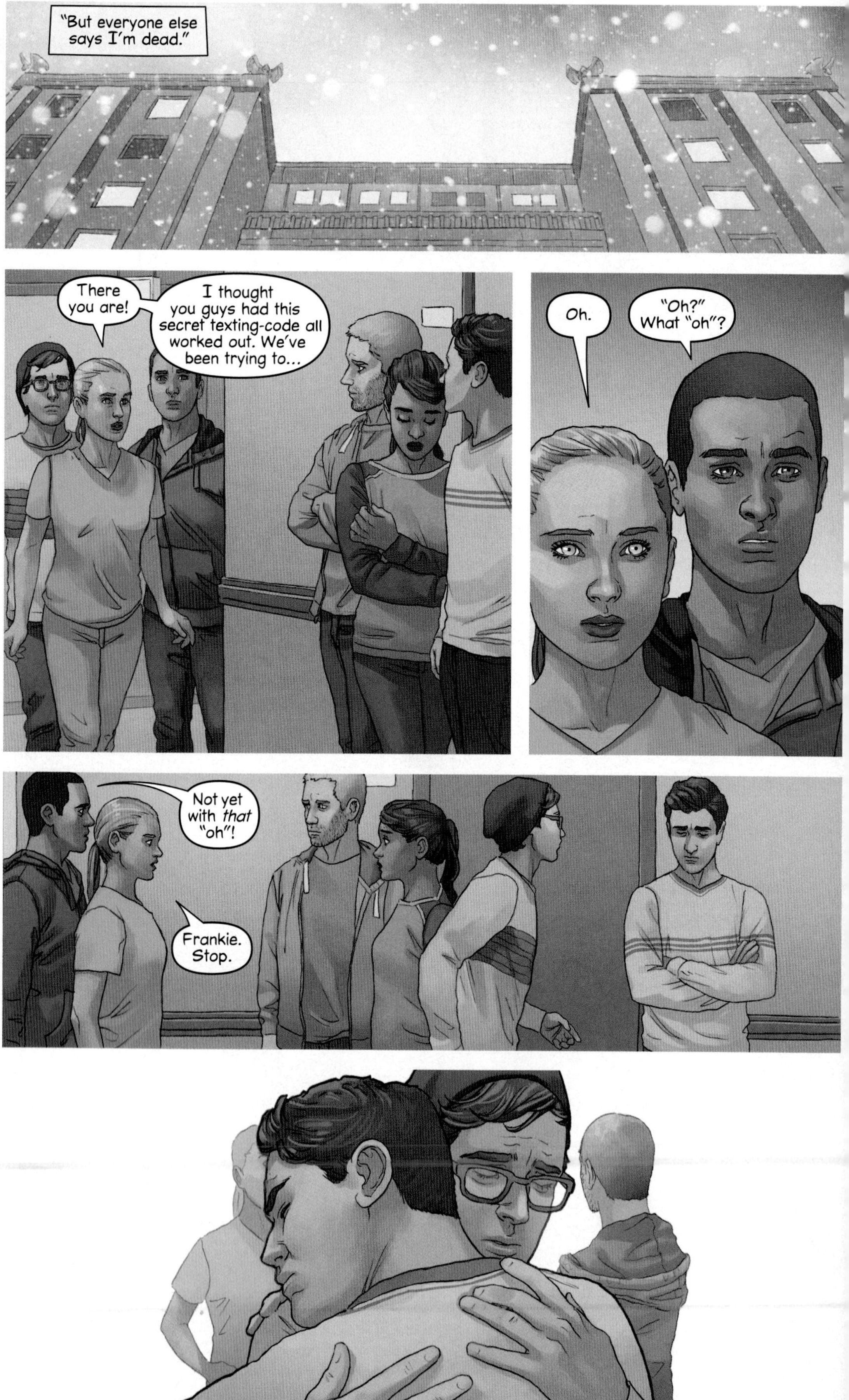
"But everyone else says I'm dead."
There you are!
I thought you guys had this secret texting-code all worked out. We've been trying to...
Oh.
"Oh?" What "oh"?
Not yet with *that* "oh"!
Frankie. Stop.

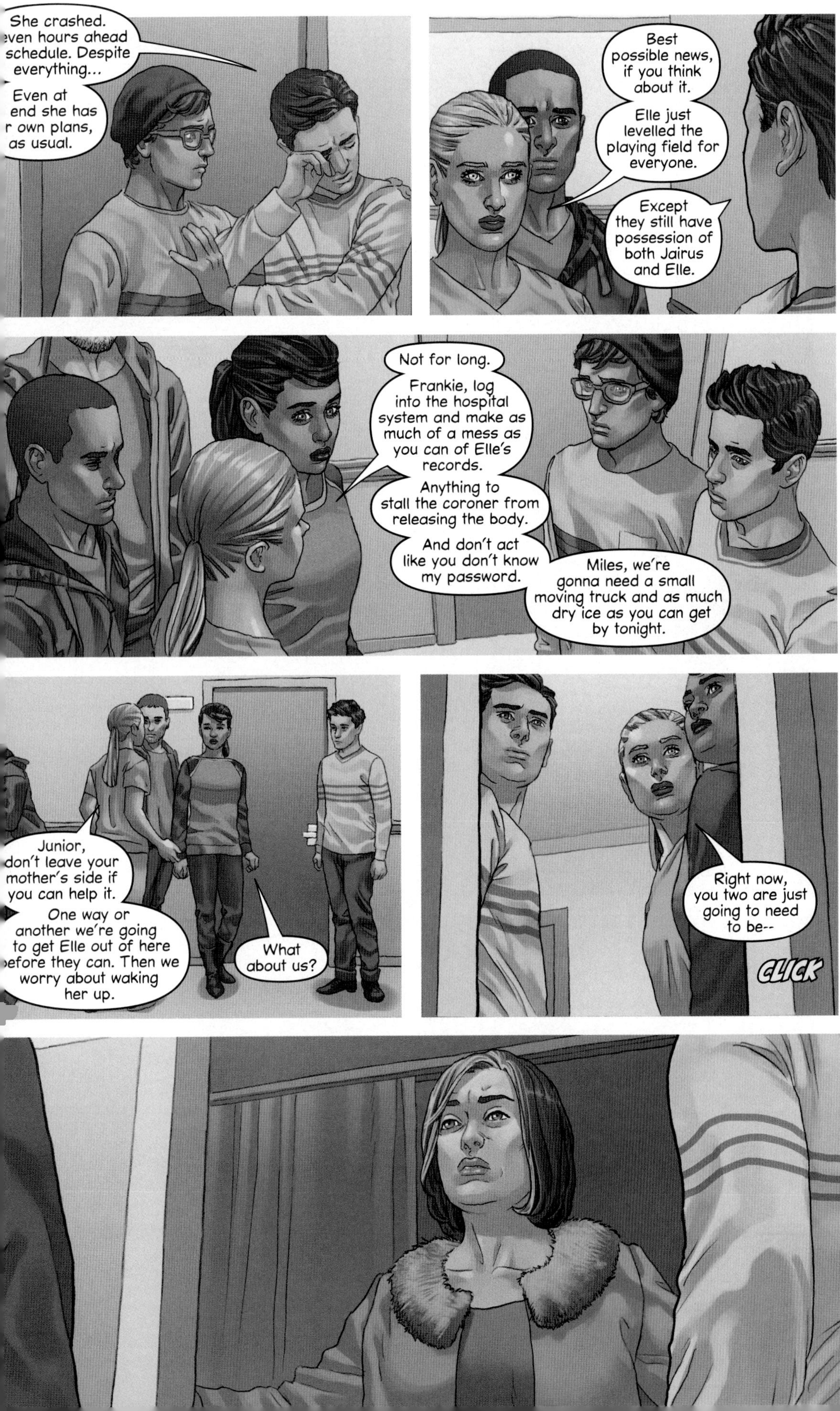
She crashed. ›ven hours ahead schedule. Despite everything...
Even at end she has r own plans, as usual.
Best possible news, if you think about it.
Elle just levelled the playing field for everyone.
Except they still have possession of both Jairus and Elle.
Not for long.
Frankie, log into the hospital system and make as much of a mess as you can of Elle's records.
Anything to stall the coroner from releasing the body.
And don't act like you don't know my password.
Miles, we're gonna need a small moving truck and as much dry ice as you can get by tonight.
Junior, don't leave your mother's side if you can help it.
One way or another we're going to get Elle out of here ›efore they can. Then we worry about waking her up.
What about us?
Right now, you two are just going to need to be--
CLICK

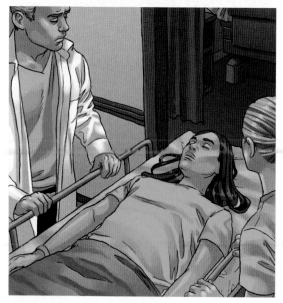
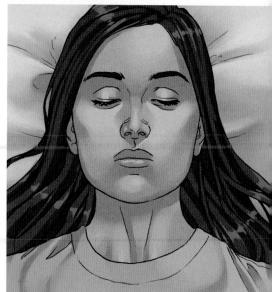

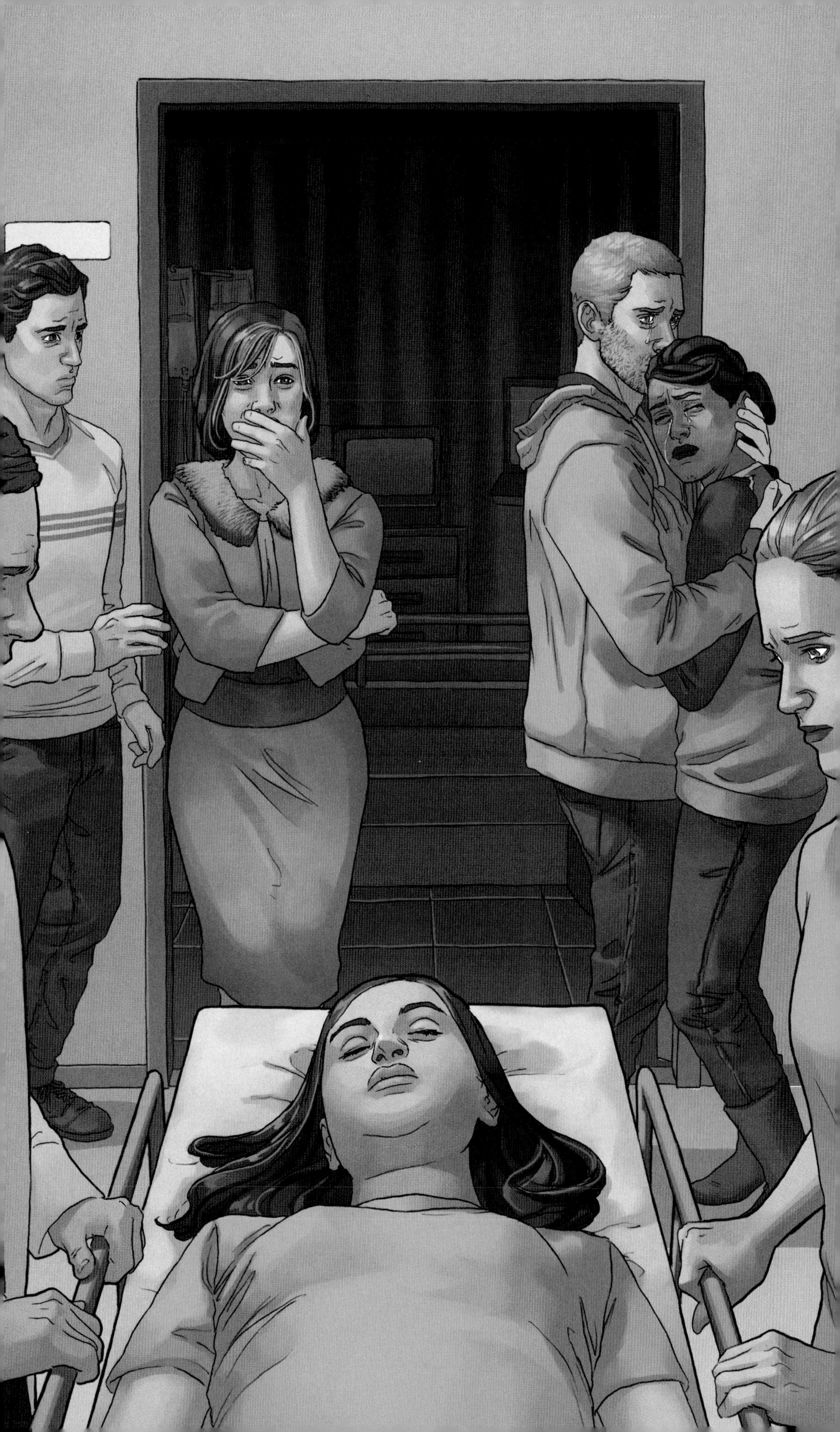

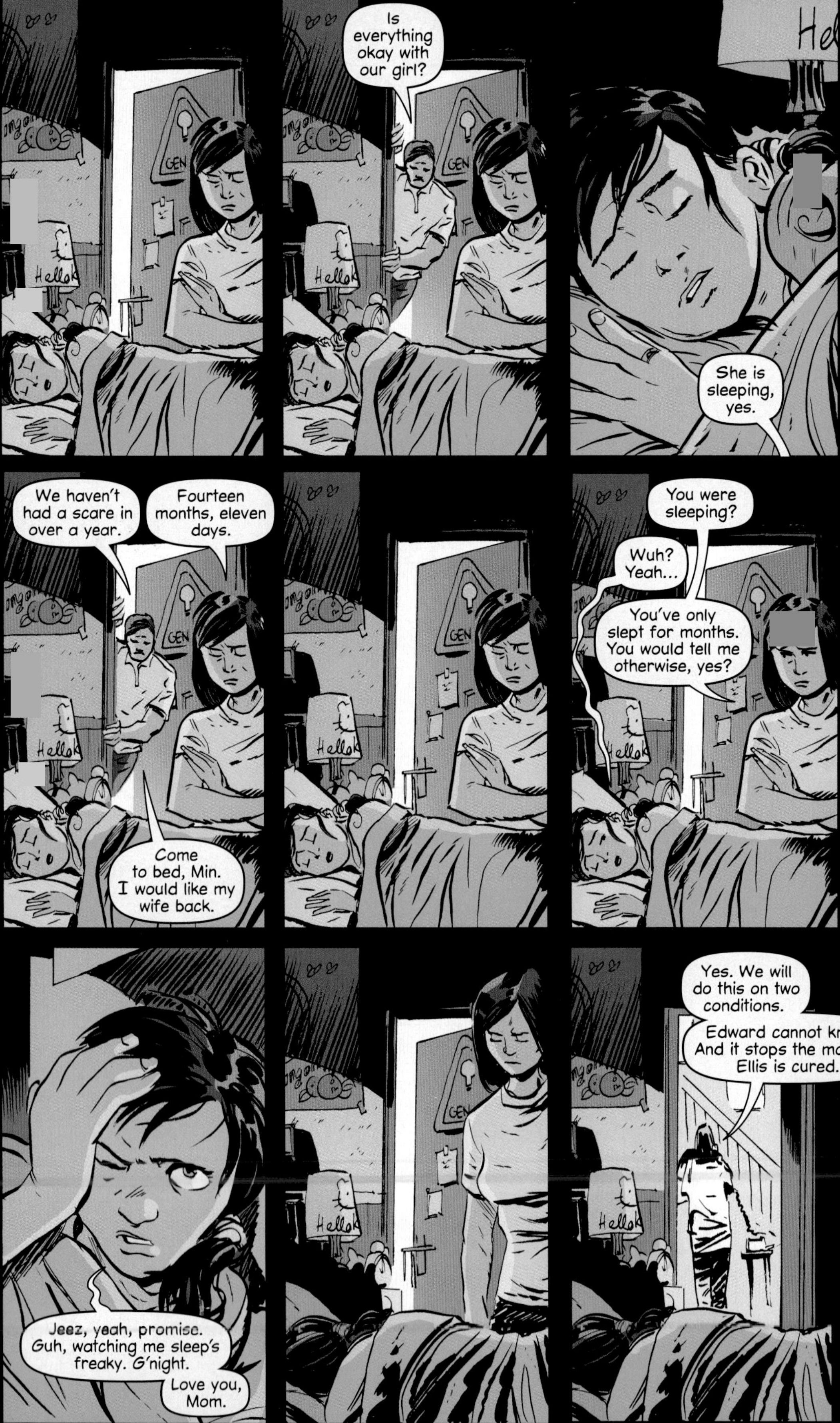
Is everything okay with our girl?
She is sleeping, yes.
We haven't had a scare in over a year.
Fourteen months, eleven days.
Come to bed, Min. I would like my wife back.
You were sleeping?
Wuh? Yeah...
You've only slept for months. You would tell me otherwise, yes?
Jeez, yeah, promise. Guh, watching me sleep's freaky. G'night.
Love you, Mom.
Yes. We will do this on two conditions.
Edward cannot know
And it stops the mome
Ellis is cured.

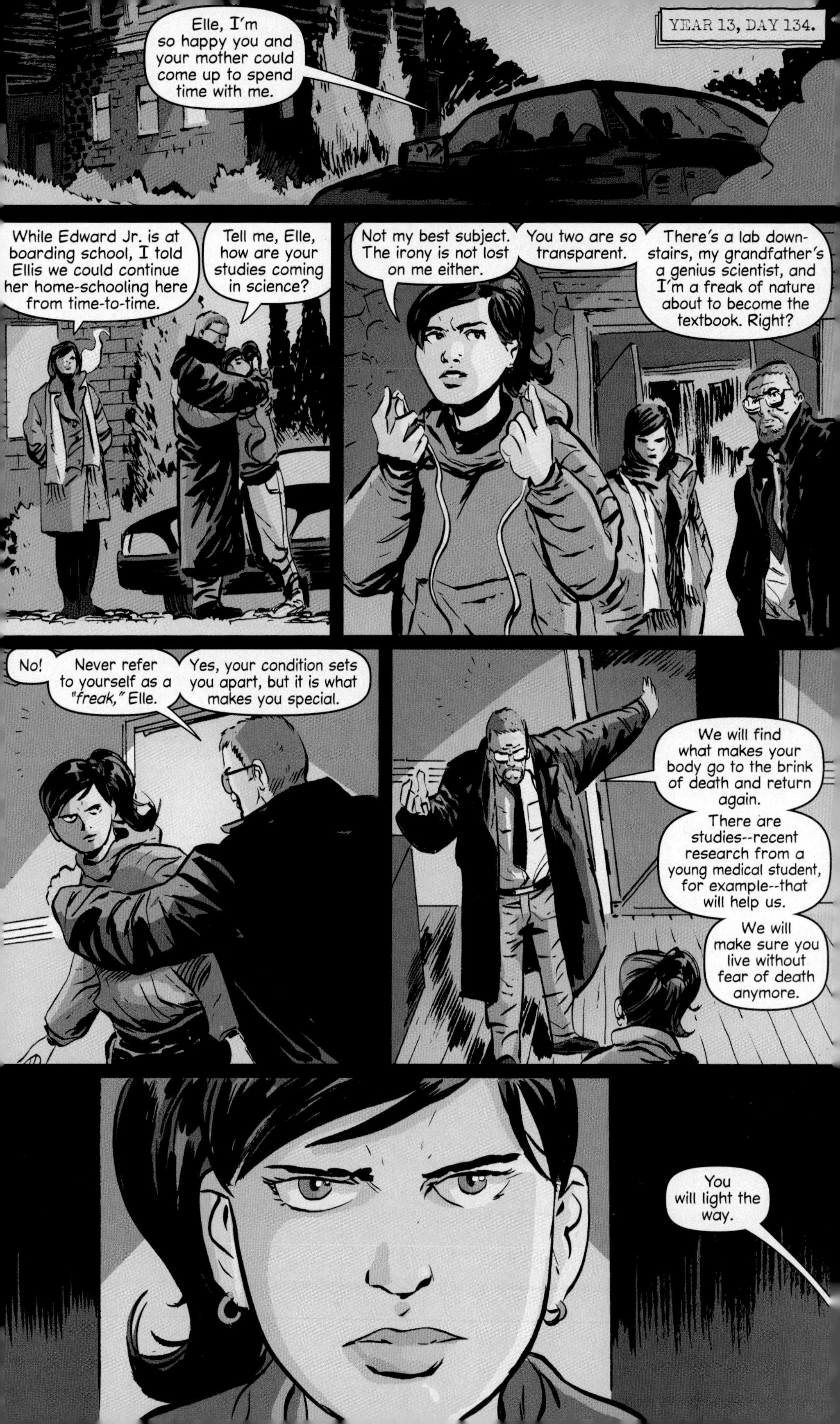
YEAR 13, DAY 134.
Elle, I'm so happy you and your mother could come up to spend time with me.
While Edward Jr. is at boarding school, I told Ellis we could continue her home-schooling here from time-to-time.
Tell me, Elle, how are your studies coming in science?
Not my best subject. The irony is not lost on me either.
You two are so transparent.
There's a lab down-stairs, my grandfather's a genius scientist, and I'm a freak of nature about to become the textbook. Right?
No!
Never refer to yourself as a "freak," Elle.
Yes, your condition sets you apart, but it is what makes you special.
We will find what makes your body go to the brink of death and return again.
There are studies--recent research from a young medical student, for example--that will help us.
We will make sure you live without fear of death anymore.
You will light the way.

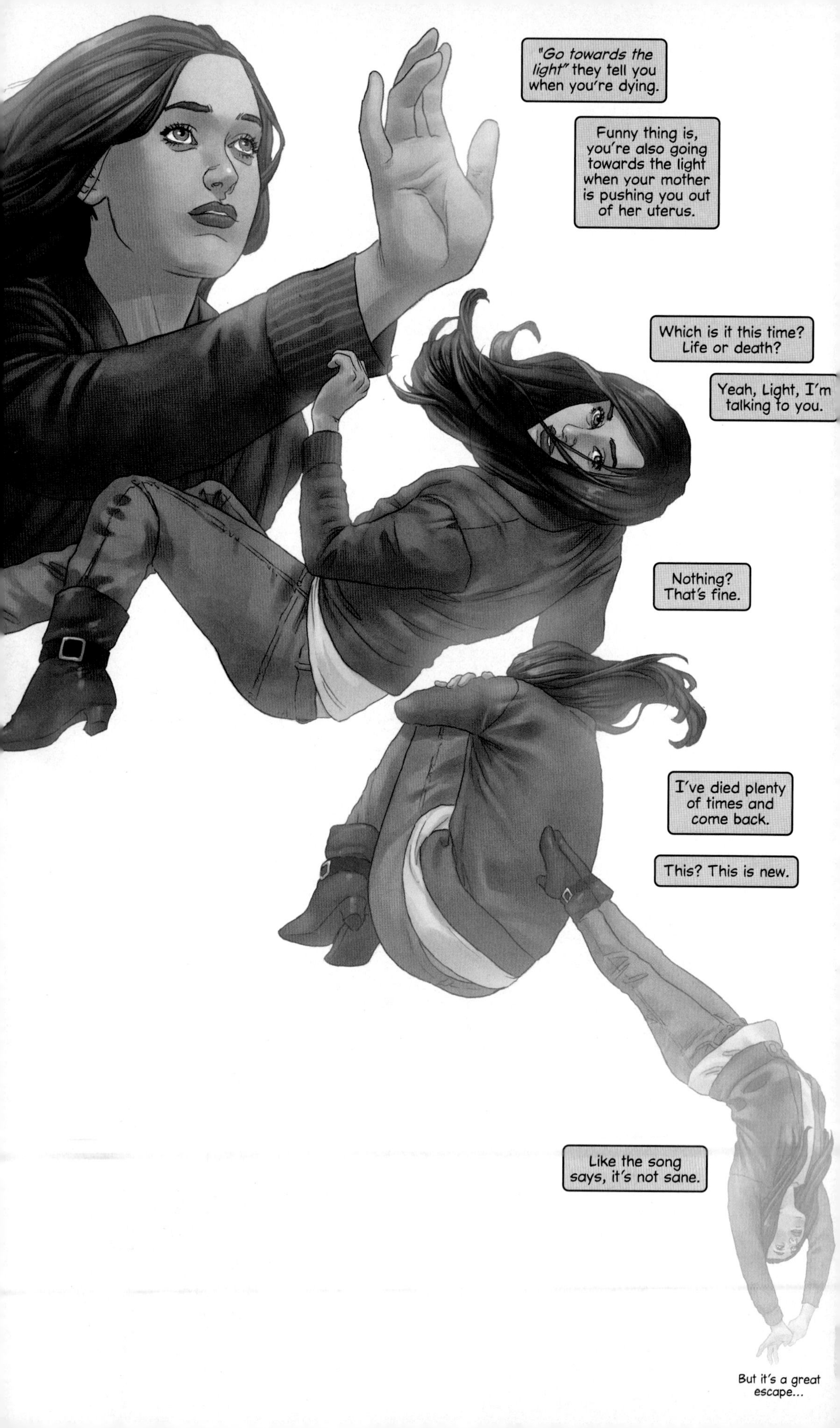
"Go towards the light" they tell you when you're dying.
Funny thing is, you're also going towards the light when your mother is pushing you out of her uterus.
Which is it this time? Life or death?
Yeah, Light, I'm talking to you.
Nothing? That's fine.
I've died plenty of times and come back.
This? This is new.
Like the song says, it's not sane.
But it's a great escape...

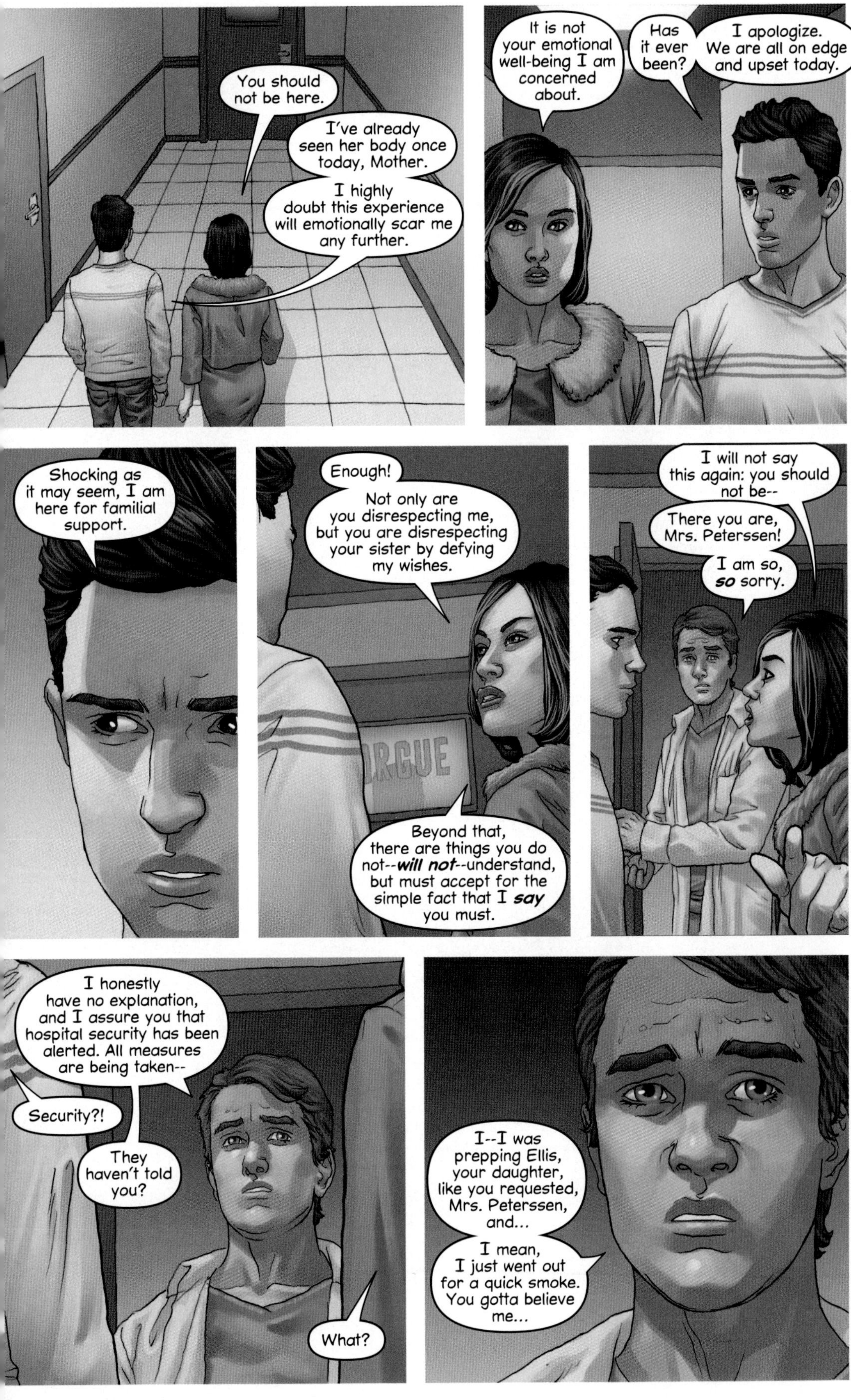
You should not be here.
I've already seen her body once today, Mother.
I highly doubt this experience will emotionally scar me any further.
It is not your emotional well-being I am concerned about.
Has it ever been?
I apologize. We are all on edge and upset today.
Shocking as it may seem, I am here for familial support.
Enough!
Not only are you disrespecting me, but you are disrespecting your sister by defying my wishes.
ORGUE
Beyond that, there are things you do not--*will not*--understand, but must accept for the simple fact that I *say* you must.
I will not say this again: you should not be--
There you are, Mrs. Peterssen!
I am so, *so* sorry.
I honestly have no explanation, and I assure you that hospital security has been alerted. All measures are being taken--
Security?!
They haven't told you?
What?
I--I was prepping Ellis, your daughter, like you requested, Mrs. Peterssen, and...
I mean, I just went out for a quick smoke. You gotta believe me...

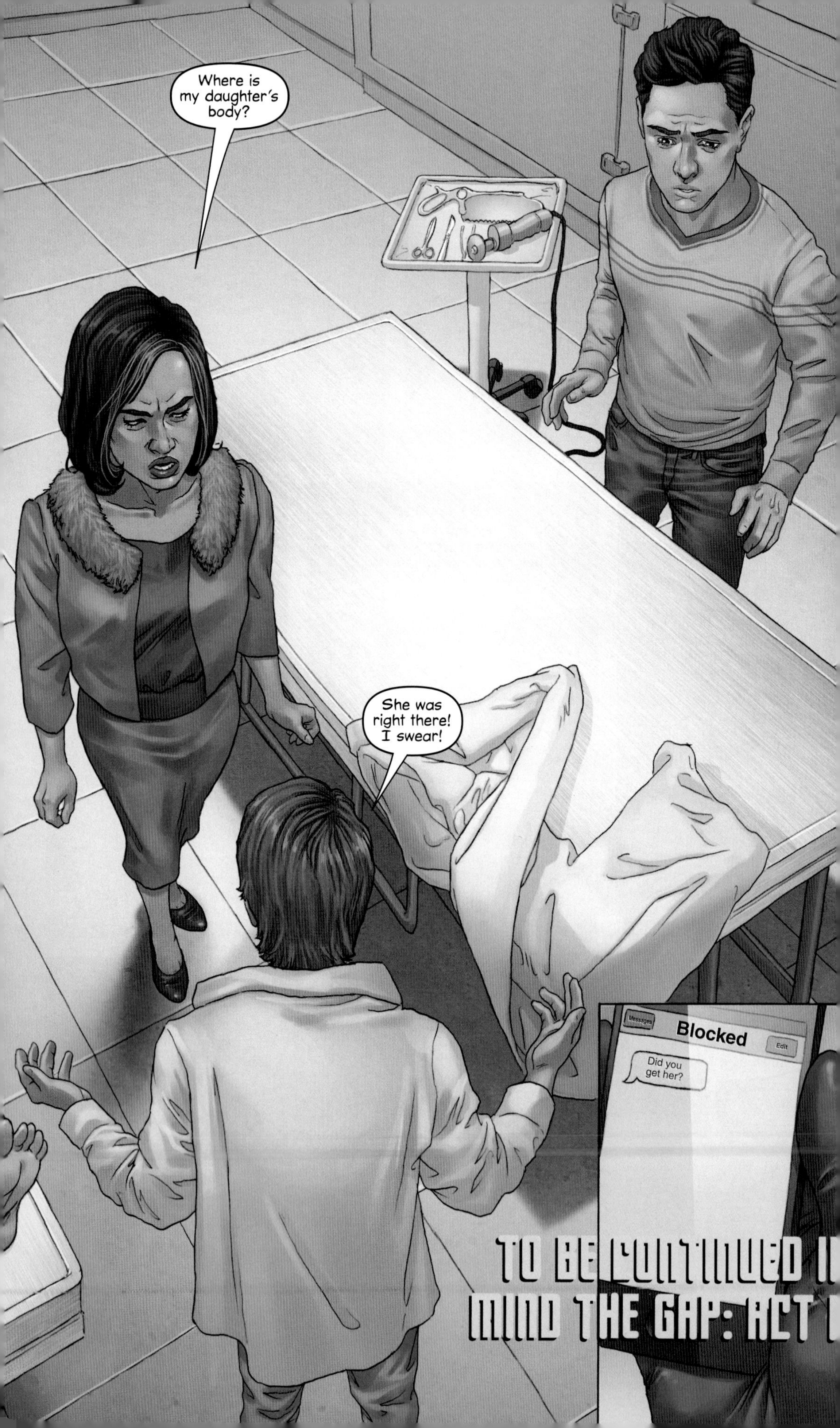
Where is my daughter's body?
She was right there! I swear!
Messages
Blocked
Edit
Did you get her?
TO BE CONTINUED I
MIND THE GAP: ACT I

"You can chain me, you can torture me, you can even destroy this body, but you will never imprison my mind."

- Mahatma Gandhi

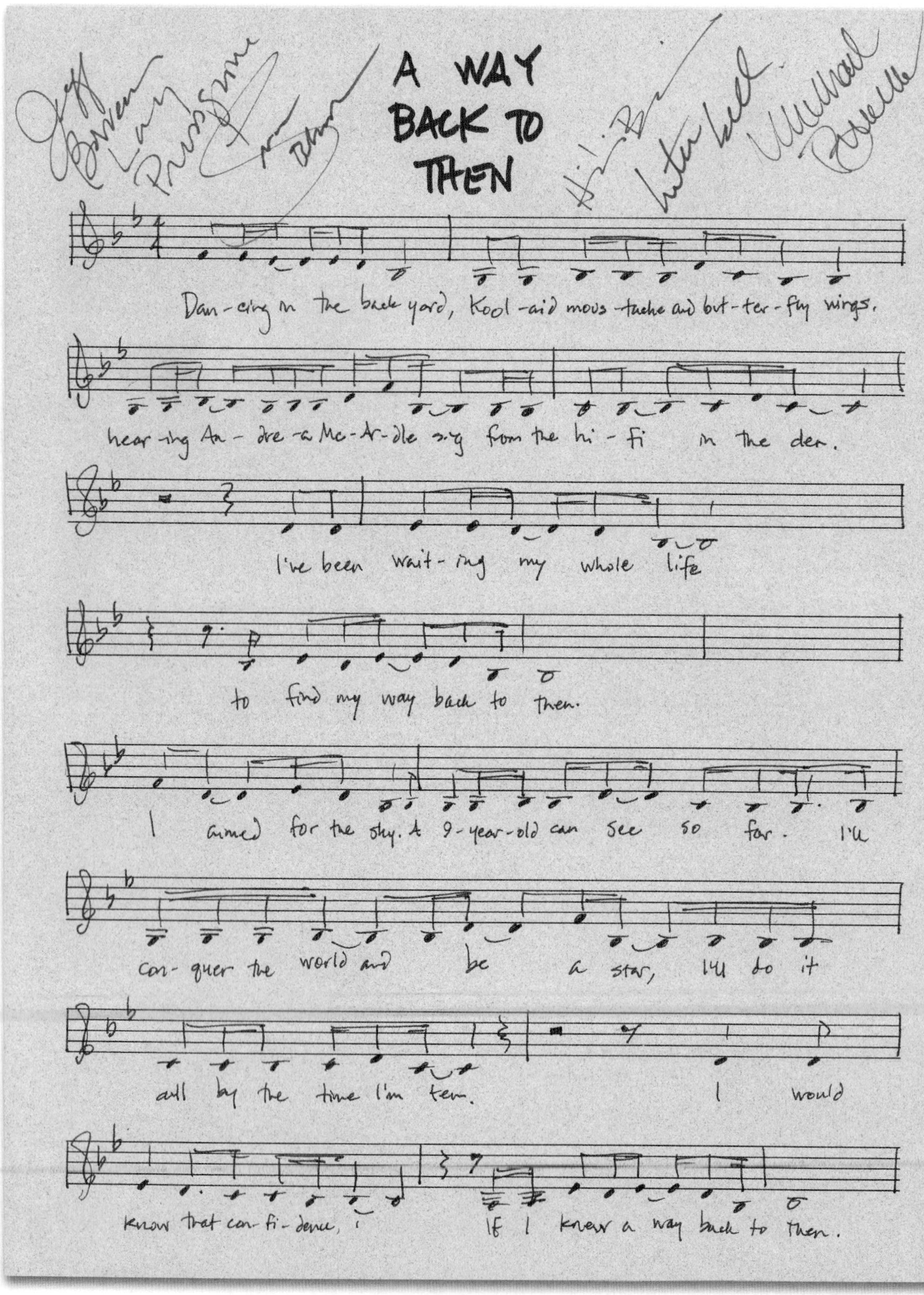
A WAY BACK TO THEN
Dan-cing in the back yard, Kool-aid mous-tache and but-ter-fly wings.
hear-ing An-dre-a Mc-Ar-dle sing from the hi-fi in the den.
I've been wait-ing my whole life
to find my way back to then.
I aimed for the sky. A 9-year-old can see so far. I'll
con-quer the world and be a star, I'll do it
all by the time I'm ten. I would
know that con-fi-dence, if I knew a way back to then.

A handwritten page of sheet music from A WAY BACK TO THEN from [title of show], signed by the original cast, director, and musical director. This hangs on my wall as an inspiration piece. The song and show itself has played an integral role in the lives of Elle, Jo, and Dane. Thanks for letting me play in your sandbox, [tos]sers!

BRIDGING THE GAP: *"Inspired by a true story"*

Here's the secret to MIND THE GAP. The hidden truth. What you only kind of see in the corner of your eye as you read the book and look for the Rosetta Stone that will reveal the part of the mystery that's nagging at you.

I am Elle Peterssen.

In a way, the secret to Elle, the Jairus project, and especially what just unfolded, all of these things are inspired by a true story: mine. No, I've never been in a coma, I'm not from an insanely wealthy family, and I've certainly never shot up anything on a subway platform—or anywhere (just to clarify, for my family who may be reading). I'm not the great-grandson of a not-Nazi scientist, either. However, Elle & I share one thing in common that greatly influenced this story and shaped everything you've read so far (and things to come).

I died three times shortly after being born very prematurely.

Okay, "died" is strong, but I stopped breathing and had to be resuscitated. See, I was born about two months early and my lungs weren't fully developed. I had what was then called Hyaline Membrane Disease (now known as respiratory distress syndrome). I was quickly transferred from one hospital to Vanderbilt Children's Hospital in Nashville, TN. Born Catholic, I was given both Baptism and Last Rights by an EMT in the ambulance en route. I needed blood and my grandfather, who was riding along, donated his. He said they "took a thimble-full, Jimbo, you were so tiny." Now, whether that part is true or not, we'll never know.

My grandfather was the original Storyteller of the family. Every year, without fail, on my birthday he would call and recount a different part of my birth. Some parts were always spot-on consistent, and others were…well, he was a storyteller, after all. But he was one of the many people who saved my life.

The other key person is a woman named Dr. Mildred Stahlman, known as "the creator of world's first newborn intensive care unit."
Dr. Stahlman initiated a program of high-risk newborn care in Tennessee in 1973 at Vanderbilt, one year before I was born. She had been studying premature and high-risk newborns for years. In fact, she was one of the doctors who tried to save Patrick Kennedy, the premature baby of Jacqueline and President John K Kennedy a decade before. Patrick also suffered from hyaline membrane disease and was born about as premature as I. Sadly, he passed away after two days.

I spent sixty-four days in Vanderbilt, under the observation of Dr. Stahlman and the other doctors and nurses at the NICU. I, along with other preemies at Vandy, were part of Dr. Stahlman's research in the care and treatment of infants with damaged lungs.

After I came home, I was just like every other kid, except a bit on the smaller/skinnier side, a lot of which is just genetic. I went back to Vanderbilt on my birthday for the first number of years to see Dr. Stahlman for tests as part of her continuing study. As far as I knew, at the time, every kid went to the doctor on their birthday. My 13th birthday was the last time I saw her.

According to her biography, Dr. Stahman's study led to her starting Vanderbilt's Neonatology Fellowship Training Program and has helped train more than 80 post-doctoral fellows from about 20 countries in research and high-risk newborn care.

All of that is a far cry from what the fictional world of MIND THE GAP is doing and the purpose of Jairus, but I think you can get the picture.

I wanted to take the time in these pages to acknowledge the achievements of and give thanks to Dr. Mildred Stahman who, as of this writing, is still alive and associated with Vanderbilt University. I also want to encourage people to visit http://www.childrenshospital.vanderbilt.org and check out the amazing work they do there. You can also donate through their site to help keep their research going.

Lastly, I would like to dedicate this to my own grandfather, who not only did his own part in saving my life when I was born, he helped inspire this story and so many more. His blood runs through mine, literally. So, to the man I am named after, to the Raconteur, the Original Storyteller, Pop-Pop, to James Andrew McCann I, who I know is looking down and probably telling anyone who'll listen "That's my grandson! Did I tell you about the time the nurses cheered the first time he pooped?", this story is for you. Love, Jimbo.

--Jim McCann

9/8/13

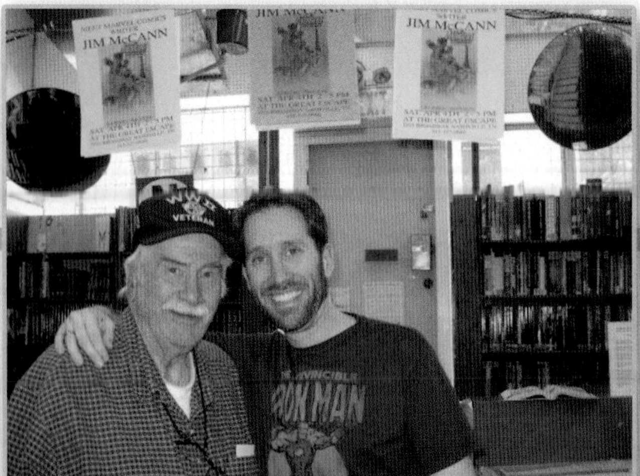
JIM McCANN
JIM McCANN

MIND

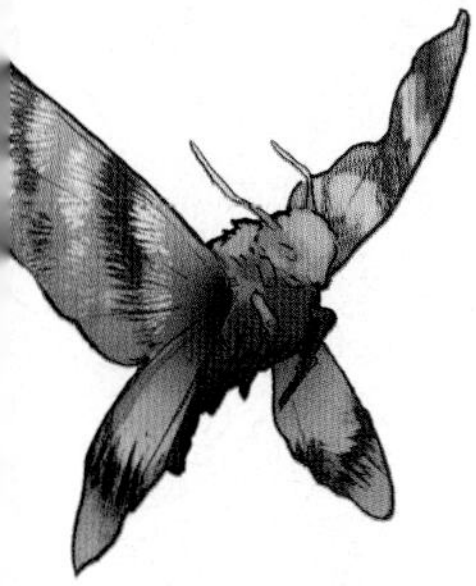

VARIANT COVERS
FOR ISSUES
11 & 12
BY MICHAEL GAYDOS

VARIANT GALLERY

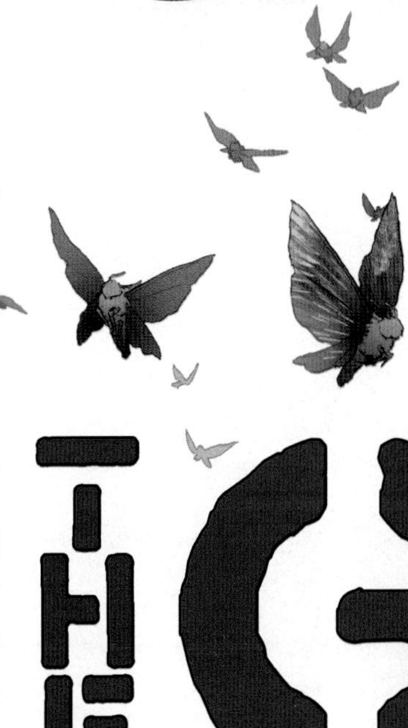

VARIANT COVERS
FOR ISSUES
13, 14, 15 & UNUSED 14
BY DAN McDAID
WITH DEBORAH McCUMISKEY ON 15

THE GAP

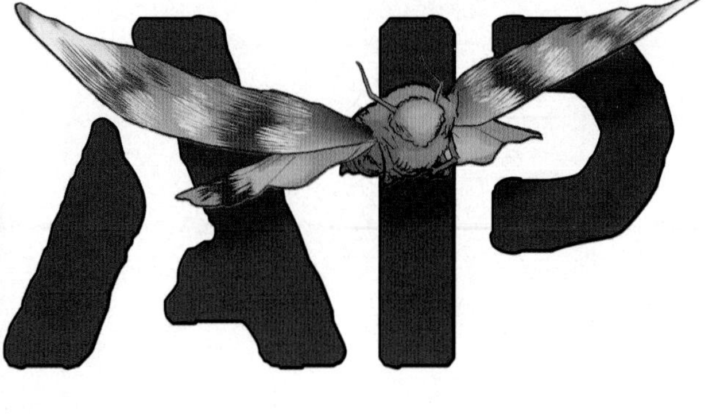

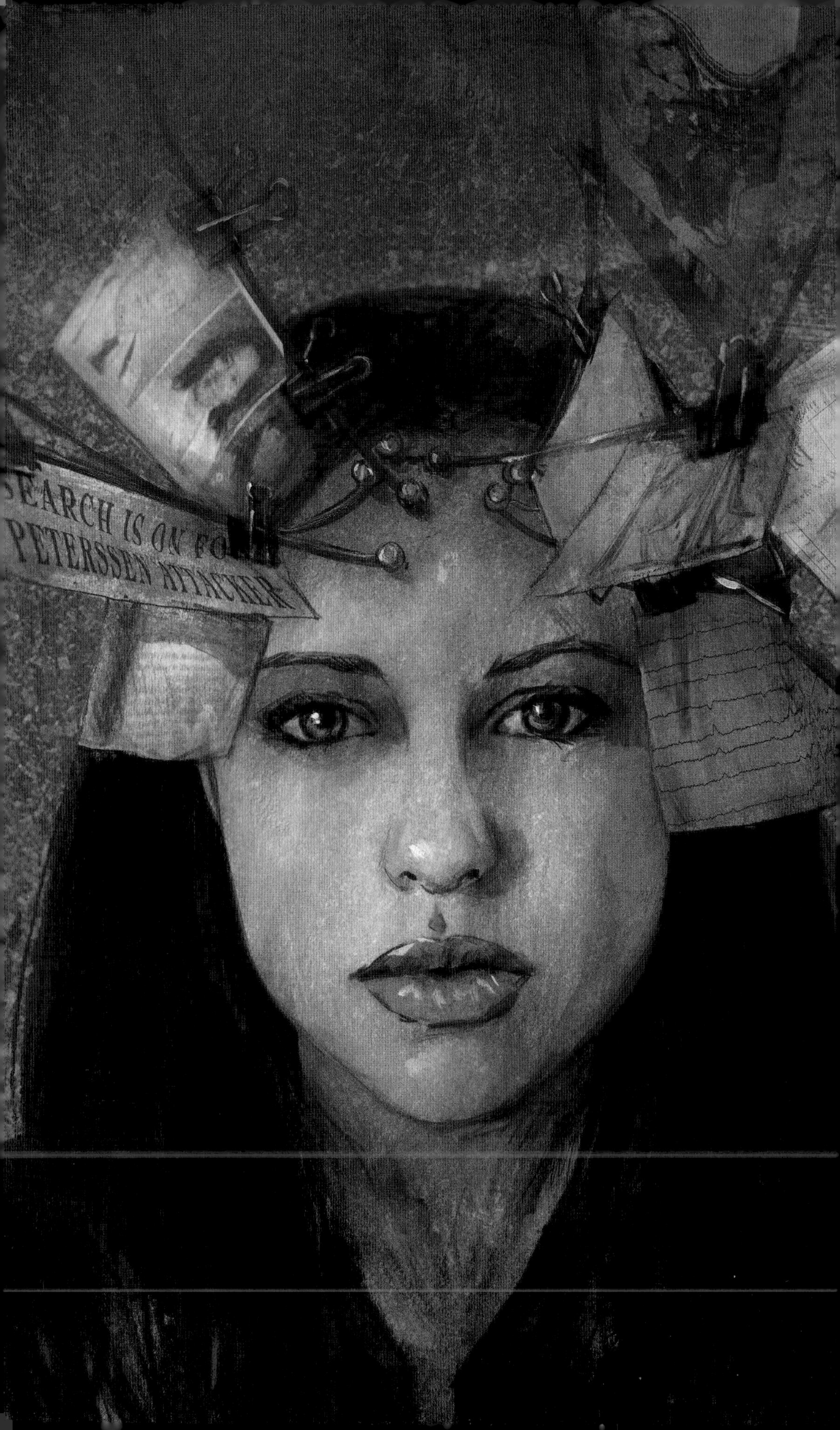
SEARCH IS ON
PETERSSEN ATTACKER

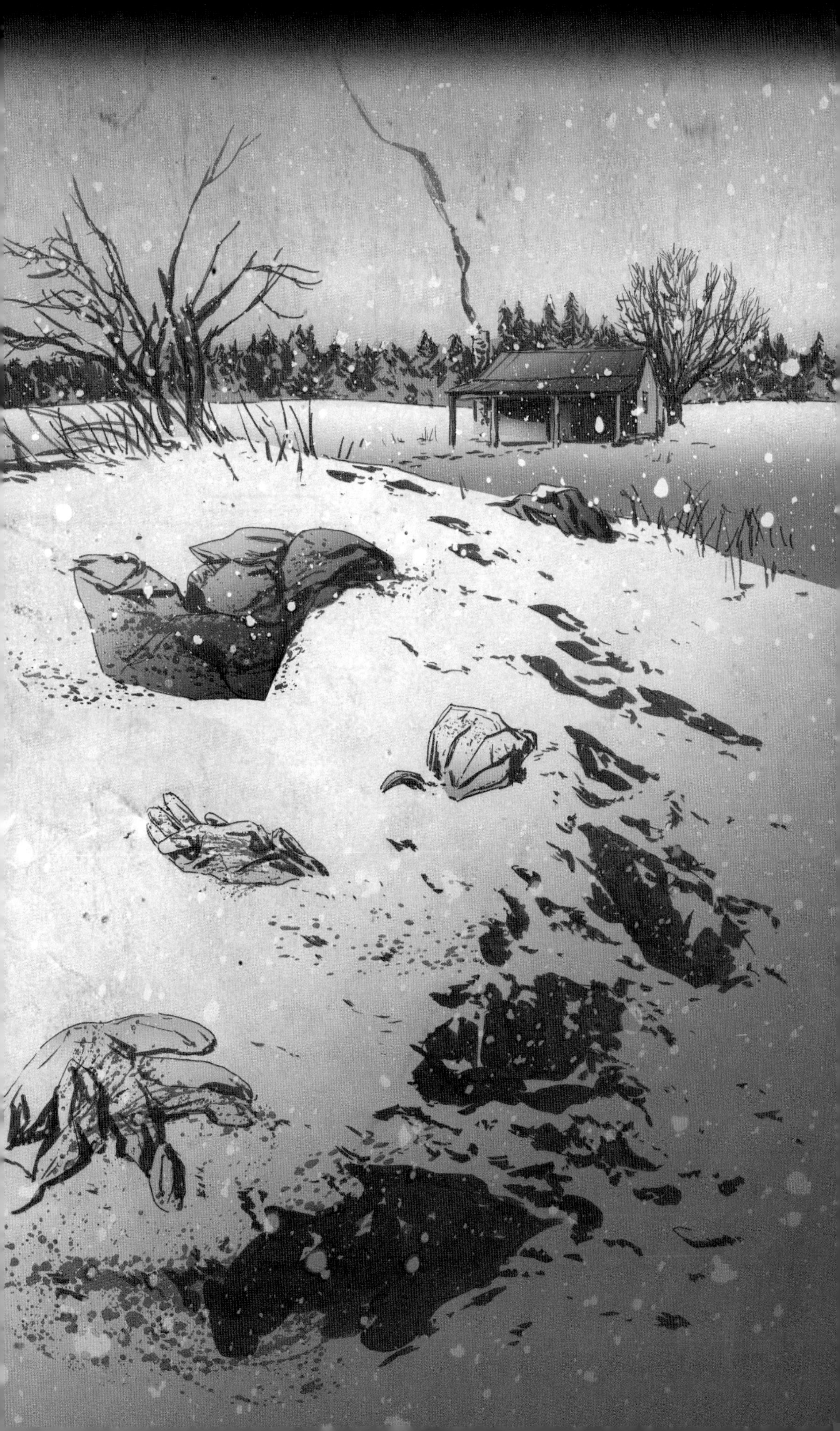

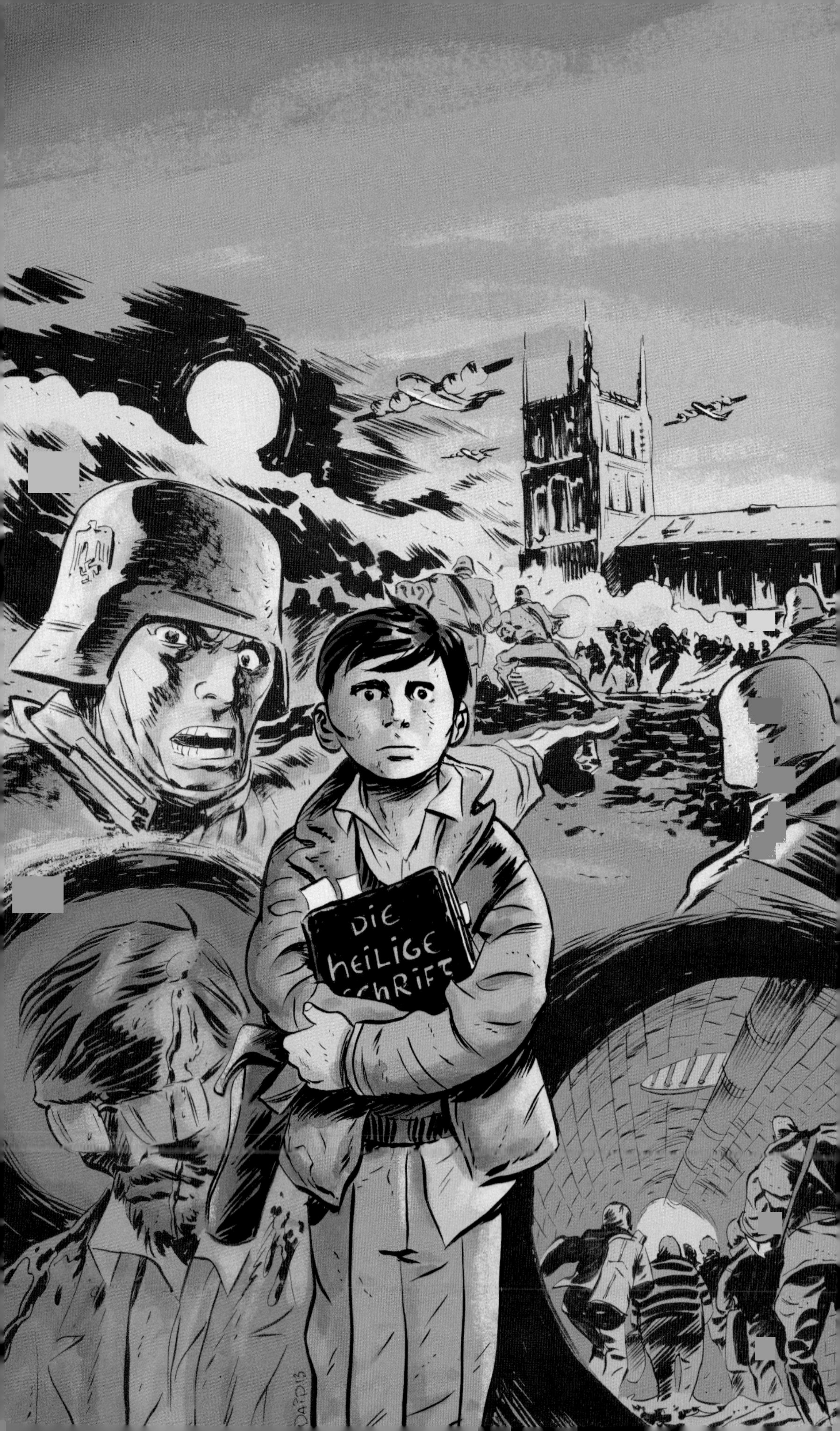
DIE
heiLIGE
schrift

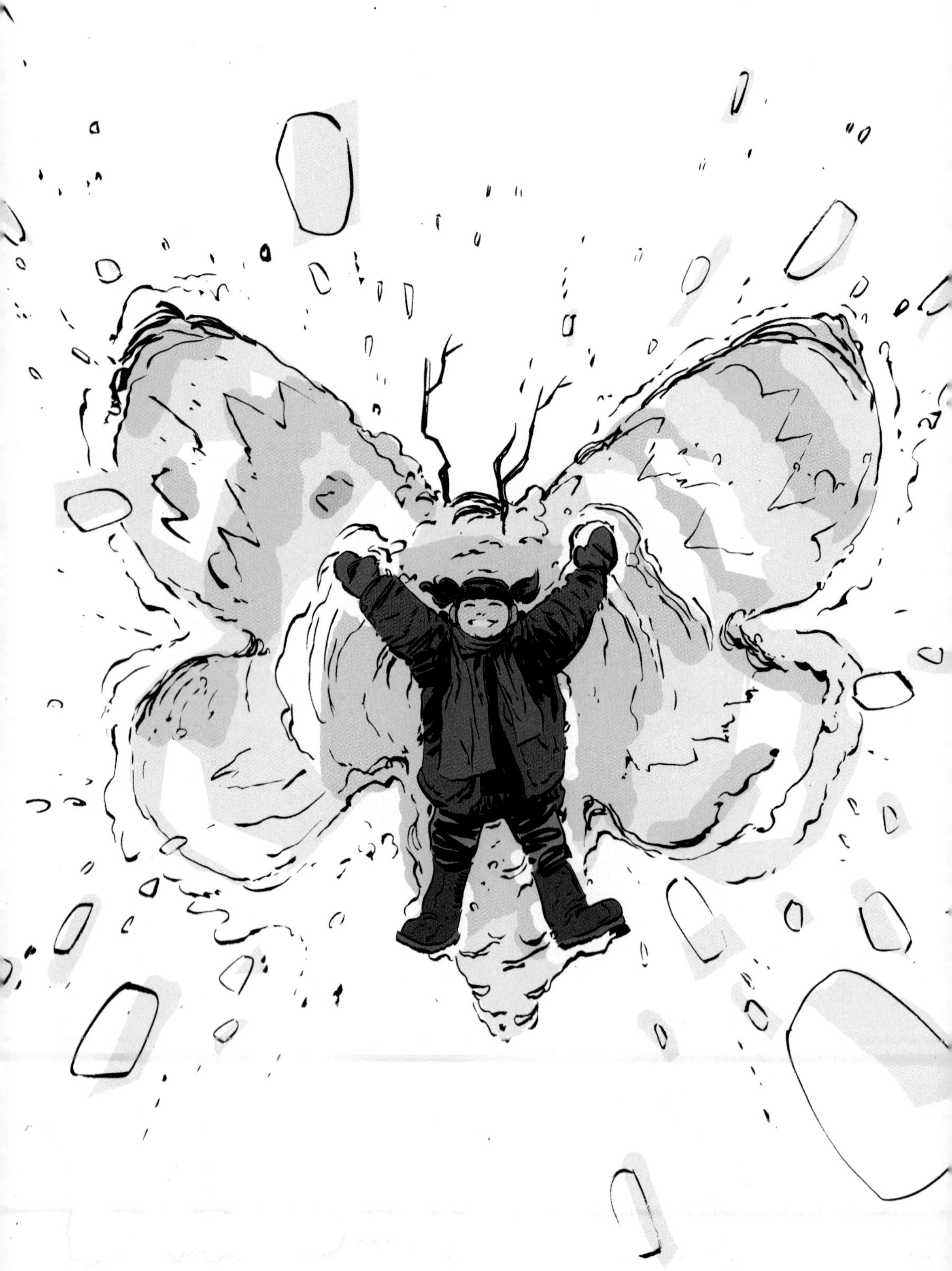
McDAID 2013

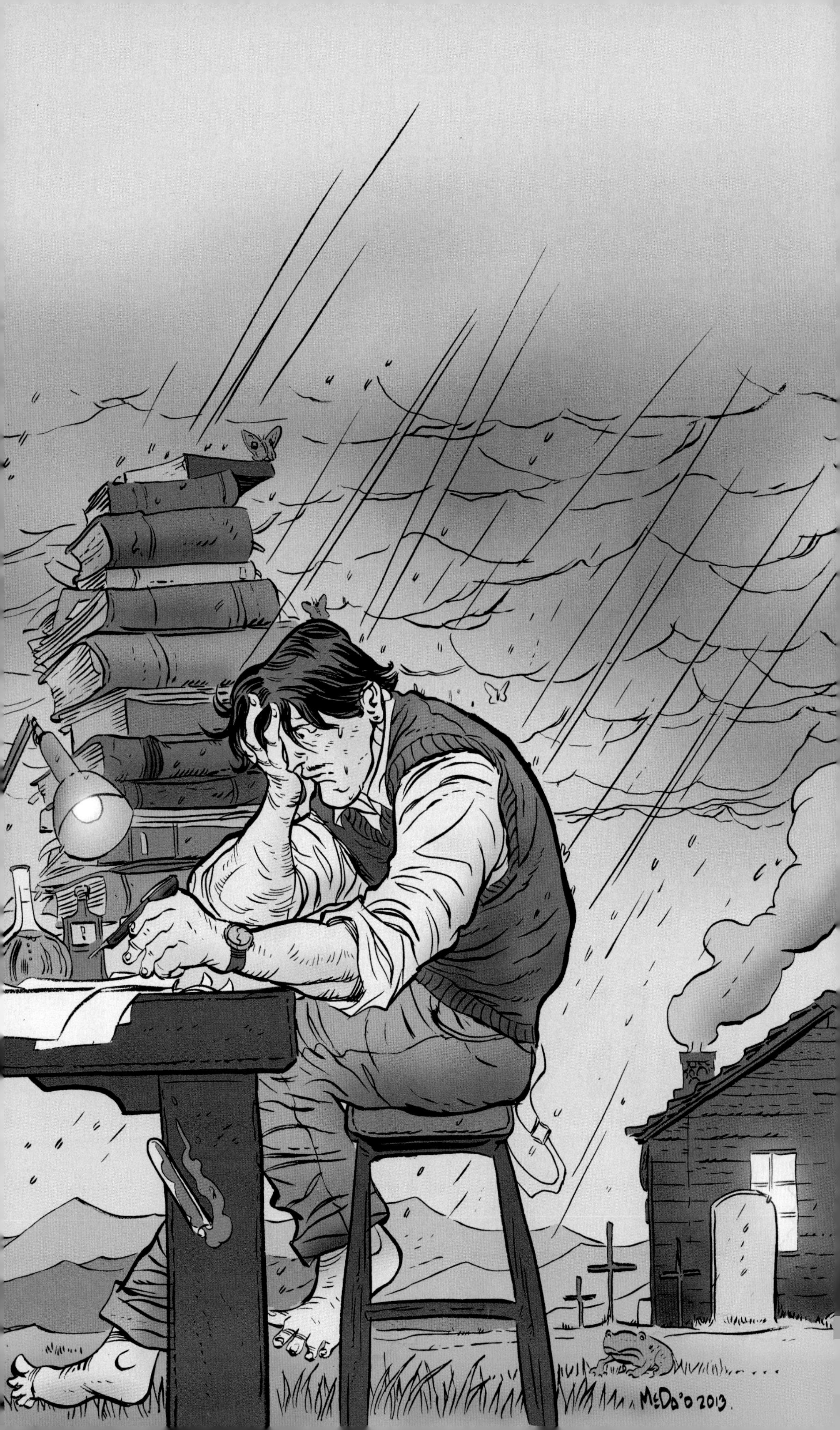
McDo'o 2013.

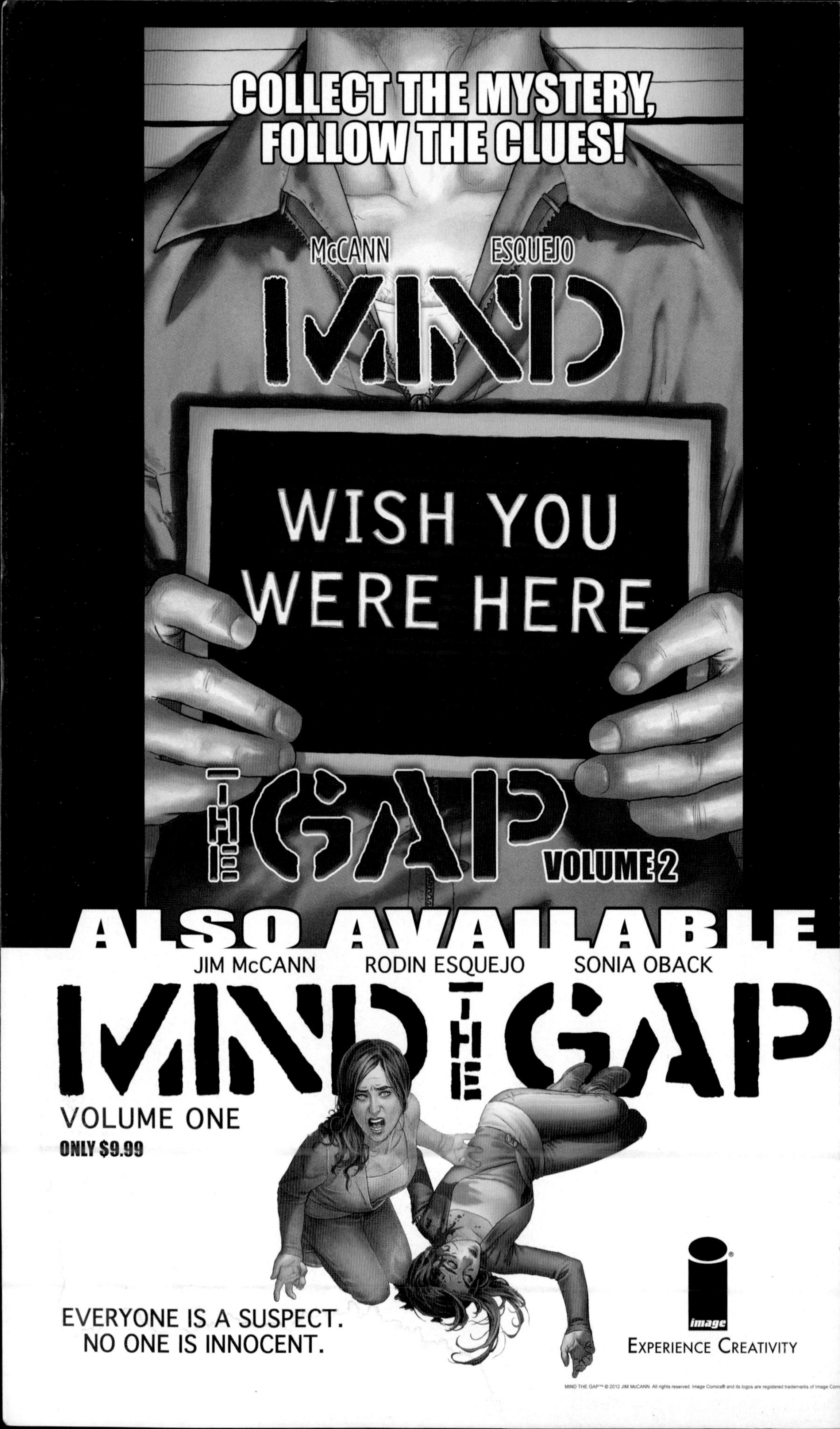

COLLECT THE MYSTERY, FOLLOW THE CLUES!
McCANN
ESQUEJO
MIND
WISH YOU WERE HERE
THE GAP
VOLUME 2
ALSO AVAILABLE
JIM McCANN
RODIN ESQUEJO
SONIA OBACK
MIND THE GAP
VOLUME ONE
ONLY $9.99
EVERYONE IS A SUSPECT.
NO ONE IS INNOCENT.
image
EXPERIENCE CREATIVITY
MIND THE GAP™ © 2012 JIM McCANN. All rights reserved. Image Comics® and its logos are registered trademarks of Image Comi

EVERYONE
IS
A SUSPECT

NO ONE
IS
INNOCENT

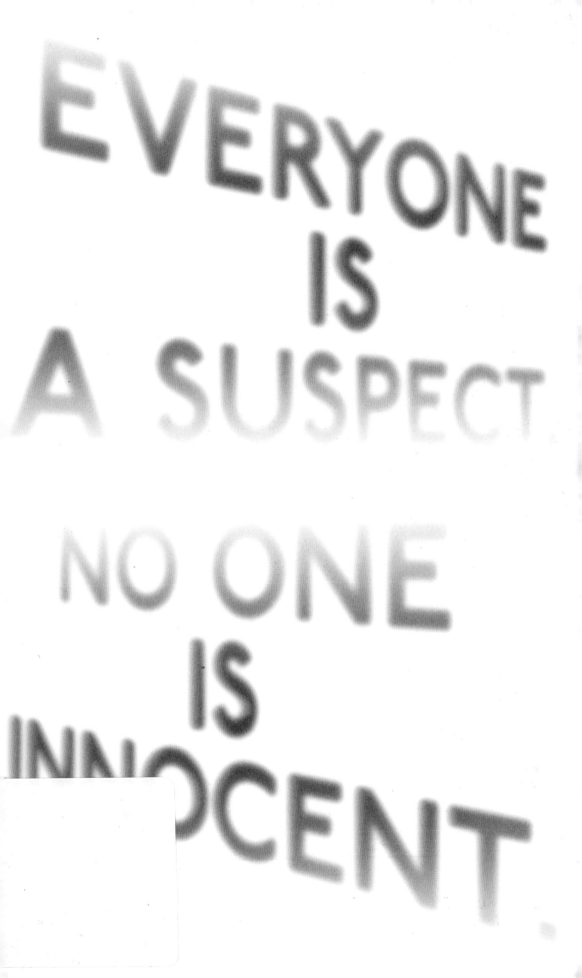

"The #1 Ongoing Series currently published by Image Comics. *Mind The Gap* is an amazing exercise in storytelling, and really unique idea. Quite simply, Jim McCann is writing a masterpiece." - Geekality

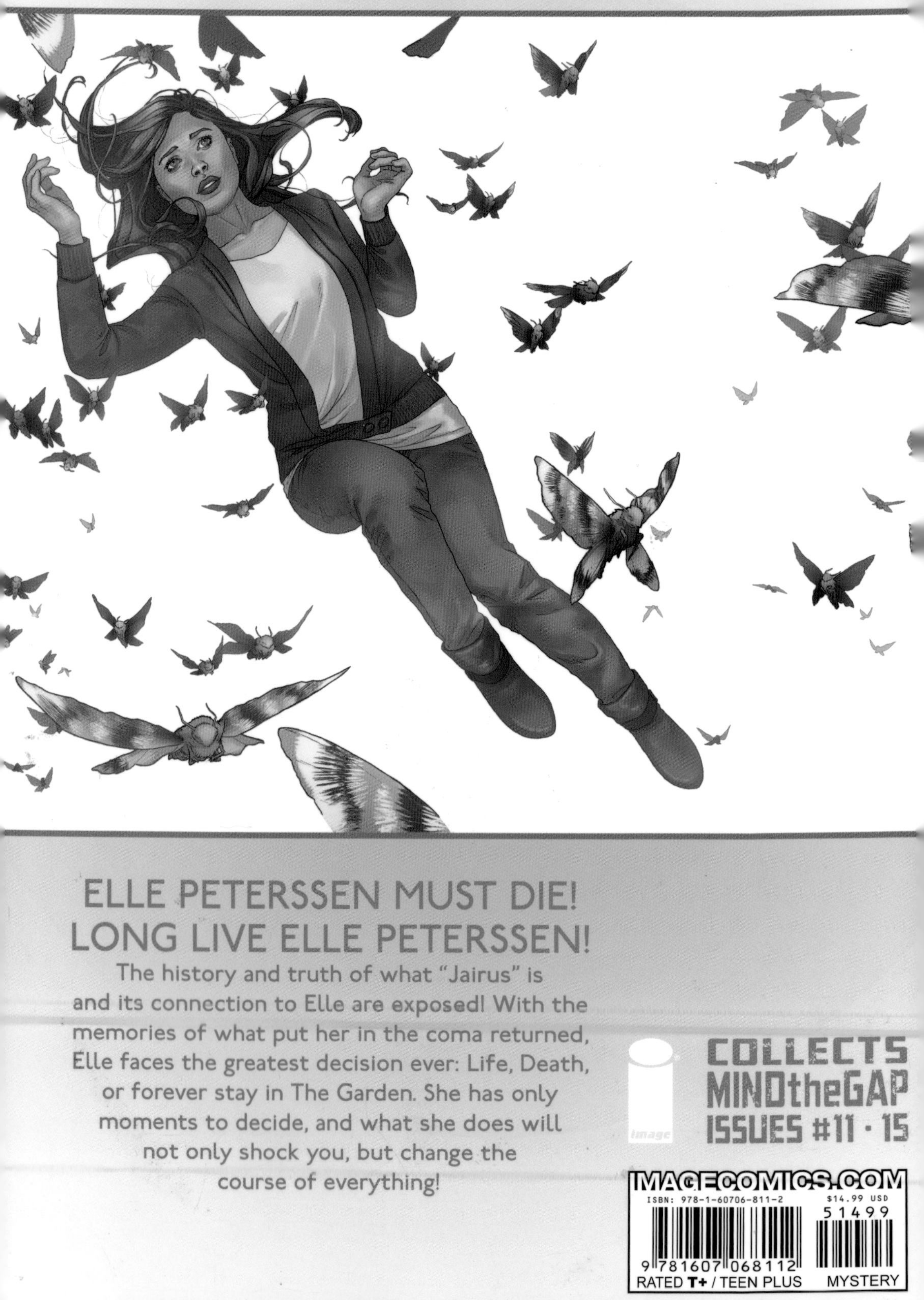

ELLE PETERSSEN MUST DIE! LONG LIVE ELLE PETERSSEN!

The history and truth of what "Jairus" is and its connection to Elle are exposed! With the memories of what put her in the coma returned, Elle faces the greatest decision ever: Life, Death, or forever stay in The Garden. She has only moments to decide, and what she does will not only shock you, but change the course of everything!

COLLECTS MIND the GAP ISSUES #11 - 15

IMAGECOMICS.COM
ISBN: 978-1-60706-811-2
$14.99 USD
51499
9 781607 068112
RATED T+ / TEEN PLUS
MYSTERY

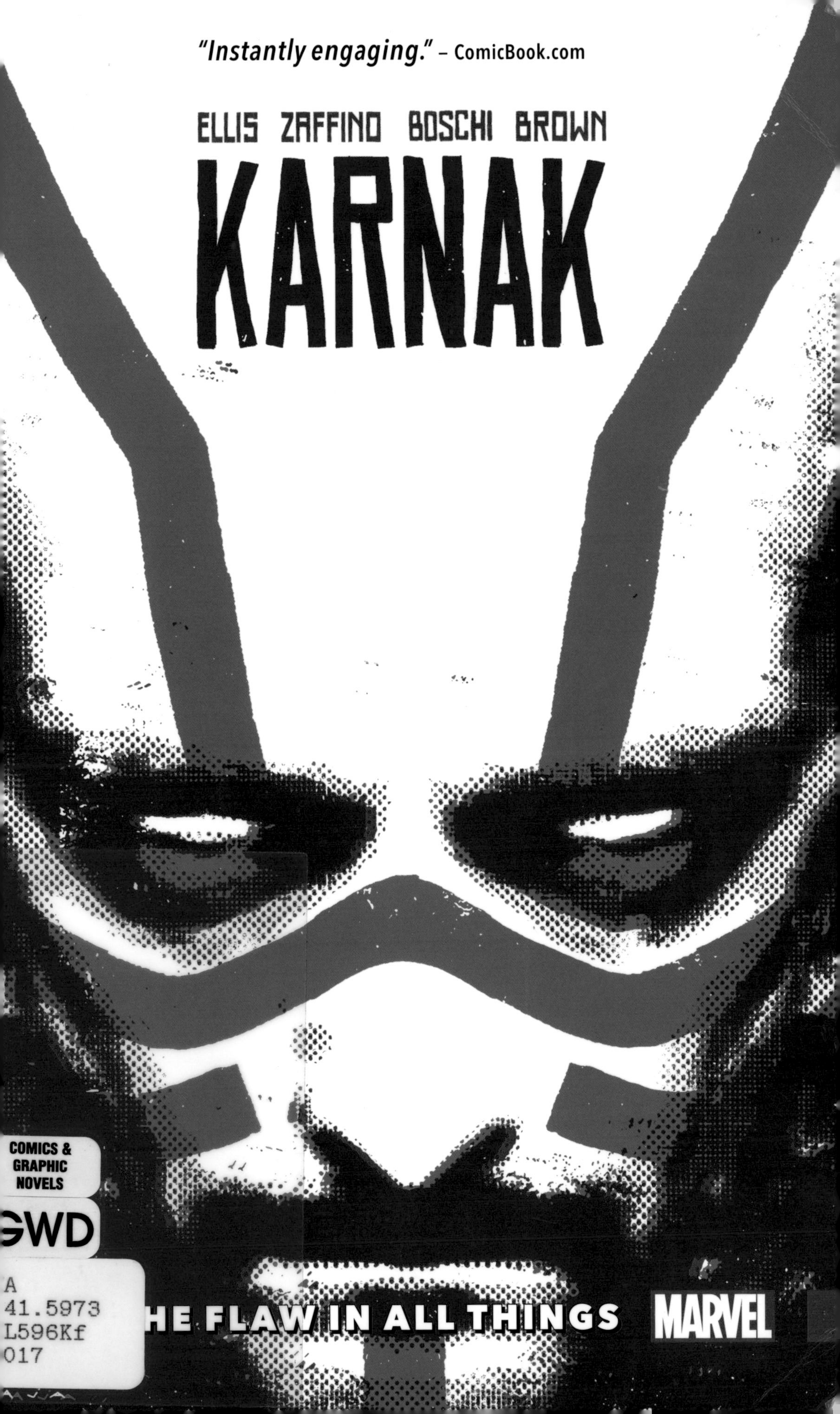
"Instantly engaging." – ComicBook.com
ELLIS ZAFFINO BOSCHI BROWN
KARNAK
HE FLAW IN ALL THINGS
MARVEL
COMICS & GRAPHIC NOVELS
GWD
A
41.5973
L596Kf
017

Collected Editions

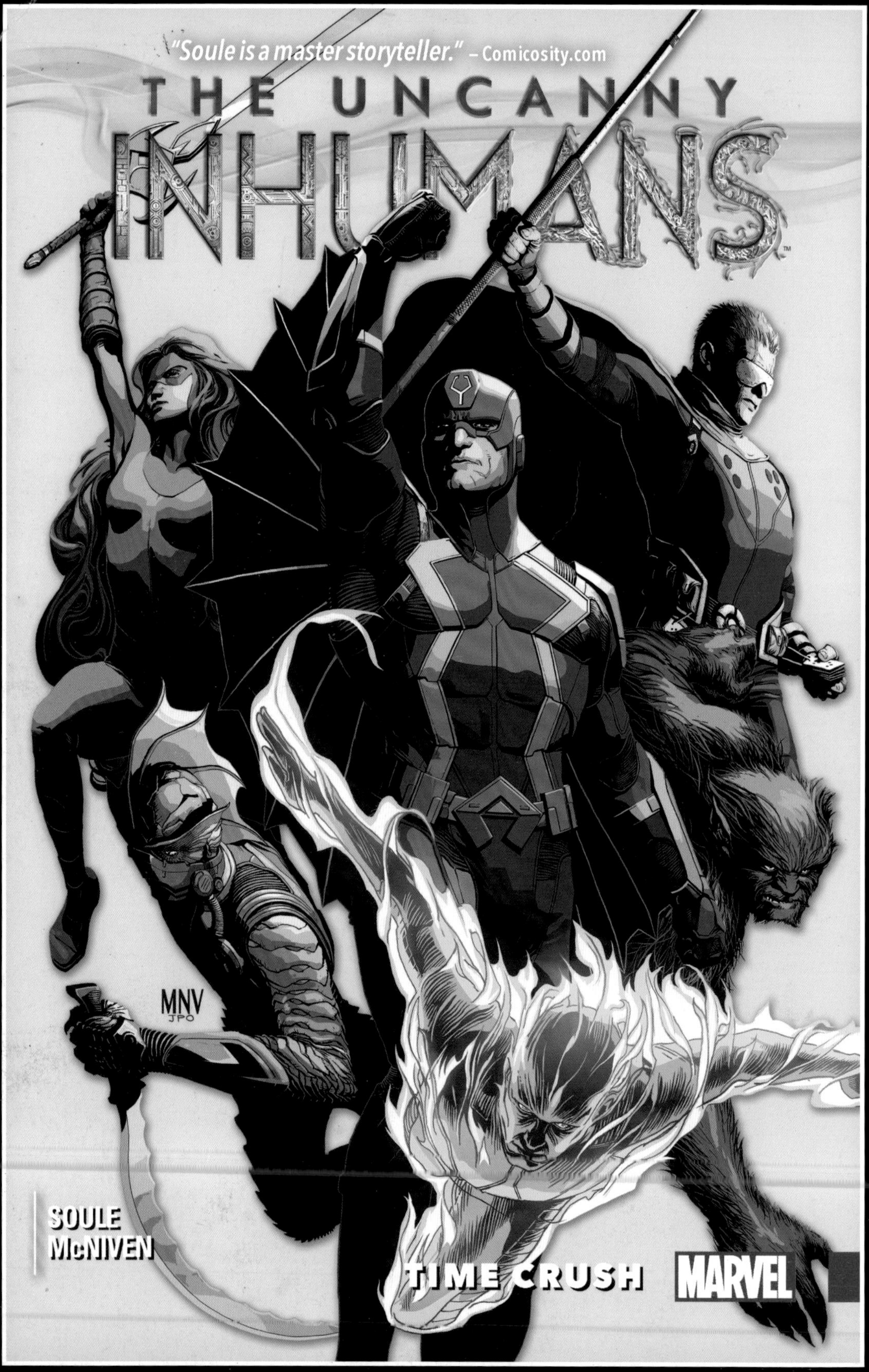
"Soule is a master storyteller." – Comicosity.com
THE UNCANNY
INHUMANS
SOULE
McNIVEN
TIME CRUSH
MARVEL

Uncanny Inhumans Vol. 1: Time Crush

ISBN 978-0-7851-9706-5